ALSO BY ARIEL BLOCH

Die Hypotaxe im Damaszenisch-Arabischen (Sentence Subordination in Damascene Arabic)

Damaszenisch-Arabische Texte (Damascene Arabic Texts)

A Chrestomathy of Modern Literary Arabic

Studies in Arabic Syntax and Semantics

ALSO BY CHANA BLOCH

A Dress of Fire: Poems by Dahlia Ravikovitch (translation)

The Secrets of the Tribe (poetry)

Spelling the Word: George Herbert and the Bible

The Selected Poetry of Yehuda Amichai (translation, with Stephen Mitchell)

The Window: New and Selected Poems of Dahlia Ravikovitch (translation, with Ariel Bloch)

The Past Keeps Changing (poetry)

THE
SONG
OF
SONGS

Afterword by Robert Alter

RANDOM HOUSE
NEW YORK

THE SONG OF SONGS

A NEW TRANSLATION

with an Introduction and Commentary

ARIEL BLOCH
AND
CHANA BLOCH

 Published in the United States by Random House, Inc., New York, and simultaneously in Canada by Random House of Canada Limited, Toronto.

Library of Congress Cataloging-in-Publication Data

Bible. O.T. Song of Solomon. Hebrew. 1995.
The Song of songs : a new translation with an introduction and commentary / [by] Ariel Bloch and Chana Bloch;
afterword by Robert Alter.
p. cm.
Contains Hebrew text and English translation of the Song of Solomon.
Includes bibliographical references and index.
ISBN 0-679-40962-9
1. Bible. O.T. Song of Solomon—Commentaries. I. Bloch, Ariel
II. Bloch, Chana. III. Bible. O.T. Song of Solomon.
English. Bloch-Bloch. 1994. IV. Title.
BS1483.B56 1994
223'.9077—dc20 93-33249

Manufactured in the United States of America

2 4 6 8 9 7 5 3

Book design by Carole Lowenstein

For our sons,
Benjamin and Jonathan,
with love

Acknowledgments

In the course of our work on the Song of Songs, we have come to appreciate the truth of the Jewish saying, "From all my teachers have I learned." Any interpretive study dealing with the Hebrew Bible must take account of generations of scholarship. This is particularly true for a text like the Song, which has elicited a wealth of exegesis from antiquity to the present day. Our scholarly debts are recorded in the Commentary and the Bibliography.

Here it is a special pleasure to thank the many friends and colleagues who have helped us. Everyone we turned to responded with uncommon generosity, and we wish to acknowledge our deep appreciation. If we have inadvertently omitted anyone's name, we hope to have expressed our gratitude in person.

Robert Alter championed this undertaking from the start. He read the translation with us, line by line, discussing problems of interpretation, and commented on the Introduction, "In the Garden of Delights." His support has meant a great deal to us. Stephen Mitchell helped with his subtle criticism and steadfast encouragement. In fact, it was he who first suggested over lunch one day that we collaborate on a new translation of the Song. The project seemed immediately appealing; at that time, we had no idea it would engage us both for years.

Our heartfelt gratitude to Sally Belfrage, Josephine Carson, Stanley Moss, Shirley Kaufman, Chana Kronfeld, and Peter Dale Scott, who read the translation closely at various stages; their criticism enabled us to come closer to the spirit of the Song. Our thanks also to Marilyn Chandler, Shirley Kaufman, and Cynthia Scheinberg for their comments on the Introduction. Most of all, we are grateful to Anita Barrows, who followed the translation and Introduction in draft after draft; we have benefited immeasurably from her poetic intuition, her critical acuity, and her unstinting generosity.

JoAnne Bernstein, David Biale, Daniel Boyarin, Kenneth Cohen, Julius Held, Thomas Rosenmeyer, Andrew Stewart, and David Winston answered queries in their respective fields. Michael Fox, Moshe Greenberg, and Carol Meyers corresponded with us about specific points. Indran Amirthanayagam, Yael Chaver, Michael Chyet, Betsy Dubovsky, Stuart Friebert, Tess Gallagher, Joanna Harris, Richard Moore, and Susan Rattray offered suggestions or advice. With their lively skepticism, the participants in the Bible study group chaired by Jacob Milgrom constituted an ideal sounding board. We are also obliged to the editors of *Equinox, The Forward, Judaism, The Iowa Review,* and *Poetry,* where some of these lyrics and portions of the Introduction and Commentary first appeared.

We have been fortunate in our agent, Georges Borchardt, who offered wise counsel and staunch support, and in our editor at Random House, Jason Epstein, whose enthusiasm for this project was an inspiration to us.

We began the translation at Yaddo in 1990, and the Introduction and Commentary at the MacDowell Colony in 1992. Both of these artists' colonies offered us comfortable working conditions in idyllic surroundings. They even provided the deer in the field and the little foxes—an unexpected gift.

Finally, we wish to thank each other. This project was truly a collaborative effort. We worked together on the translation, debating—sometimes fiercely—the meaning of the Hebrew text and the multitude of possibilities offered by English; then Chana wrote the Introduction and Ariel the Commentary, each of us consulting with the other and editing the other's many drafts. Neither one of us could have completed this work without the devoted assistance of the other.

ARIEL BLOCH and CHANA BLOCH
Berkeley, spring 1994

Contents

IN THE GARDEN OF DELIGHTS

THE SONG OF SONGS is a poem about the sexual awakening of a young woman and her lover. In a series of subtly articulated scenes, the two meet in an idealized landscape of fertility and abundance—a kind of Eden—where they discover the pleasures of love. The passage from innocence to experience is a subject of the Eden story, too, but there the loss of innocence is fraught with consequences. The Song looks at the same border-crossing and sees only the joy of discovery.

The poem is set in early spring, with its intimations of ripening. The rains of the winter season have just ended, the vines are in blossom, the air is alive with scents and birdsong. Since the poem speaks through metaphor, this setting reveals something essential about the lovers, who live in harmony with the natural world. The images of spring reflect their youth, and the innocent freshness of their passion.

The woman appears to be very young, probably just past puberty. Her brothers call her their "little sister" and think of her as a child—"We have a little sister / and she has no breasts," they say—though she is more grown-up than they admit: since by her own account her breasts are developed, she has reached sexual maturity (8:8–10).[1] The Shulamite, as she is called, is presented in relation to her close family, her mother and her brothers, as well as a group of young women, the daughters of Jerusalem. She and her lover meet secretly in the countryside at night and part at daybreak, so it is clear that they are not married.

For centuries, exegetes have considered their relationship chaste, ignoring the plain sense of the Hebrew. The word *dodim*, which occurs six times in the Song, including the opening verse—"Your *dodim* are better than wine"—is almost always translated as "love," though it refers specifically to sexual love.[2] Moreover, the metaphors of feasting

[1]Compare Ezek. 16:7–8: "Your breasts were well-formed. . . . I saw that you had reached the age of lovemaking" (*'et dodim*). See Moshe Greenberg, *Ezekiel, 1–20*, vol. 22 of *The Anchor Bible* (Garden City, N.Y.: Doubleday, 1983), pp. 270, 276–77.

[2]Song 1:2, 1:4, 4:10 (twice), 5:1, 7:13; compare Prov. 7:18, Ezek. 16:8, 23:17. Unless otherwise specified, references to the Bible are to the standard English translations; occasionally the numbering differs from the Hebrew by a verse or two.

suggest fulfillment, particularly when they are in the perfect tense, and the verb "to come into" or "to enter" often has a patently sexual meaning in biblical Hebrew:

> I have come into my garden, . . .
> I have gathered my myrrh and my spices,
> I have eaten from the honeycomb,
> I have drunk the milk and the wine. (5:1)

All this strengthens our conviction that the sexual relationship between the two lovers is not just yearned for—as has often been assumed—but actually consummated. In this respect, our understanding of the Song differs crucially from that of most commentators in the past, and indeed some even in our own day.

How can a poem so voluptuous be so full of innocent delight? For one thing, since it relies on metaphor rather than explicit statement, the language of the Song is restrained and delicate even where it is most sensuous. And because the lovers seem new to love, tender and proud and full of discovery, their words have a kind of purity—a "cleanly wantonness," in the phrase of the seventeenth-century English poet Robert Herrick.

In the Bible, written for the most part from a male point of view, women are by definition the second sex. History is traced through the line of the fathers, as in the priestly genealogies ("And Enoch begat Methuselah"), and the typical formulas for sexual relations ("he knew her," "he came in unto her," "he lay with her") make the woman seem passive and acted upon. But in the Song, where the lovers take turns inviting one another, desire is entirely reciprocal. Both are described in images that suggest tenderness (lilies, doves, gazelles) as well as strength and stateliness (pillars, towers). In this book of the Bible, the woman is certainly the equal of the man.

Indeed, she often seems more than his equal. Most of the lines are hers, including the first word in the poem—"Kiss me"—and the last. As a rule, she is the more forceful of the two; her lover describes her as *'ayummah*, "daunting" (6:4, 10). Only the Shulamite makes dramatic statements about herself: "I am dark, and I am beautiful!" (1:5), "I am a wall / and my breasts are towers" (8:10), and only she commands the elements: "Awake, north wind! O south wind, come, / breathe upon my garden" (4:16). She isn't shy about pursuing her lover: she goes out into the streets of Jerusalem at night to search for him—bold and unusual behavior for an unmarried woman (3:1–4, 5:6–7). She finds him, and makes it perfectly clear that she intends to keep him: "I held him, I would not let him go / until I brought him to my mother's house" (3:5).

Her invitations to love are more outspoken than his: "Let my lover come into his garden" (4:16); "There I will give you my love" (7:13); "I would give you . . . / my pomegranate wine" (8:2). She is the one who takes the initiative in their lovemaking: "I awakened you," she reminds him with some pride (8:5). In 6:11–12 he goes down to the walnut grove in an expectant mood ("to see if the vine had budded"), and there, to his surprise, she anticipates and rewards him. When she asks him to be true to her forever—"Bind me as a seal upon your heart" (8:6)—she phrases the wish in her own characteristically emphatic way.

It is the Shulamite who pronounces the great truths about love:

For love is as fierce as death,
its jealousy bitter as the grave.
Even its sparks are a raging fire,
a devouring flame. (8:6)

And she is the one who teaches that love must not be roused carelessly:

Daughters of Jerusalem, swear to me
by the gazelles, by the deer in the field,
that you will never awaken love
until it is ripe. (2:7, 3:5, 8:4)

The wisdom here may sound like Ecclesiastes ("Everything under the heavens has its time and its season: . . . a time to embrace, and a time to refrain from embracing," 3:1, 5) but the spirit that informs it is very different: not a bleak determinism but the inner logic of the passions. And the voice is her own—urgent, insistent, filled with awe at love's power.

The Shulamite's lively presence has been obscured by two millennia of translations and interpretations that, for the sake of propriety, have presented her as a sweet young thing, chaste and demure and properly bridal. In most translations (the King James Version is a notable exception), she wears a veil, a reading not supported by the Hebrew. That incongruous veil, like the fig leaf of Renaissance painting and sculpture, is a sign of the discomfort of the exegetes. When we lift the veil from her face, the Shulamite is revealed as a passionate young woman, as spirited and assertive as Juliet.

Apart from the Shulamite, women are given an unmistakable prominence in the Song. There is no mention of a father or a "father's house," the usual biblical term for "family," while mothers are referred to repeatedly. The Shulamite is her mother's favorite (6:9); when she speaks of her brothers, she calls them, in the Hebrew, "my mother's sons" (1:6); she wishes her lover were as close to her as a brother "who nursed at [her] mother's breast" (8:1). She brings her lover home to her "mother's house," perhaps to signify a more binding relationship (3:4, 8:2). She declares that she awakened her lover in the very place where his mother conceived and gave birth to him (8:5). Even King Solomon's mother appears in the poem, crowning her son on his wedding day (3:11). Though the history of the tribe is shaped by the fathers, the traditions of love, in the Song at least, are handed down by the mothers.

The daughters of Jerusalem act as a kind of chorus, a foil to the Shulamite and an audience. She addresses her feelings about love to them, and turns to them for help; they are invoked, and perhaps even present, during some of the couple's intimate dialogues. Like the young women who accompany Jephthah's daughter in her mourning, or the women of Bethlehem who come out to greet Naomi, the daughters of Jerusalem represent the social milieu in which the lovers move, answering their need for public testimony and public validation. The young man's companions, mentioned briefly in 1:7 (and perhaps 5:1 and 8:13), may serve a similar purpose, though unlike the daughters of Jerusalem they are given no voice in the poem. The lovers in the Song are certainly unlike the many star-crossed couples of other literary traditions who languish in tragic isolation.

The brothers and the watchmen provide whatever friction there is in the poem. From the beginning, the Shulamite's brothers are watching her; as one would expect in a biblical text, they are their sister's keepers. In 1:6 we learn that they have rebuked her, possibly for her sexual behavior—that is, if "guarding the vineyard" is understood metaphorically. The enigmatic "Catch us the foxes" (2:15), which has been assigned to a variety of speakers, belongs most plausibly to the brothers; in their proprietary way, they are worrying about the young "foxes" who may be despoiling "their" vines (the vineyard is associated with the Shulamite throughout the poem). Later they consider how to deal with their little sister when she is old enough for suitors (8:8–9). We are not surprised that the Shulamite has the last word in these deliberations (8:10).

When the watchmen first come upon the Shulamite in the streets of Jerusalem at night, they seem harmless enough, but later they assault her physically (3:3, 5:7). Whether or not this incident reflects reality, its primary purpose in the poem is to create dramatic tension. By their opposition, the brothers and the watchmen provoke the Shulamite to reveal her resolve and assurance in love. And their presence serves as a contrast to the sweet flowing milk and honey and myrrh, which to some readers might otherwise seem cloying.

Despite the brothers and watchmen, the Song has none of the dark complication of many familiar love stories. For Romeo and Juliet, love is wedded to loss and death; for Tristan and Isolde, or for Heathcliff and Catherine, love itself is a form of suffering. The word "passion" comes from the Latin *patior,* "to suffer," and passionate love is often regarded as a consuming disease, its symptoms being (in Sappho's diagnosis) a fluttering heartbeat, a burning sensation, a drumming in the ears, a cold sweat, paleness, and trembling. But apart from one episode of rapid heartbeat (5:4), the lovers in the Song exhibit few of the usual symptoms. They don't suffer love, they savor it.

The Song has its moments of anxiety or yearning, to be sure, but the prevailing mood is one of celebration. Hopelessness is not among its charms. The young, in each other's arms, sing a sensual music, their theme the transforming experience of falling in love. Like the blossoming wildflowers, they take no thought for the morrow. Sufficient unto the day is its own delight.

The lovers are fervent, impetuous, filled with an unwavering headlong intensity. "Take me by the hand, let us run together!" in 1:4 proclaims their exuberance. Hyperbole is their natural language. Dramatic and self-dramatizing, the Shulamite sings out:

> Let me lie among vine blossoms,
> in a bed of apricots!
> I am in the fever of love. (2:5)

And her lover matches her extravagance:

> Oh come with me, my bride,
> come down with me from Lebanon. . . .
> from the mountains of the leopards,
> the lions' dens. (4:8)

A moment later, they are tender and playful with each other; they vie in the gallantries of praise; she interrupts him lovingly to complete his thought. He in particular is fond of affectionate epithets: "my love," "my friend," "my sister, my bride," "my dove," "my perfect one." Both of them delight in the sound of the first person plural: "our bed," "our roofbeams," "our rafters," they say, "our wall," "our land," "our doors," taking possession, as a couple, of the world around them.

Shakespeare was right about lovers: they have such seething brains, such fantasies. To be in love is to be caught up in the power of fantasy. "Be like a gazelle," the Shulamite commands (2:17), as if the words themselves had the power to transform reality. In her mind her lover can as easily become a king. When she calls him "the king," or when he calls her "nobleman's daughter," they are dressing up in borrowed robes, playing at King-Solomon-and-his-court. And though they seem, at least from this distance, convincingly pastoral, it may be that they are only playing at being shepherds; apart from 1:7–8, the images of pasturing (2:16, 6:2–3), like those of the vineyard, are erotic double entendres. Perhaps, like Marlowe's Passionate Shepherd, or Shakespeare's Rosalind, they are really just lovers in shepherds' clothing.

Jerusalem is at the center of their world ("Shulamite" probably means "woman of Jerusalem"), but the geography of their imagination reaches from the mountains of Lebanon to the oasis of Ein Gedi, from Heshbon in the east to Mount Carmel on the sea—the four points of their compass. The garden of delights in the Song is a fantasy garden, filled with precious and exotic spices:

> flowering henna and spikenard,
> spikenard and saffron, cane and cinnamon,
> with every tree of frankincense,
> myrrh and aloes,
> all the rare spices. (4:13–14)

Henna and saffron grew in ancient Israel, but myrrh, cinnamon, and cane probably did not, while frankincense, aloes, and spikenard were imported from faraway Arabia, India, Nepal, and China.[3] With what abandon these lovers inhabit their fantasies! But that is precisely what makes them seem so convincing. The Song of Songs offers us an imaginary garden—with real lovers in it.

[3]Yehuda Feliks, *Song of Songs: Nature, Epic and Allegory* (Jerusalem: Israel Society for Biblical Research, 1983), pp. 22–26.

Elsewhere in the Bible, nature is the mirror of God, reflecting His power and sublimity, and man, that paragon of animals, is glorified as the crown of Creation:

> You have made him master
> over all the works of Your hands,
> You have set the world at his feet.
> (Ps. 8:6; compare Gen. 1:28)

The notion of man's preeminence was very likely formed in reaction to the neighboring pagan cultures with their animal gods, and it is as rooted in biblical thought as the archetypal oppositions of day and night, light and darkness, sea and dry land. But in the Song the name of God does not even appear, and there is no opposition between human and animal, no hierarchy, no dominion. Nature is the mirror of the human lovers.

The lovers discover in themselves an Eden, thriving and abundant, a Promised Land of vines and fig trees, pomegranates, wheat, milk and honey. The poet's metaphors keep shifting between the actual landscape, suffused with erotic associations, and the landscape of the body. The Shulamite waits for her lover in a garden, but she herself is a garden; the two of them go out to the fragrant vineyards to make love, but she herself is a vineyard, her breasts like clusters of grapes, and their kisses an intoxicating wine.

The Song is filled with wonder for what the poet Denise Levertov calls "animal presence." When the lovers are compared to animals, it is in tribute to their beauty and undomesticated freedom. Both lovers have dovelike eyes, and both are associated with deer and gazelles. At moments they seem almost transformed into those graceful creatures. The Shulamite, hiding behind a wall, is a rock dove in the craggy ravines (2:14); the young man bounding over the mountains is a gazelle, a stag (2:9). When she asks him to "be like a gazelle, a wild stag" (2:17, 8:14), she is sweeping aside the biblical hierarchies, and we are reminded that animals were once venerated for their power and beauty. It is not by chance that the Shulamite asks her friends to swear "by the gazelles, by the deer in the field." In an oath, precisely where we might expect to find the name of God, we find instead the names of two animals that are frequently associated with the lovers. This oath makes plain the secular boundaries of the lovers' world. Divinity lives within them and their landscape; the earth is all of paradise they need to know.

KING SOLOMON is a central figure in the lovers' fantasies, not a character in the poem, as commentators once assumed. His reign is invoked as a symbol of legendary splendor that enhances and ennobles the two young lovers. The account of Solomon in the Book of Kings, even if largely historical, appears to incorporate elements of legend. Solomon "exceeded all the kings of the earth in riches and in wisdom" (1 Kings 10:23). He controlled the caravan trade in gold and spices, and his merchant fleet brought back sandalwood, precious stones, gold, silver, ivory, apes, and peacocks (9:26–28; 10:11, 14–15, 22). He imported horses from Cilicia and chariots from Egypt for sale to the kings of the Hittites and Aram, while building his own force of twelve thousand horses and fourteen hundred chariots (10:26, 28–29). Women he imported, too, one might say—from the Moabites, Ammonites, Edomites, Phoenicians, and Hittites—for his harem of seven hundred wives and three hundred concubines (11:1–3). He was a master builder, famous for the Temple in Jerusalem; his elaborate palace complex boasted a separate dwelling for the daughter of Pharaoh, the most politically consequential of his wives (6:38–7:1, 8). His throne was made of ivory overlaid with the finest gold: "Nothing like it was ever made in any kingdom," and all his drinking vessels were of gold: "None were of silver; nobody valued silver much in the days of Solomon" (10:18–21). One can almost hear the chronicler's gasp of admiration.

Now, kings are regarded with a skeptical eye elsewhere in the Bible, and wealth is often suspect. The "Law of the King" in Deuteronomy 17:14–20, apparently formulated with Solomon in mind, stipulates that a king shall not "multiply" horses, wives, silver, and gold (listed, yes, in that order). The author of Kings admits that Solomon's love of foreign women led to idolatry and the dissolution of the kingdom (1 Kings 11:1, 4, 9–11). And in the Book of Ecclesiastes, the king contemplates his vast possessions—gold and silver, herds and flocks, houses, gardens, vineyards, orchards—with the weariness of the jaded connoisseur, and declares them all "vanity" (2:4–11).

But in the Song, King Solomon is a sign and a wonder. Whenever the poet alludes to queens and concubines, horses and chariots, the cedars of Lebanon, gold, ivory, and spices, the reader is imaginatively invited into

King Solomon's court. The geographical range of the Song suggests the extent of his empire, which stretched from the Red Sea to the Euphrates. Even the formulas of counting—threescore queens, fourscore concubines, a thousand pieces of silver, ten thousand men—owe something to the rhetoric of glorification in the Book of Kings. The Song lingers appreciatively over that world of opulence—that is, until the final lyrics, when wealth and possessions are weighed in the balance by the two lovers, and found wanting. The Shulamite scorns the wealthy fool who would try to buy love (8:7), and her lover grandly dismisses the king along with his vineyard, and his need to keep watch (8:11–12). Solomon in all his glory, as Jesus will later say, is eclipsed by the lilies of the field. In the Song, even that magnificent king is no match for the lovers, who feast in splendor.

A POEM about erotic love would seem out of place in Holy Scripture, particularly if one's point of reference is the antipathy to sexuality in the New Testament. But sex is no sin in the Old Testament. As a matter of fact, sexual attraction is counted as one of the wonders of the world in the Book of Proverbs:

> Three things I marvel at,
> four I cannot fathom:
> the way of an eagle in the sky,
> the way of a snake on a rock,
> the way of a ship in the heart of the sea,
> the way of a man with a woman.
> (Prov. 30:18–19)

The image in Genesis of man and wife "cleaving" to each other and becoming "one flesh," at once mythic and anatomically precise, sees that union as healing the primal wound of separation (Gen. 2:23–24). It is a husband's duty to provide food, clothing, and "conjugal rights" (*'onah*) to his wife (Exod. 21:10). And since fertility is a central concern—God's blessing over Adam and Eve is "Be fruitful and multiply" (Gen. 1:28)—sex within its ordained bounds is almost a sacred calling.

In images that recall the Song, the Book of Proverbs recommends erotic pleasure as a remedy against temptation, a way of keeping a good man out of trouble:

Drink water from your own cistern,
fresh water from your well. . . .

Let your fountain be blessed;
take delight in the wife of your youth,
a loving doe, a graceful gazelle.

Let her breasts fill you with pleasure,
be entranced always by her love.
(Prov. 5:15, 18–19)

And even the skeptical speaker of Ecclesiastes sees love as a God-given consolation for the dreariness of existence:

Go eat your bread with joy, then,
and drink your wine with a merry heart,
for God has already approved what you do.

May you always be clothed in white
and never lack oil to anoint your head.

Enjoy life with a woman you love
all the fleeting days that are granted you
under the sun,
all your fleeting days.

For this is your portion in life,
to repay your toil here under the sun.
(Eccles. 9:7–9)

But sex is sanctioned only in marriage; on this point the Old Testament laws are unequivocal. Outside the pale of marriage there are only crimes and punishments, catalogued in exhaustive detail. A young woman was assumed to be a virgin when she married; according to Deuteronomy, her parents had to produce the proof of her virginity (that is, the bloodstained garment) before the town elders in the event that her husband accused her. In the absence of such evidence, she could be stoned for "playing the whore in her father's house" (Deut. 22:13–21). This severe penalty is typical of the laws regulating sexuality—though, of course, the laws do not tell us how people actually behaved. And it is worth noting that sex between unmarried people, though hardly approved of, is not considered a flagrant transgression like incest and adultery (the technical term for such offenses is *gilluy 'arayot*, "uncovering someone's nakedness").[4] If a

[4]Rachel Biale, *Women and Jewish Law* (New York: Schocken Books, 1984), p. 175. This attitude was maintained by the rabbis; *see* pp. 191–2.

man forced a young woman to have sex with him, he was required to marry her, paying the bride-price of fifty shekels of silver to her father, and forbidden to divorce her (Deut. 22:28–29). At issue here is not premarital sex but property: an unmarried woman's sexuality was the property of her father, and a married woman's, of her husband.

The perils of sex are dramatized in the Book of Proverbs. In one passage, an adulterous woman goes after her poor victim in the city streets at night, kissing him openly and seducing him with honeyed words:

> I have spread my couch
> with dyed Egyptian linen,
> sprinkled my bed
> with myrrh, aloes, and cinnamon.
> Come, let us drink our fill of love,
> let us make love all night long!
> (Prov. 7:16–18)

This passage may remind us of the Song in its naming of fragrant spices and the association of wine and lovemaking, but while it makes plain the irresistible appeal of sex, it is intended, of course, as a stern warning.

In the prophetic books, the whore and adulteress are contemptuous metaphors for Israel. Hosea, Jeremiah, and Ezekiel conceive of the covenant between God and Israel as a marriage—or rather, when Israel goes astray, as a marriage on the rocks, with God as the wronged husband and Israel as the unfaithful wife—and their images for illicit sexuality bristle with revulsion.[5] There is an element of horror at female sexuality in Jeremiah's picture of Israel as a she-camel "snuffing the wind in her lust; who can restrain her when she is in heat?" (Jer. 2:23–24). Certainly, Ezekiel's talk of donkeys and stallions (23:20) makes the very notion of sex seem degrading.

The biblical narratives openly acknowledge the role of sexuality in human existence. Samson and Delilah, David and Bathsheba—tales like these have led sober citizens to declare the Bible unfit reading for children. Women behave with a surprising boldness in some of these stories. Tamar, dressed as a prostitute, tricks her father-in-law, Judah, into sleeping with her; Ruth anoints herself, puts on her best clothing and lies down at the feet of Boaz on the threshing floor at night (in one interpretation, she seduces him). But for all their sexual aggressiveness, Tamar

[5]Hosea 1–3, Jer. 2–3, Ezek. 16.

and Ruth are interested only in perpetuating the family line. They make themselves whores for the sake of heaven, one might say; they are not sexual beings but the handmaidens of history.

It is possible that the unconstrained relation between the young lovers in the Song is not so remote from daily life in ancient Israel as one might think. The biblical laws, after all, are prescriptive, and they do not necessarily reflect reality. Still, we must be as tentative in drawing inferences about social behavior from literature as we are from the legal codes. The Song is after all a work of the imagination, a work unique in its unabashed celebration of erotic love. Its theme is the wonder of a woman with a man—an unmarried woman, with no concern about perpetuating the family line and no motive but pleasure. In it, eros is its own reward. One might be tempted to call the Song subversive, were it not the least polemical of books. No wonder the pious exegetes of synagogue and church were so quick to marry off the young lovers.

THE LANGUAGE of the Song is at once voluptuous and reticent. "Let my lover come into his garden / and taste its delicious fruit" (4:16) is characteristic both in what it boldly asserts and in what it chooses to leave unexpressed. We can appreciate its restraint by comparing this verse with, say, the invitation of Inanna, the goddess of love and fertility, to Dumuzi in the sacred marriage rite of Sumer: "Plow my vulva, my sweetheart."[6] In the Song, sexuality is evoked primarily by metaphors such as the vineyard and garden, mountain of myrrh, hill of frankincense, a mound of wheat edged with lilies, the sweet fruit of the apricot tree. The Shulamite describes her lover as a shepherd pasturing among lilies (2:16, 6:2–3); he anticipates an erotic encounter by saying he will go to the mountain of myrrh (4:6). The use of metaphor that both reveals and conceals has the effect of enhancing the Song's eroticism, while the suggestive play of double entendre suffuses the whole landscape with eros.

In celebrating love and lovers, the Song proclaims the power of the imagination. The verb *damah* ("to be like") occurs with particular frequency; in one of its conjugations, *dimmah*, it means "to liken, to

[6]S. N. Kramer, trans., "Sumerian Sacred Marriage Texts," in *Ancient Near Eastern Texts Relating to the Old Testament*, ed. James B. Pritchard, 3rd ed. (Princeton: Princeton University Press, 1969), p. 643.

compare," but also "to conjure up a mental image, to imagine, to fantasize." The lover imagines the Shulamite as a mare (the verb here is *dimmitik̄*, 1:9) and a palm tree (*dametah*, 7:8); she imagines him as a gazelle or a stag (*domeh*, 2:9), and tells him to "be like" a gazelle or a stag (*demeh lek̄a*, 2:17, 8:14). In using these verbs, as Robert Alter has observed, the poet is "flaunting the effect of figurative comparison,"[7] deliberately calling attention to the workings of simile and metaphor, and by extension, the workings of the imagination. We have already noticed the role of fantasy in the Song. It is often hard to tell what is real and what imagined; for that reason, many readers have found the poem to be dreamlike, with a freedom of movement, a dizzying fluidity, that conveys the intoxication of the senses.

Similes and metaphors from nature alternate with images from art and architecture in the four formal set-pieces where the lovers single out for praise the parts of each other's bodies; these poems belong to a genre often referred to by the Arabic term *waṣf*. The images are not literally descriptive; what they convey is the delight of the lover in contemplating the beloved, finding in the body a reflected image of the world in its freshness and splendor.

There is a striking Egyptian example of the form almost a thousand years older than the Song, which may have been known in ancient Israel:

> One alone is [my] sister, having no peer:
>   more gracious than all other women.
> Behold her, like Sothis rising
>   at the beginning of a good year:
> shining, precious, white of skin,
>   lovely of eyes when gazing.
> Sweet her lips [when] speaking:
>   she has no excess of words.
> Long of neck, white of breast,
>   her hair true lapis lazuli.
> Her arms surpass gold,
>   her fingers are like lotuses. . . .
> Lovely of [walk] when she strides on the ground,
>   she has captured my heart in her embrace.[8]

[7]Robert Alter, *The Art of Biblical Poetry* (New York: Basic Books, 1985), p. 193.
[8]Michael V. Fox, *The Song of Songs and the Ancient Egyptian Love Songs* (Madison: University of Wisconsin Press, 1985), p. 52; from poem no. 31. Fox makes a good case for the possible transmission of Egyptian love poetry to ancient Israel.

This genre was to have a long history. It later became a favorite of the troubadour poets and the Elizabethan sonneteers, but Shakespeare effectively put an end to it with his satirical "My mistress' eyes are nothing like the sun."

If the first *waṣf* (4:1–7) seems fairly conventional in its itemized account of the young woman's body, each of the others is given an inventive twist. In 5:10–16, the Shulamite offers an impassioned description of her lover's uniqueness in response to the daughters of Jerusalem, who have asked what makes him so special, the framework of question and answer adding a note of dramatic urgency. In 6:4–10, the allusions to King Solomon's court, and the hyperbolic comparisons, invest the form with a mythic grandeur. Here the expected simile or metaphor about the eyes is replaced by an exclamation, "Your eyes! Turn them away / for they dazzle me" (6:5), and the final verse is couched as the extravagant tribute of Solomon's court:

> Every maiden calls her happy,
> queens praise her,
> and all the king's women:
>
> "Who is that rising like the morning star,
> clear as the moon,
> bright as the blazing sun,
> daunting as the stars in their courses!" (6:9–10)

Finally, in 7:2–7, the Shulamite is dancing as the audience cheers her on: "Again, again!" (7:1). This time the traditional order of praise, from the head down, is reversed: starting appropriately with her graceful dancing feet, the Shulamite's body, in intimate detail, is surveyed in her lover's gaze. Reading these four *waṣfs* together, we can appreciate both the homage paid to convention and the poet's virtuoso variations.

Though the Song is not a drama, as some critics have assumed, it is dramatic in effect, since many of the poems are either monologues spoken in the presence of an audience or dialogues between the lovers. In 1:15–17 and 2:1–3, where the lovers admire one another, part of the pleasure of the dialogue is in their quickness and verve as they outdo each other in praise. In 7:8–11 the dialogue is handled with great charm and imaginative freedom. The young man is confessing to the Shulamite how she once seemed to him inaccessible, a lofty palm tree:

> I said in my heart,
> Let me climb into that palm tree
> and take hold of its branches.

And oh, may your breasts be like clusters
of grapes on a vine, the scent
of your breath like apricots,
your mouth good wine—

when she interrupts him with a knowing endearment, completing his sentence:

That pleases my lover, rousing him
even from sleep.

I am my lover's,
he longs for me,
only for me.

That playful interruption beautifully captures the intertwining speech of lovers.

Though most of the Song is devoted to the lovers' words, the poet also lets us hear their inner voices. What the young man confesses in the passage just quoted are his secret fantasies: how he daydreamed, how he yearned from afar. We hear the lovers musing aloud about their intentions: "I must rise and go about the city, / . . . till I find / my only love" (3:2); "I will hurry to the mountain of myrrh, / the hill of frankincense" (4:6). The refrain "His left hand beneath my head, / his right arm / holding me close" (2:6, 8:3) is a moment of inwardness, a rapt meditation compounded of memory and desire. The Shulamite's emotions are the subject of 5:2–8, when, ardent and impatient, the young man comes to her door at night. She coyly pretends reluctance, though her heart is beating fast. As soon as he leaves, she is filled with regret and longing: "How I wanted him when he spoke!" With economy and precision, the poet evokes passion, coquetry, self-reproach, and yearning, letting us see the tension between the Shulamite's feelings and her words.

The lovers take turns seeking one another: he invites her or "goes down" to her (2:8–13, 5:2–6, 6:2, 6:11); she goes looking for him or invites him (3:1–4, 5:6–7, 7:12–14). They move from desire to anticipation to fulfillment and back to desire; sexual consummation, expressed in 5:1 and 6:12, is an episode in the poem, not its grand finale, and it doesn't appease their hunger for very long. A number of strategically placed refrains punctuate the Song:

I am in the fever of love. (2:5, 5:8)

His left hand beneath my head,
his right arm
holding me close. (2:6, 8:3)

Daughters of Jerusalem, swear to me. . . . (2:7, 3:5, 5:8, 8:4)

My beloved is mine and I am his. (2:16, 6:3; cf. 7:11)

Who is that rising from the desert! (3:6, 8:5; cf. 6:10)

The incremental repetition of refrains and motifs such as these, and the densely exfoliating metaphors, have the effect of binding the lyrics to one another, reinforcing the impression of artistic design.

The lovers' relations to each other and to the daughters of Jerusalem, the brothers, the mother, and the watchmen add up to a kind of "plot," like the narrative thread in a Schubert song cycle. There is a perceptible symmetry between the first and last chapters: in both we hear about Solomon (1:5, 8:11–12), the vineyard (1:6, 8:11–12), the brothers (1:6, 8:8), and the lovers' companions (1:3–4, 1:7, 8:13). The Shulamite's spirited response to her brothers in 8:10 resolves the tensions implied in 1:6, 8:8–9, and perhaps 2:15. The elements of a plot are available, and we can hardly help wanting to link them, though plot seems the least of our poet's concerns. The Song of Songs is a sequence of lyric poems, episodic in its structure—not a narrative, and not a drama. The so-called gaps and discontinuities in the text are problematic only for those who attempt to read it as one or the other.

The Song doesn't begin at the beginning, and it doesn't have a "proper" ending. It starts at a pitch of intensity that implies an already existing erotic relationship. And it doesn't conclude, as some might have wished, with the dramatic declaration of 8:5–7, scored for trumpets and high-sounding cymbals. Instead, it ends quietly, with the Shulamite's "Run away!" (Hebrew *beraḥ*, "flee") in 8:14:

> Hurry, my love! Run away,
> my gazelle, my wild stag
> on the hills of cinnamon.

This resonantly open ending reveals the poet's delicacy of touch. We know the lover will return, as he did after the Shulamite's almost identical words in 2:17:

> Run away, my love!
> Be like a gazelle, a wild stag
> on the jagged mountains.

Like a musical da capo, the parting in 8:14 inevitably implies another meeting. The lack of closure at the end of the poem has the effect of prolonging indefinitely the moment of youth and love, keeping it, in Keats's phrase, "forever warm."

THE SONG OF SONGS is a work of subtlety and sophistication, remarkable for its artistic control and elegant finish. Because of its consistency of characterization, themes, images, and poetic voice, it asks to be read as a unified sequence.[9] The Song is set in springtime, in the city of Jerusalem with its outlying vineyards and pastures. The two lovers are recognizably the same throughout, as are the daughters of Jerusalem, the mother, the brothers, and the watchmen. Eros is celebrated as the most powerful of human pleasures; other conceptions of love—as irrational and destructive, say, or spiritually improving—are not even contemplated.

It is of course conceivable that the Song was composed by a school of poets sharing certain values and recurring motifs, like the poets of courtly love. And one might imagine, too, that its unity and consistency were the work of a redactor who collected love poems of others, stringing them together with refrains and repetitions and multiple cross-references. But it is equally plausible, and rather more attractive, to assume that the Song was the work of a poet—one who, as so often in the Bible, would have found it perfectly natural to incorporate quotations and adaptations of material already in circulation. Indeed, if a redactor was responsible for shaping the poem as we now have it, then he or she was a literary artist of the highest caliber, and fully deserves to be called a poet.

Some scholars, pointing to the shifts of scene or image or address, have argued that the Song lacks cohesiveness and cannot be regarded as a unified work of art. There are those who see it as an anthology of love poems in a variety of genres—lyrics of yearning or fulfillment, poems in praise of the beloved, duets of mutual praise, etc. A more extreme view takes it to be a patchwork of epigrammatic poems, some of which merely "fill up space in one column of the scroll so that a new, longer poem can begin in a new column."[10] This approach bears the stamp of nineteenth-century biblical scholarship, which was typically concerned with breaking the text down into its constituent units. We have only to

[9]Among those who argue persuasively for this view are Roland E. Murphy, "The Unity of the Song of Songs," *Vetus Testamentum* 29 (1979): 436–43; and Fox, *Song of Songs*, pp. 202–26.

[10]Franz Landsberger, "Poetic Units Within the Song of Songs," *Journal of Biblical Literature* 73 (1954): 212.

compare the Song with such anthologies as the Psalter and the Book of Proverbs to see just how unified it is. The Song is more of a piece too than Ecclesiastes, which purports to be the work of a single author and encompasses a variety of material, from prosaic to gnomic to high poetic.

It makes no sense to judge lyric poetry by the standards of logical discourse, requiring a systematic progression from A to B to C and thence to a conclusion, with every link soldered firmly into place, as some exegetes do. None of the poems in the Bible would fit such a model. Even a short lyric like the Twenty-third Psalm brings together disparate elements: "He makes me lie down in green pastures" and "You spread a table for me in full view of my enemies," shifting abruptly from shepherd to host and from the third person to the second. Apparently the biblical poets had a more flexible notion of unity and structure than many scholars have recognized.

One source available to the poet may have been folk lyrics or secular love poems performed at banquets and festivals and transmitted orally for perhaps hundreds of years. Indeed, much of the poetry in the Bible originated in the oral tradition, and circulated in the mouths of the people long before it was written down.

Singing to the accompaniment of flute, timbrel, or lyre was as much a part of the good life in ancient Israel as drinking wine or anointing oneself with fine oils; we know this in part from the scathing denunciations of the prophets. Ezekiel, for one, hopeless about ever getting through to the rich and pampered, compares himself with bitter irony to "a singer of bawdy songs who has a sweet voice and plays skillfully."[11] One would like to know what was sung on festive occasions; perhaps something like 5:1 in our poem, which has been called a drinking song:

> Feast, friends, and drink
> till you are drunk with love!

And it may be that some version of 3:11 was sung at weddings before it was incorporated into the Song. But there is no way of knowing which lyrics would have circulated in this fashion, or to what extent they were modified by our poet.

The prominence of women in the Song, and the unusually sympathetic rendering of a woman's perspective, has led some readers to wonder

[11]Ezek. 33:32; cf. Amos 6:5–6, Isa. 5:11–12, 24:8–9.

whether the author might have been a woman. This question is being asked with increasing frequency about many of the anonymous works of antiquity, particularly those that reveal a sensitive understanding of women characters. For example, there has been much speculation (some of it rather irresponsible) about whether "J," one of the major prose documents of the Pentateuch, was written by a woman.[12] In the case of the Song, the question arises naturally, since women are associated to some extent with poetry and song in the Bible. Women traditionally sang songs of victory (1 Sam. 18:6–7; compare Exod. 15:20–21) and mourning (2 Chron. 35:25, Jer. 9:17–22), probably composing them as well. The rousing victory poem in Judges 5 was attributed to Deborah; though this may have come about because Deborah was a great political leader, the very fact of the attribution is of some significance. One would suppose that professional women singers (*šarot, mešorerot*) also sang love songs, particularly when they performed at banquets and festivals (2 Sam. 19:36, Eccles. 2:8, Ezra 2:65). Whether or not they composed love songs is anyone's guess. A poet would not have had to be literate. Most of the population was illiterate; it is only in the modern age that we associate literary composition with writing.

It is possible, then, that some of the individual lyrics of the Song were composed by women, or that a woman poet was the author of the final version. This is a hypothesis that will appeal to many readers today. Perhaps it would help to explain why the Song is so remarkably different in spirit from much of the Bible. But ultimately, it must be said, there is no way to determine the gender of an author on the basis of style or content. Any statement about the gender of our poet is necessarily conjectural—and as impossible to verify as whether the poet was young or old, from Jerusalem or the countryside, from the north or the south.

It was a common practice in antiquity to attribute works of literature to eminent figures from the past—the Torah to Moses, for example, and many of the Psalms to David. In this way the Song of Songs, the Book of Proverbs, and Ecclesiastes all came to be associated with

[12] Harold Bloom and David Rosenberg, *The Book of J* (New York: Grove Weidenfeld, 1990). See the review by Chana Bloch, "Shakespeare's Sister," in the *Iowa Review* 21 (1991): 66–77, and the other pieces in that issue's "Forum on *The Book of J*," pp. 11–86.

Solomon, who was known as a poet and a sage: according to the Book of Kings, he was the author of three thousand proverbs and a thousand and five songs (1 Kings 4:32). The stages of Solomon's literary career were worked out by Rabbi Jonathan, who deduced that the Song was an early effort: "When a man is young he composes songs; when he grows older he makes sententious remarks; and when he becomes an old man he speaks of the vanity of things."[13] The biblical view of Solomon as a poet, and son of a poet, which persisted until the nineteenth century, is captured in a stanza of English doggerel:

> King David and King Solomon lived very wicked lives,
> with half a hundred concubines and quite too many wives.
> But when old age came creeping on, they both were filled
> with qualms,
> so Solomon wrote the Proverbs, and David wrote the Psalms.

No one takes the attribution in 1:1 seriously today, though some scholars still date the Song early, linking the images of wealth and luxury, and the joyous spirit of the poem, to the Golden Age of Solomon, "the only really happy reign of an Israelite king"[14]—as if happiness were the exclusive property of the tenth century BCE. Like many great leaders, Solomon became a figure of legend, and the stories about him continued to flourish long after his time. In Ecclesiastes, probably a work of the third century BCE, he is presented as the type of the most fortunate man; in the Hellenistic age, Solomon with his riches and wisdom came to be regarded as a kind of Jewish counterpart to the Ptolemaic kings.[15] The Talmud, later, contains tales about Solomon's mother, his wedding day, his magnificent throne, and the like, all fanciful elaborations of the biblical text.[16] The Song uses extrabiblical mate-

[13]Maurice Simon, trans., "Canticles Rabbah," in vol. 9 of *Midrash Rabbah*, ed. H. Freedman and Maurice Simon (1930; reprint, London: Soncino Press, 1983) p. 17.

[14]M. H. Segal, "The Song of Songs," *Vetus Testamentum* 12 (1962): 483.

[15]Francis Landy, *Paradoxes of Paradise: Identity and Difference in the Song of Songs* (Sheffield: Almond Press, 1983), p. 29; Martin Hengel, *Judaism and Hellenism: Studies in their Encounter in Palestine during the Early Hellenistic Period*, trans. John Bowden (London: SCM Press, 1974), vol. 1, pp. 129–30. Hengel speculates about the fascination with Solomon in the Hellenistic age and later, citing the many writings attributed to him. Apart from the Book of Proverbs, Ecclesiastes, and the Song, these include the Psalms of Solomon, the Wisdom of Solomon, and the Testament of Solomon. Hengel suspects the intention was to demonstrate the antiquity and superiority of Jewish wisdom to that of Greece.

[16]Louis Ginzberg, *The Legends of the Jews* (Philadelphia: Jewish Publication Society, 1909–38), vol. 4, pp. 125–76; vol. 6, pp. 277–303; compare Matt. 6:29.

rial about Solomon and treats it as if it were familiarly known. In 3:11, for instance, Solomon's mother crowns him on his wedding day, yet neither the crowning nor the wedding appears in any of the biblical texts, suggesting that the poet was drawing on the folklore tradition. The references to Solomon, then, do not exclude a date of composition long after the Solomonic age.

The most reliable criterion for dating the Song is language. After the Babylonian Exile in the sixth century BCE, Hebrew gradually came to be replaced by Aramaic as the major language of communication in Palestine. Hence the Aramaic portions in the late Old Testament books of Ezra and Daniel, and the traces of Aramaic even in the Greek New Testament. Historically, the language of the Song represents a transitional stage between classical Biblical Hebrew and the Hebrew of the Mishnah, a collection of oral law edited around 200 CE, which likewise shows the imprint of Aramaic.

If a language changed at a constant rate, the date of the later biblical texts could be assessed with some accuracy by measuring their Aramaic content—a kind of linguistic carbon dating. Although this method is imprecise, it gives us a fairly reliable gauge of how far along Hebrew was in the process of change when the Song came to be written down. The following are examples of forms and expressions either patterned after or influenced by Aramaic:

'eyk̄ah in the locative sense, "where" (1:7)
šallamah "lest" (1:7), after the Aramaic *di le-mah*
'ad še- "before, until, while" (1:12), corresponding to the Aramaic *'ad di*
rahiṭenu "our rafters" (1:17) from the root *rhṭ*, as in *rehṭā* in Syriac (a language belonging to the Aramaic family)
berotim "cypresses" (1:17), as in the Syriac *berutā*, for the Hebrew *berošim*
miṭṭato še-li-šelomoh (literally "his bed that is to Solomon," 3:7); this syntax occurs only here in the Bible, but becomes standard in Mishnaic Hebrew
'aḥuzey ḥereb̄ "skilled in warfare" (3:8), after an Aramaic idiom
me'av referring to the surface of the belly (5:14), as in the Aramaic *me'ohi* (Dan. 2:31), rather than to the entrails, as in Hebrew

The frequency of Aramaisms, reflected not only in vocabulary but also in morphology, idiom, and syntax, clearly points to a late date.

Like the Mishnah, the Song contains many new Hebrew words that do not appear in earlier texts or that replace older words:

naṭar "to guard" (1:6, 8:11–12), used for the older *naṣar*
kotel "wall" (2:9) for *qir*
ḥarakkim "crevices" (2:9)
setav "winter, rainy season" (2:11)
pag "unripe fig" (2:13)
semadar "blossoms or blossoming of the grapevine" (2:13, 15, 7:13)
ṭannep̄ "to soil, dirty" (5:3)
qevuṣṣot "hair, bunches of hair" (5:11)
ginnah "garden" (6:11)
'omman "craftsman" (7:2) for *ḥaraš*
mezeg "mixed wine" (7:3)
sugah "surrounded by" (7:3)

More than any other text in the Old Testament, the Song appears to reflect the vernacular idiom; one scholar calls it "the first text in the Bible that makes spoken Hebrew fit for literature, including poetry."[17] Some examples:

še- becomes an all-purpose conjunction, largely replacing the relative *'ašer* ("who, which," etc., 1:7, 3:1–4, 3:11, 4:1–2, 6:5), *ki* ("that," 1:6, 5:8) and *ki* ("because," 5:2, 6:5), and forming compound conjunctions, *'ad še-* (1:12, 2:7, 2:17, 3:5, 8:4) and *kim'aṭše-* ("no sooner than," 3:4).

The masculine form replaces the feminine in the plurals of pronouns and verbs (2:7, 3:5, 4:2, 5:3, 6:6, 8:4).

There is a major change in the tense system: the perfect becomes the regular tense for the narrative past, replacing the classical *waw*-conversive.

Finally, there are words of Persian or Greek origin in the Song, *pardes* "orchard" (4:13), from which the English "paradise" is derived, and the enigmatic *'appiryon*, "pavilion, palace[?]"(3:9). All these factors taken

[17]Abba Bendavid, *Leshon Miqra u-Leshon Ḥak̄amim* (Biblical Hebrew and Mishnaic Hebrew) (Tel Aviv: Dvir, 1967), vol. 1, p. 74. The only exceptions to these innovative tendencies are the deliberately archaizing uses in 1:1 *'ašer li-šelomoh*, 3:11 *ṣe'eynah u-re'eynah*, 4:11 *tiṭṭop̄nah*, and 6:9 *va-ye'aššeruhah . . . va-yehalleluhah.*

together—the Aramaic influence, the similarity to Mishnaic Hebrew, the influence of the spoken idiom, the foreign loan-words—suggest that the Song was written down in post-Exilic times, most likely in the Hellenistic period, around the third century BCE.[18]

A Hellenistic date raises some intriguing questions about the relation of the Song to Greek literature and art. After Palestine came under the sway of Alexander in 332 BCE, Greek culture began to be widely diffused there. Greek was the language of administration and commerce, and was known to the upper classes. Thirty Hellenic cities were established, most of them along the Mediterranean coast or near the Sea of Galilee, and were settled by Greek officials, soldiers, and merchants. In a jumble of languages—Hebrew, Aramaic, Greek—a new culture began to evolve, an eclectic mélange of East and West. The precise extent of Greek influence in the early Hellenistic period is the subject of some debate, given the fragmentary nature of the evidence. According to one authority, the works of the Greek poets and philosophers were available in Palestine, and "the man who wished to acquire Greek learning could probably achieve his object to a certain degree in the Greek towns of the country."[19]

Scholars have long pointed out parallels between the Song and the pastoral idylls of Theocritus, court poet to Ptolemy Philadelphus at Alexandria in Egypt, who wrote in the first half of the third century BCE. Among the examples usually cited are the reference to a dark beauty, the comparison of a graceful woman to a horse, and the image of foxes raiding a vineyard,[20] but the affinities go beyond this handful of slender correspondences, which may well have come from the common stock of Mediterranean culture. The Song resembles Greek pastoral poetry in its central conceit—the lovers as shepherds in a setting of idyllic nature—and its celebration of innocent pleasures in highly sophisti-

[18]See H. L. Ginsberg, "Introduction to the Song of Songs," in *The Five Megilloth and Jonah* (Philadelphia: Jewish Publication Society, 1969), p. 3; Fox, *Song of Songs*, pp. 186–90.

[19]Victor Tcherikover, *Hellenistic Civilization and the Jews*, trans. S. Applebaum (Philadelphia: Jewish Publication Society, 1959), p. 114.

[20]For Song 1:5, compare Idyll X.26-27: "Charming Bombyca, all call thee . . . sun-scorched, and I alone, honey-hued"; for Song 1:9, compare Idyll XVIII.30-31: "As some . . . Thracian steed [adorns] the chariot it draws, so rosy Helen adorns Lacedaemon"; for Song 2:15, compare Idyll I.48-49: "one [fox] goes to and fro among the vine-rows plundering the ripe grapes," and Idyll V.112-13: "the foxes with their bushy tails that come ever at evening and plunder Micon's vineyard." These translations are from A. S. F. Gow, ed. and trans., *Theocritus* (Cambridge: Cambridge University Press, 1950), vol. I.

cated art. As in pastoral, the lovers exist in a world of leisure and delight, untroubled by the wind and the rain of a real shepherd's life, a world conjured up by the poet's idealizing imagination. The Song is informed by an entirely new sensibility, unique in the Bible. Given the temper of the times, it is possible that the poet of the Song had some knowledge of the themes of Greek poetry, just as the author of Ecclesiastes seems to have been aware, in a general way, of questions debated by the Stoic and Epicurean philosophers.

One can more confidently assume borrowing in areas that were commonly accessible, such as the visual arts. We know that Attic pottery decorated with Dionysiac scenes has been found at a number of archaeological sites. And what would our poet have seen on a visit to the coast cities of Ptolemais (Acre), Joppa (Jaffa), Ascalon (Ashkelon), and Gaza, or to Marissa, Scythopolis (Beth She'an), or Gadara, with their buildings and shrines, gymnasia and theaters? A statue of a nude Aphrodite was found a few decades ago in the area of Mount Carmel.[21] The nude Aphrodite was "an astonishing novelty" in Hellenistic art.[22] While archaic and classical Greek sculpture explored the beauty of the unclothed male body, the female form was draped, with very few exceptions. It is only with the work of Praxiteles—in particular, his much-imitated Aphrodite of Knidos (ca. 350 BCE)—that the female nude comes into its own as a subject of Greek sculpture. There is nothing comparable in Jewish art, given the Second Commandment (Exod. 20:4), which effectively ruled out the physical representation of the human body. One can imagine what it would have meant for a Hebrew poet to see for the first time, in a public setting, the sculpture of a nude body—and a woman's body, at that. The lyrics in the Song praising the lovers' physical beauty may well owe something to the encounter with Greek art. As in the case of Greek pastoral poetry, the argument does not rest on exact correspondences, and here again we are, of course, in the realm of conjecture.

[21] Elias J. Bickerman, "The Historical Foundations of Postbiblical Judaism," in *The Jews: Their History, Culture, and Religion*, ed. Louis Finkelstein, 3rd ed. (New York: Jewish Publication Society, 1960), vol. 1, p. 93. See the photograph of a nude Aphrodite found at Mount Carmel, dated fourth to third century BCE, in Cecil Roth's article "Art: Antiquity to 1800," in *Encyclopedia Judaica*, 1971 ed., vol. 3, col. 510. The evidence is unfortunately limited because the Maccabees in their iconoclastic zeal destroyed pagan sites, and the Romans carted away much of artistic value; moreover, many sites are yet to be excavated.

[22] R. R. R. Smith, *Hellenistic Sculpture* (London: Thames and Hudson, 1991), p. 79.

A Hellenistic date for the Song is a hypothesis, and it is still controversial. In ancient history, there are no certainties, and more questions than answers. But it is clear that much of the Song is anomalous in the biblical context, and calls for explanation: the concern with the private life as opposed to the public and communal, the frank interest in sexual experience, the idealization of pastoral innocence, the aesthetic appreciation of the human body. All of this would suggest that the Song was composed in a Hellenized atmosphere.

READERS TODAY often ask, with some puzzlement, how the Song ever managed to "get into" the canon of Holy Scripture. It is, after all, an emphatically secular book: the name of God is never once mentioned. Nor is there any reference to Israel's history, or to the national themes that figure so importantly in the rest of the Bible. The erotic joy of the two lovers, the human body presented as an object of admiration, the beauty of nature appreciated for its own sake—all seem out of place in the Bible.

We tend to think of Holy Scripture as a single volume, soberly bound in black, with each verse numbered, and with cross-references up and down the margins. But in ancient Israel, "the Bible" was a collection of scrolls written on papyrus and stored in a room or cave. The Song was first written down in an age when literacy was not yet widespread and copying by hand laborious; the perishable papyrus needed to be carefully stored if it was to survive in the harsh Near Eastern climate. Under such conditions, no work of literature could last very long unless it had acquired a devoted following, an audience that would wish to preserve it.

Most people assume that the criteria for canonization were strictly religious, and that they reflected an orthodox point of view. In fact the Hebrew Bible, an anthology of works composed over the period of nearly a millennium, is a very heterogeneous collection. The word "Bible" comes from the Greek *ta biblia*, meaning "the books," appropriately a plural noun. Not every book meets the test of piety: Job and Ecclesiastes, for example, challenge the fundamental beliefs that human beings are the crown of Creation, or that evil is punished and virtue rewarded, yet they found a place in the canon. Some books may have been preserved for reasons of national pride, or because they were numbered among the literary treasures of the Jewish people—the Song, in this instance, because it is one of the most beloved works of ancient Hebrew literature.

There is barely any evidence about how the canon of the Hebrew Bible was formed: who made the decisions, what criteria were employed, and when the canon was closed. Scattered bits of information in the Apocrypha, Pseudepigrapha, Talmud, and Midrash, and in writers like Josephus, are cryptic and ambiguous. The Song is found in the third section of the Hebrew Bible—the *Ketubim* ("Writings" or Hagiographa), a miscellany including Wisdom literature, poetry, and history—that was granted canonical status centuries after the Torah and the Prophets. The scholarly consensus is that the canon was probably closed sometime before the end of the first century CE; many scholars believe that at the Council of Jamnia in 90 CE the rabbis simply gave their sanction to writings that had already been accepted as authoritative.

There was apparently some controversy about admitting the Song to the canon, as there was about Ecclesiastes and the Book of Esther. Rabbi Akiva (d. 135 CE), who read the Song allegorically, insisted that there had never been any doubt about its canonical status:

> God forbid! No man in Israel ever disputed the status of the Song of Songs . . . for the whole world is not worth the day on which the Song of Songs was given to Israel; for all the writings are holy, but the Song of Songs is the holiest of the holy.[23]

From this denial of denials, we may conclude that there were still reservations about the Song even in his day.

It may be that the attribution to Solomon in the title (1:1) was a factor for admission to the canon. A book believed to have been written by one of Israel's admired kings, and preserved for a thousand years, would certainly have been difficult to exclude. (That this attribution was added by an editor, possibly for the express purpose of preserving the book, was recognized only much later.) It is generally assumed that the allegorical interpretation of the Song, which may have gained currency around this time, played a role as well.

On the other hand, it is entirely possible that the allegorical interpre-

[23]Mishnah, Yadayim 3:5, as translated in Sid Z. Leiman, *The Canonization of Hebrew Scripture: The Talmudic and Midrashic Evidence*, 2nd ed. (New Haven: Transactions of the Connecticut Academy of Arts and Sciences, 1991), p. 121.

tation and the final imprimatur of the rabbis came after the Song had already attracted a popular following. We know that secular or even pagan customs of holidays like Passover or Christmas were often sacralized by the religious authorities because they were widely established in popular practice. It is not hard to imagine a similar process at work in the official reception of the Song, bestowing upon this most secular of books an aura of sanctity. At all events, by virtue of its place in the canon, the Song demanded interpretation. The Jewish and Christian exegetes, an imaginative and industrious lot, had their work cut out for them.

FOR A BOOK of only eight chapters, the Song has elicited a prodigious volume of commentary. There is hardly a line of the Song that does not present some difficulty, and no other book of the Bible has called forth such wildly divergent interpretations.[24] The difficulties arise in part from the compactness and concentration of the poetic form. While the narrative prose of the Bible is fairly straightforward and accessible, biblical poetry is compressed and elliptical, sometimes to the point of unintelligibility. The language, too, is very often obscure. The Song has an unusually high proportion of *hapax legomena* (words occurring only once), as well as rare words and constructions. A hapax is almost as frustrating for the interpreter as a lacuna: even where the context provides some clues, it is difficult to establish the precise meaning of such a word. Verses like "King Solomon built an *'appiryon*" (3:9) or "your *šelaḥim* are an orchard" (4:13) or "a king is caught in the *rehaṭim*" (7:6) must finally remain a riddle.

Actually, the Song itself is a kind of hapax, for it is the only example of secular love poetry from ancient Israel that has survived. Other love poems must have been composed in biblical times, including poems about courtship, marriage, or unrequited love, but if they were written down at all, they have since vanished. There is something to be learned

[24]For a more detailed summary of the history of exegesis, see H. H. Rowley, "The Interpretation of the Song of Songs," in his *The Servant of the Lord and Other Essays on the Old Testament* (Oxford: Basil Blackwell, 1965), pp. 197–245; Marvin H. Pope, *Song of Songs*, vol. 7c of *The Anchor Bible* (Garden City, N.Y.: Doubleday, 1977), pp. 89–229; and Roland E. Murphy, *The Song of Songs* (Minneapolis: Fortress Press, 1990), pp. 11–41.

by comparing the Song with poems from ancient Egypt or Hellenistic Greece, but because it is one of a kind, the Song is in many respects an enigma.

Early audiences would have had no trouble understanding the Song in its literal sense; even in rabbinic times there were those who still understood it in this way. Rabbi Akiva warned, "Whoever warbles the Song of Songs at banqueting houses, treating it like an ordinary song, has no portion in the World to Come,"[25] the emphatic prohibition making it perfectly clear just what people were doing, and where. Rabbi Simeon ben Gamaliel (late first century CE) recounted that twice a year, on the fifteenth of Av and the Day of Atonement, the young women of Jerusalem would dress in white and go out to dance in the vineyards, calling out to prospective husbands, "Young man, lift up your eyes and see what you would choose for yourself," and reciting verses from the Book of Proverbs and the Song of Songs.[26] These rabbinic passages are the earliest testimony we have about the popular understanding of the Song. For the young men in the tavern, or the young women in the vineyard, the Song needed no interpretation, whatever the theologians were saying.

But the theologians prevailed: for twenty centuries, the Song was almost universally read as a religious or historical allegory. The allegorical interpretation found its first great champion in Rabbi Akiva, who taught that the Song was about the love of God and the people of Israel, an interpretation elaborated in various ways by Jewish commentators such as Rashi (d. 1105) and Ibn Ezra (d. 1168). The Church Fathers, following Origen (d. 254), applied this reading to the relations between Christ and his Bride the Church, or Christ and the soul of the believer. For the rabbis and Church Fathers the "spiritual" meaning is inherent in the text; to read it as "carnal" is to miss its deeper truth. They found support in the Old Testament metaphor of God's marriage to Israel and the New Testament image of Christ as a Bridegroom[27]—though nothing in the Song itself calls for such an interpretation.

The rabbis and the Church Fathers were committed to an allegorical interpretation, moreover, because in their world the very fact of sexuality had become problematic. The rabbis associated the *yeṣer ha-ra‘* ("evil impulse") primarily with sexuality; on the other hand, they never saw

[25]Tosefta, Sanhedrin 12:10, as quoted in Fox, *Song of Songs*, p. 249.
[26]Mishnah, Ta‘anith 4:8, as quoted in Fox, *Song of Songs*, p. 229.
[27]Isa. 54:5, Jer. 2:2, Hosea 2:14–20; Matt. 9:15, 25:1–13, John 3:29.

celibacy as an ideal, but instead advocated marriage and "the sober duty of procreation."[28] The Church Fathers were rather more extreme: Origen took Christ literally—not allegorically, alas!—and made himself a eunuch for the kingdom of heaven's sake; Jerome (d. 420) believed that a man who too ardently desires his own wife is an adulterer; Augustine (d. 430) wistfully imagined procreation in Eden, when the body obeyed the will without the vexation of lust. These men genuinely believed that in reading the text allegorically they were serving a higher purpose. They sought to spiritualize the Song, to purge its mortal grossness, the way some Greek philosophers interpreted away the carnality of the Homeric gods, or Philo converted the legends of Genesis into a series of philosophical and moral truths. This kind of exegesis requires considerable ingenuity and linguistic acrobatics, and some of its more extravagant "findings" now seem very curious: the Shulamite's two breasts as Moses and Aaron, or the Old and New testaments; her navel as the Great Sanhedrin or the order of holy preachers.

Allegories that reconstructed the intimate passion of the lovers as political or religious history now seem particularly misconceived. The Targum, a seventh-century paraphrase in Aramaic, saw in the Song an account of God's relations with Israel from the Exodus till the coming of the Messiah. Luther read it as Solomon's thanksgiving to God for his divinely ordained and peaceful kingdom; one twentieth-century exegete read it as an Essene manifesto, with the Pharisees playing the role of watchmen. And as recently as 1992 a Jesuit theologian wrote a commentary arguing that the Song is "a text in code" about "the restoration of the Davidic monarchy in Judah after the exile." A major discovery of his is a "hitherto unsuspected" meaning of the word "love." Commentators have invariably understood this word to refer to the affection between the lovers, a reading he finds "reductionist" and "sentimental." On the basis of his study of the treaty literature of the ancient Near East, he concludes that "love" is a technical term for the sociopolitical alliance between the house of David and the Jewish community.[29] One cannot help thinking of those learned, old, respectable scholars in Yeats's poem who "shuffle" and "cough in ink" as they annotate the lines of the young Catullus.

[28]David Biale, *Eros and the Jews: From Biblical Israel to Contemporary America* (New York: Basic Books, 1992), pp. 40, 43–44.

[29]Luis Stadelmann, *Love and Politics: A New Commentary on the Song of Songs* (New York: Paulist Press, 1992), pp. 2, 16, 23.

In the abundance and generosity of the Song, a lily is a lily is a woman's body is a man's lips is a field of desire. The allegorists, intent on delivering a spiritual equivalent for every last physical detail, read the Song as if they were decoding a cryptogram. From their perspective, of course, they were not imposing an arbitrary reading but searching out the hidden soul of the text. The allegorical interpretation now seems to us constrained and often absurd, but it may well have played a vital role in safeguarding the text. When we remember how many great works of antiquity have been lost—the poems of Sappho, for example, have come down to us only in fragments—we must be grateful for the protective wrap of allegory, if indeed it helped to preserve the Song intact.

The Song fared better at the hands of the mystics, Jewish and Christian, who honored its literal meaning as symbolic of the human longing for union with God. The *Zohar* (a mystical commentary on the Pentateuch written in the late thirteenth century) speculated about intercourse between the male and female aspects of God, believing that this could actually be influenced by the way in which human sexual relations were conducted; for this exalted purpose, the Cabbalists were encouraged to have intercourse with their wives on Sabbath eve.[30] Christian mystics like Bernard of Clairvaux in the twelfth century, or St. Teresa of Avila and the poet St. John of the Cross in the sixteenth, contemplating the love of God and the soul, found in the Song a source and inspiration for their ecstatic spirituality. St. Bernard, who wrote eighty-six sermons on the first two chapters of the Song, set the tone: "O strong and burning love, O love urgent and impetuous, which does not allow me to think of anything but you. . . . You laugh at all considerations of fitness, reason, modesty and prudence, and tread them underfoot."[31] The mystics read the Song allegorically, to be sure, but they remained true to its intensity and passion, its emotional power.

All along, there were those who favored a literal interpretation, though they had to pay dearly for their views. Theodore, Bishop of Mopsuestia (d. 429), who read the Song as a poem by Solomon in defense of his marriage to Pharaoh's daughter, was condemned in his own day, and again after his death by the Second Council of Constantinople in 553—sufficient deterrent for any commentator with

[30]Gershom Scholem, *Major Trends in Jewish Mysticism* (1941; 3d rev. ed., New York: Schocken Books, 1961), pp. 225–35; Biale, *Eros and the Jews*, pp. 109–13.

[31]"Sermon 79," in *Bernard of Clairvaux: On the Song of Songs*, trans. Irene Edmonds, Cistercian Fathers Series, no. 40 (Kalamazoo, Mich.: Cistercian Publications, 1980), p. 137.

like inclinations. Among the Protestant Reformers, the humanist and Bible translator Sebastian Castellio considered the Song a "lascivious and obscene poem in which Solomon described his indecent amours";[32] Castellio thought it had no spiritual value and should be excluded from the canon. For this and other offenses, he was forced to leave Geneva.

As the allegorical approach lost ground at the end of the eighteenth century, Protestant exegetes began to expound the literal sense, while attempting in one way or another to defend the Song against charges of indecency. In the Victorian era, some commentators who supported the popular "dramatic theory" spun out of the poem a scenario with three principal characters: King Solomon, a beautiful country maiden, and her shepherd-lover. The King carries the maiden off to Jerusalem, and tries to convince her to exchange her humble station for a life at court, but the Shulamite, a paragon of virtue and devotion, steadfastly resists his blandishments and remains true to her rustic swain. This soap opera is embellished with a complicated plot line and a moral purpose, neither of which has any foundation in the text. One famous scholar of Semitics, the author of an influential introduction to the Old Testament, defended this interpretation—"the triumph of plighted love over the seductions of worldly magnificence"—as having "real ethical value," lending the Song "a purpose and an aim," thereby saving it from the reproach of being "purely sensuous."[33] So much for Victorian sermonizing. But even in our day there are exegetes who take an apologetic stance. Although the Song is no longer seen as the "erotic effluvia of the unchaste Oriental mind which calls a spade a spade,"[34] there are still commentators who prefer to think of the lovers as a married couple, or who declare their love unconsummated.

A new theory was advanced at the turn of the century, based on research by the Prussian consul in Damascus, who saw the Song as a collection of poems like those sung at peasant weddings in Syria. In festivities lasting for seven days, the bride and bridegroom were crowned as king and queen, and their beauty proclaimed in formal songs

[32]According to Calvin's account, quoted in Roland H. Bainton, "The Bible in the Reformation," in *The Cambridge History of the Bible: The West from the Reformation to the Present Day*, ed. S. L. Greenslade (Cambridge: Cambridge University Press, 1963), pp. 8–9.

[33]S. R. Driver, *An Introduction to the Literature of the Old Testament* (1913; reprint; Cleveland: Meridian, 1956), p. 445.

[34]Max L. Margolis, "How the Song of Songs Entered the Canon," in *The Song of Songs: A Symposium*, ed. Wilfred H. Schoff (Philadelphia: Commercial Museum, 1924), p. 9. Margolis is characterizing the views of his contemporaries in 1924.

of praise; war songs were sung, and the bride performed a sword dance. But the "wedding-week theory" doesn't really fit the details of the Song: though the young man is addressed as "king," the woman is never called a "queen"; the dance in 7:1 is not a sword dance, and apart from 3:11, the poem has nothing to do with a wedding ceremony. Still, it is conceivable that popular customs such as those in Syria may have had their analogue in ancient Israel, and may shed light on the composition of some of the Song's lyrics. And this theory at least recognized the love of ordinary mortals as the subject of the Song.

More recently, scholars have associated the Song with Near Eastern fertility rites that were celebrated with music and ecstatic poetry in Sumer from the third millennium BCE, and later adopted by the Akkadians, the Canaanites, and, some believe, the ancient Hebrews. Each spring the king and a priestess, representing Dumuzi and Inanna (Tammuz and Ishtar), would participate in this "sacred marriage rite" for the purpose of restoring life to nature.[35] Some of the images and motifs in the ancient Mesopotamian poems, detached from their original ritual context, may indeed have left their traces on the Song; an example of such an image is "Your right hand you have placed on my vulva, / Your left stroked my head."[36] But fertility, the central concern of the cultic rite, is of no concern in the Song. And since the prophets emphatically denounced the fertility rites of Israel's neighbors, it is unlikely that the Song would have found its way into the canon if it had anything to do with the copulation of the gods; human kisses were problem enough for the rabbis.

The commentaries on the Song are, as Polonius might have said, the best in the world, whether literal, philosophical, ecclesiastical, allegorical-historical, comical-allegorical, or tragicomical-mystical-eschatological. They define the subject of the Song variously as the love of God and Israel, Christ and the Church, or Christ and the believer's soul; the chaste love of the Virgin Mary; the marriage of Solomon and Pharaoh's daughter, or of the active and the passive intellect; the discourse of Solomon with Wisdom; the trials of the people of Israel; or the history

[35]The clearest explanation may be found in Samuel Noah Kramer, *The Sacred Marriage Rite: Aspects of Faith, Myth, and Ritual in Ancient Sumer* (Bloomington: Indiana University Press, 1969), pp. 49–106.

[36]Ibid., p. 105. See also the Mesopotamian clay plaque of lovers embracing in a similar posture in Diane Wolkstein and Samuel Noah Kramer, *Inanna, Queen of Heaven and Earth: Her Stories and Hymns from Sumer* (New York: Harper and Row, 1983), pp. 43, 187.

of the Church—and that's only a partial list. Commentators have praised the Song for teaching chastity, fidelity, and virtue, or denounced it as lewd and injurious to morals. Of course, every reading of the Song necessarily bears the imprint of the interpreter's time, personal outlook, and taste. But whatever its ideological bias, this voluminous scholarship has advanced the understanding of the text, and no student of the Song can afford to ignore it.

In some respects, the Song seems very accessible to readers now, more so than it has been for some two thousand years. The Shulamite, with her veil off, is a figure all of us recognize, and we find the frankness about erotic love more natural than did earlier audiences. In our day it is the innocence of the Song, its delicacy, that has the power to surprise. Perhaps that very innocence is one source of the poem's continuing attractiveness. To read the Song is to recover, through the power of art, a freshness of spirit that is now all but lost to us. The Eden story preserves a memory of wholeness and abundance from the beginning of time; the prophets look forward to a peaceable kingdom at the End of Days. The Song of Songs locates that kingdom in human love, in the habitable present, and for the space of our attention, allows us to enter it.

About the Translation

THE TRANSLATION presented here follows the Masoretic (or established) Text of the Leningrad Codex, the oldest extant manuscript of the entire Hebrew Bible (early eleventh century CE), which is reproduced in the standard editions of the *Biblia Hebraica*. We have taken into account variant readings in the major translations of antiquity—the Greek Septuagint, the Syriac Peshitta, and the Latin Vulgate—which occasionally reflect manuscript traditions differing from the Masoretic Text. Since the Masoretic Text of the Song is very reliable, we have found it necessary to emend only one verse, 6:12.

Like most contemporary translations, we print the Song as poetry (the King James Version prints it as prose). In dividing the Song into separate lyrics, we have followed the internal logic of the text as we see it, taking note of changes of speaker or scene; the grapevine ornament marks the beginning of each new lyric. We sometimes differ from other translators in determining where one poem ends and another begins. For example, we separate 3:6 from 3:7–11 because, contrary to what is generally assumed, 3:6 is not a question, and 3:7 not an answer. Line breaks and stanza divisions reflect our understanding of the poem and our judgments about the demands of English verse. The Hebrew and English are presented on facing pages, the Hebrew in lines of verse corresponding to the English, along with chapter and verse numbers, as a help to the reader who wishes to compare our translation with the original or with other translations. The Hebrew includes the traditional cantillation marks.

For the sake of clarity, four typefaces are used in this translation to indicate the different speakers: roman for the young man, and italics for the young woman; boldface roman for the brothers, and boldface italics for the daughters of Jerusalem. Although there are no formal indications in the Hebrew text assigning the verses to different speakers such as one finds in many translations ("The Shulamite speaks," "The shepherd-lover replies"), the text itself often supplies clues about who is speaking. For example, the participants in a dialogue are usually identifiable because Hebrew distinguishes gender formally in the second person: *hinnak̄ yap̄ah* (feminine) versus *hinnek̄a yap̄eh* (masculine), both of which mean "You are beautiful" (1:15–16). In some cases the identification of the speaker depends on one's interpretation of the context. Exegetes and translators therefore differ widely in assigning verses such as 2:15, 3:6, 3:7–11, 5:1b ("Feast, friends"), 6:11–12, 7:10b ("That pleases my lover") and 8:5a ("Who is that"). The reader is invited to consult the Commentary for our rationale in identifying the speakers of these verses.

Our highest priority has been fidelity to the spirit of the Hebrew text; for that reason our translation is by no means a free re-imagining of the poem. Every line in the English is based on scrupulous research, explained in detail in the Commentary. At the same time, as one would expect in a poetic translation, we have chosen to translate freely when a word-for-word rendition would have been awkward, pedantic, or untrue to the spirit of the Song. In such cases, the reader will find the literal sense recorded in the Commentary. On a few occasions we have adopted a felicitous phrasing that we admired in the King James Version, the Jewish Publication Society Bible, the New English Bible, or the translations of T. Carmi, Marcia Falk, Peter Jay, and Diane Wolkstein; such borrowings are noted in the Commentary. More frequently, however, we will be found to differ, sometimes substantially, from the commonly accepted readings.

The Song is one of the most enigmatic books in the Bible. Line by line and word by word, it is far more obscure and problematic than a reader of English might suppose, in part because it contains a higher proportion of rare locutions—the technical term is *hapax legomena*—than any other book of the Bible. A few examples, explained at greater length in the Commentary, will suggest how we went about deciphering the text.

In resolving interpretive cruxes, our practice has been to look first to the internal evidence of the Song itself. Since the Song is consistent in its language and imagery, words or expressions or grammatical constructions in one chapter often help to interpret difficulties in another. For example, the notion of "spreading" implied in *rep̄idato* (3:10) elucidates the rare verb *rapped*, which we understand as "to make or spread a bed" (2:5). Similarly, the notion of height implied in *dagul* "towering" (5:10) suggests a possible meaning for *nidgalot*, literally "the elevated ones" (6:4,10), which we interpret as "stars."

As a second step, we turned to other books of the Bible for help. A crucial instance is the word *dodim*, a comprehensive term for lovemaking, including kisses and caresses as well as intercourse. This meaning could not be determined on the basis of the Song alone. However, the word occurs three other times in the Bible, in each case referring to sexual love. In Proverbs 7:18 an adulterous woman invites a young man: "Come, let us drink our fill of *dodim* [*nirveh dodim*], let us make love all night long, for my husband is not at home." This sense of the word is found also in Ezekiel 16:7–8, "Your breasts were well-formed. . . . I saw that you had reached the age of lovemaking [*'et dodim*]," and 23:17, "They came to her into the bed of love [*miškab̄ dodim*] and defiled her with their lust." Given these uses of *dodim*, we can be quite certain that the word also refers to sexual love in the Song—something a reader would not know from most translations, which render it simply as "love."

An example that has a significant bearing on our view of the Shulamite is the word *ṣammah*, which occurs three times in the Song (4:1,3; 6:7); this has been translated either as "hair" or "veil." Some medieval Jewish commentators understood the word as "hair" (the King James Version, accordingly, has "locks"), but the reading "veil," which appeared as early as the Septuagint, made its way into most modern versions. Again, the meaning of *ṣammah* cannot be established on the basis of its occurrences in the Song alone. But the word is found once more in the Bible, in a passage of Isaiah which proves to be decisive. There, in a series of sarcastic imperatives, the prophet tells the Virgin Daughter of Babylon that she will have to bare parts of her body in public, exposing herself to shame:

> Take the millstones, and grind meal:
> uncover thy locks [*galli ṣammatek̄*];
> make bare the leg, uncover the thigh [*galli šok*], . . .
> Thy nakedness shall be uncovered,
> yea, thy shame shall be seen.
>
> (Isa. 47:2–3, King James Version)

In this passage, "thigh" and *ṣammah* are both governed by the same verb, *galli* ("lay bare," not "remove"). *Galli šoq* means "lay bare [your] thigh" (obviously not "remove your thigh"!), and therefore *galli ṣammatek̄* can only mean "lay bare your *ṣammah*." This verse in Isaiah clearly tilts the scales in favor of the meaning "hair." One can understand why "veil" was adopted by translators in earlier centuries: a Shulamite who hides her seductive charms with a veil, as befits a chaste maiden of Israel, best served the apologetic approach to the Song—what may be called the "pious bias" in biblical exegesis.[1] It is surprising, however, that the Shulamite still remains veiled in most contemporary versions of the Song, which are not governed by that bias. But as so often in the history of translation, a misreading, once established, tends to be perpetuated in version after version.

Only after carefully weighing the internal biblical evidence did we consider that of the surrounding cultures. For example, the straightforward Hebrew meaning of *diglo 'alay 'ahab̄ah* in 2:4 is "his flag over me is love." We consider this an exuberant metaphoric expression of the Shulamite's delight in the young man's love. There is no need to resort to Akkadian *diglu* "glance, intent," from *dagalu* "to look," and to explain this as "his intent towards me is love," as some scholars have done. It isn't likely that biblical Hebrew would have borrowed such a basic verb as "to look," for which it has its own words (*ra'ah, hibbiṭ*). Finding a verbal root in a cognate language is not in itself a solution to a problem in the text; the field of Semitic languages is filled with roots, not every one worth digging up. To our thinking, the traditional Jewish principle of exegesis from within the biblical corpus (*nidrešet torah mi-tok̄ 'aṣmah*) is often methodologically more sound than the hasty resort to extrabiblical sources.

Readers tend to associate interpretive difficulties primarily with obscure words, but much of the meaning of a text is encoded in the inflections of a language: the moods and tenses of verbs, prefixes and suffixes, definite or indefinite articles, prepositions, and plural forms. Mistranslations occur when their specific functions are overlooked or edited out in unjustified emendations. It is best to proceed from the assumption that every such nuance is motivated and meaningful. For example, the tense of the verbs in 5:1 is crucial to the sense of the passage: "I have come [*ba'ti*] into my garden, I have gathered [*'ariti*] my myrrh, I have eaten [*'ak̄alti*], I have drunk [*šatiti*]." The perfect tense here implies a completed action. Translations that resort to a noncommital present tense ("I come, I gather, I eat, I drink"), or an infinitive construction ("I have come . . . to eat"), downplay the sexual implications of the image, if not by design then at least in effect.

There is no reason to ignore or explain away the possessive suffix of *susati* in 1:9, as exegetes have done for centuries. Although a straight-

[1] For another example of the "pious bias" in Bible exegesis, see Ariel Bloch, "Questioning God's Omnipotence in the Bible: A Linguistic Case Study," in *Semitic Studies in Honor of Wolf Leslau*, ed. Alan S. Kaye (Wiesbaden: Otto Harrassowitz, 1991), vol. 1, pp. 174–88.

forward reading of *susati* yields "my mare," the word has usually been translated with the indefinite article ("a mare"), and sometimes even as a collective noun ("my cavalry"). Neither reading is tenable on linguistic grounds. It may be that the erotic connotations of the image prompted the pious translators and exegetes to avoid the possessive suffix—or so at least it seems, since they certainly had no problem translating *yonati* in 2:14, which has the same syntax, as "my dove." Another reading that ought to be taken at face value is the plural *bateynu* ("our houses," 1:17); there is no need to "correct" it to "our house," as the King James and other versions have done. We read this as a metaphorical expression for the places in the countryside where the lovers meet to make love, and we translate, "Wherever we lie / Our bed is green." Similarly, *har'ini 'et mar'ayik̄* (literally "let me see your sights," 2:14) is usually rendered "let me see your face." We believe the plural form is intended, and adds a nuance worth preserving: "Let me see all of you, from every side."

In a poetic translation, tone, rhythm, and sound are naturally of crucial importance. Since the Song was almost certainly intended to be recited or sung, we have paid particular attention to the music of the poem, which is rich with assonance and alliteration, as lines like the following may suggest:

> *Nop̄et tiṭṭop̄nah śip̄totayik̄ kallah,*
> *deb̄aš ve-ḥalab̄ taḥat lešonek̄,*
> *ve-reaḥ śalmotayik̄ ke-reaḥ leb̄anon.* (4: 11)
>
> *Kep̄arim 'im neradim,*
> *nerd ve-k̄arkom, qaneh ve-qinnamon,*
> *'im kol 'aṣey leb̄onah.* (4:13–14)

Any modern translator of the Song must acknowledge the lofty achievement of the King James Version (1611). With its rich textures and resounding cadences, the King James Version's Song is magnificent English poetry, justly beloved by generations of readers. Nonetheless, significant advances in biblical scholarship during the past four centuries—not to speak of the past four decades—have shown many of its readings to be in error, including some of the best-known verses, such as "Stay me with flagons, comfort me with apples" (2:5) or "terrible as an army with banners" (6:10). And its language is often dated, as in "I am sick of love" (2:5) or "My beloved put in his hand by the hole of the door, and my bowels were moved for him" (5:4).

Taken out of its accustomed liturgical context and read as a work of art, the Song becomes a new poem, just as a painting or statue in a church looks entirely different when displayed in a secular setting. The heightened diction of the King James Version, already somewhat archaic in the seventeenth century, was conceived for liturgical purposes, and would be inappropriate in a contemporary translation. One of the major challenges facing a translator today is to find the proper register in English, neither too formal and stylized nor too breezy and colloquial—language that is fresh and urgent and passionate, and at the same time dignified. Just as earlier interpretations typically erred on the side of prudishness, contemporary translations (perhaps to atone for centuries of exegetical evasiveness) sometimes verge on crudeness, as in a recent translation by a distinguished scholar: "Your vulva [is] a rounded crater; / May it never lack punch!" (7:3) This verse alone, with its three howlers, illustrates how important it is for a translator to be sensitive to levels of style. The word *šorereḵ* means "navel," not "vulva"—and besides, the anatomical term "vulva" would be out of place in the delicately allusive language of the Song. There is a difference between sex and eros, as the poet of the Song is well aware. A translation of the Song ought to be informed by this distinction.

Translating an ancient text is in some ways analogous to the process of restoring a work of art that has been dulled by time. Not long ago, a team of conservators examined the frescoes on the ceiling of the Sistine Chapel using infrared light to penetrate the surface, and then, with meticulous care, set about removing five centuries of grime, soot, smoke, and old varnish. The work of the conservators revealed unexpectedly brilliant colors, hues of turquoise and orange that seemed quite unlike Michelangelo—that is, unlike the Michelangelo of tradition, who was thought to favor a much darker palette. Readers of this translation will discover that the colors of the Song are brighter, its music more sensuous, than they may have anticipated from other versions. Those charms of the Song are not our invention; they belong to the pleasures of the Hebrew. Our aim has been to restore in English the passion and intensity of the original.

THE SONG OF SONGS

WHICH IS SOLOMON'S

שִׁיר הַשִּׁירִים אֲשֶׁר לִשְׁלֹמֹה

א

2 יִשָּׁקֵ֙נִי֙ מִנְּשִׁיק֣וֹת פִּ֔יהוּ
כִּֽי־טוֹבִ֥ים דֹּדֶ֖יךָ מִיָּֽיִן׃

3 לְרֵ֙יחַ֙ שְׁמָנֶ֣יךָ טוֹבִ֔ים
שֶׁ֖מֶן תּוּרַ֣ק שְׁמֶ֑ךָ
עַל־כֵּ֖ן עֲלָמ֥וֹת אֲהֵבֽוּךָ׃

4 מָשְׁכֵ֖נִי אַחֲרֶ֣יךָ נָּר֑וּצָה

הֱבִיאַ֨נִי הַמֶּ֜לֶךְ חֲדָרָ֗יו
נָגִ֤ילָה וְנִשְׂמְחָה֙ בָּ֔ךְ
נַזְכִּ֤ירָה דֹדֶ֙יךָ֙ מִיַּ֔יִן

מֵישָׁרִ֖ים אֲהֵבֽוּךָ׃

1 2 *Kiss me, make me drunk with your kisses!*
Your sweet loving
is better than wine.

3 *You are fragrant,*
you are myrrh and aloes.
All the young women want you.

4 *Take me by the hand, let us run together!*

My lover, my king, has brought me into his chambers.
We will laugh, you and I, and count
each kiss,
better than wine.

Every one of them wants you.

א

5 שְׁחוֹרָה אֲנִי וְנָאוָה
בְּנוֹת יְרוּשָׁלָם
כְּאָהֳלֵי קֵדָר
כִּירִיעוֹת שְׁלֹמֹה׃

6 אַל־תִּרְאוּנִי שֶׁאֲנִי שְׁחַרְחֹרֶת
שֶׁשְּׁזָפַתְנִי הַשָּׁמֶשׁ

בְּנֵי אִמִּי נִחֲרוּ־בִי
שָׂמֻנִי נֹטֵרָה אֶת־הַכְּרָמִים
כַּרְמִי שֶׁלִּי לֹא נָטָרְתִּי׃

1 5 *I am dark, daughters of Jerusalem,*
and I am beautiful!
Dark as the tents of Kedar, lavish
as Solomon's tapestries.

6 *Do not see me only as dark:*
the sun has stared at me.

My brothers were angry with me,
they made me guard the vineyards.
I have not guarded my own.

7 הַגִּידָה לִּי שֶׁאָהֲבָה֮ נַפְשִׁי
אֵיכָה תִרְעֶה
אֵיכָה תַּרְבִּיץ בַּצָּהֳרָיִם
שַׁלָּמָה אֶהְיֶה֙ כְּעֹטְיָ֔ה
עַל עֶדְרֵי חֲבֵרֶיךָ׃

8 אִם־לֹא תֵדְעִי֙ לָ֔ךְ
הַיָּפָה בַּנָּשִׁים
צְאִי־לָ֞ךְ בְּעִקְבֵי הַצֹּאן
וּרְעִי אֶת־גְּדִיֹּתַ֔יִךְ
עַל מִשְׁכְּנוֹת הָרֹעִים׃

1 7 *Tell me, my only love,*
where do you pasture your sheep,
where will you let them rest
in the heat of noon?
Why should I lose my way among the flocks
of your companions?

8 Loveliest of women,
if you lose your way,
follow in the tracks of the sheep,
graze your goats in the shade
of the shepherds' tents.

א

9 לְסֻסָתִי֙ בְּרִכְבֵ֣י פַרְעֹ֔ה
דִּמִּיתִ֖יךְ רַעְיָתִֽי׃

10 נָאו֤וּ לְחָיַ֙יִךְ֙ בַּתֹּרִ֔ים
צַוָּארֵ֖ךְ בַּחֲרוּזִֽים׃

11 תּוֹרֵ֤י זָהָב֙ נַעֲשֶׂה־לָּ֔ךְ
עִ֖ם נְקֻדּ֥וֹת הַכָּֽסֶף׃

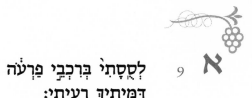

1 9 My love, I dreamed of you
as a mare, my very own,
among Pharaoh's chariots.

10 Your cheekbones,
those looped earrings,
that string of beads at your throat!

11 I will make you golden earrings
with silver filigree.

א

12 עַד־שֶׁ֤הַמֶּ֙לֶךְ֙ בִּמְסִבּ֔וֹ
נִרְדִּ֖י נָתַ֥ן רֵיחֽוֹ׃

13 צְר֨וֹר הַמֹּ֤ר ׀ דּוֹדִי֙ לִ֔י
בֵּ֥ין שָׁדַ֖י יָלִֽין׃
14 אֶשְׁכֹּ֨ל הַכֹּ֤פֶר ׀ דּוֹדִי֙ לִ֔י
בְּכַרְמֵ֖י עֵ֥ין גֶּֽדִי׃

15 הִנָּ֤ךְ יָפָה֙ רַעְיָתִ֔י
הִנָּ֥ךְ יָפָ֖ה
עֵינַ֥יִךְ יוֹנִֽים׃

16 הִנְּךָ֨ יָפֶ֤ה דוֹדִי֙
אַ֣ף נָעִ֔ים
אַף־עַרְשֵׂ֖נוּ רַעֲנָנָֽה׃
17 קֹר֤וֹת בָּתֵּ֙ינוּ֙ אֲרָזִ֔ים
רַהִיטֵ֖נוּ בְּרוֹתִֽים׃

1 12 *My king lay down beside me*
and my fragrance
wakened the night.

13 *All night between my breasts*
my love is a cluster of myrrh,
14 *a sheaf of henna blossoms*
in the vineyards of Ein Gedi.

15 And you, my beloved,
how beautiful you are!
Your eyes are doves.

16 *You are beautiful, my king,*
and gentle. Wherever we lie
our bed is green.
17 *Our roofbeams are cedar,*
our rafters fir.

ב

1 אֲנִי֙ חֲבַצֶּ֣לֶת הַשָּׁר֔וֹן
שֽׁוֹשַׁנַּ֖ת הָעֲמָקִֽים׃

2 כְּשֽׁוֹשַׁנָּה֙ בֵּ֣ין הַֽחוֹחִ֔ים
כֵּ֥ן רַעְיָתִ֖י בֵּ֥ין הַבָּנֽוֹת׃

3 כְּתַפּ֙וּחַ֙ בַּעֲצֵ֣י הַיַּ֔עַר
כֵּ֥ן דּוֹדִ֖י בֵּ֣ין הַבָּנִ֑ים
בְּצִלּוֹ֙ חִמַּ֣דְתִּי וְיָשַׁ֔בְתִּי
וּפִרְי֖וֹ מָת֥וֹק לְחִכִּֽי׃

2 1 *I am the rose of Sharon,*
the wild lily of the valleys.

2 Like a lily in a field
of thistles,
such is my love
among the young women.

3 *And my beloved among the young men*
is a branching apricot tree in the wood.
In that shade I have often lingered,
tasting the fruit.

ב

4 הֱבִיאַנִי֙ אֶל־בֵּ֣ית הַיָּ֔יִן
וְדִגְל֥וֹ עָלַ֖י אַהֲבָֽה׃

5 סַמְּכ֙וּנִי֙ בָּאֲשִׁישׁ֔וֹת
רַפְּד֖וּנִי בַּתַּפּוּחִ֑ים
כִּי־חוֹלַ֥ת אַהֲבָ֖ה אָֽנִי׃

6 שְׂמֹאלוֹ֙ תַּ֣חַת לְרֹאשִׁ֔י
וִימִינ֖וֹ תְּחַבְּקֵֽנִי׃

7 הִשְׁבַּ֨עְתִּי אֶתְכֶ֜ם בְּנ֤וֹת יְרוּשָׁלִַ֙ם֙
בִּצְבָא֔וֹת א֖וֹ בְּאַיְל֣וֹת הַשָּׂדֶ֑ה
אִם־תָּעִ֧ירוּ ׀ וְֽאִם־תְּעֽוֹרְר֛וּ אֶת־הָאַהֲבָ֖ה
עַ֥ד שֶׁתֶּחְפָּֽץ׃

2 4 *Now he has brought me to the house of wine*
and his flag over me is love.

5 *Let me lie among vine blossoms,*
in a bed of apricots!
I am in the fever of love.

6 *His left hand beneath my head,*
his right arm
holding me close.

7 *Daughters of Jerusalem, swear to me*
by the gazelles, by the deer in the field,
that you will never awaken love
until it is ripe.

ב

8 ק֚וֹל דּוֹדִ֔י הִנֵּה־זֶ֖ה בָּ֑א
מְדַלֵּג֙ עַל־הֶ֣הָרִ֔ים
מְקַפֵּ֖ץ עַל־הַגְּבָעֽוֹת׃

9 דּוֹמֶ֤ה דוֹדִי֙ לִצְבִ֔י א֖וֹ לְעֹ֣פֶר הָֽאַיָּלִ֑ים
הִנֵּה־זֶ֤ה עוֹמֵד֙ אַחַ֣ר כָּתְלֵ֔נוּ
מַשְׁגִּ֙יחַ֙ מִן־הַ֣חַלֹּנ֔וֹת
מֵצִ֖יץ מִן־הַחֲרַכִּֽים׃

10 עָנָ֥ה דוֹדִ֖י וְאָ֣מַר לִ֑י
ק֥וּמִי לָ֛ךְ רַעְיָתִ֥י יָפָתִ֖י
וּלְכִי־לָֽךְ׃

11 כִּֽי־הִנֵּ֥ה הַסְּתָ֖ו עָבָ֑ר
הַגֶּ֕שֶׁם חָלַ֖ף הָלַ֥ךְ לֽוֹ׃
12 הַנִּצָּנִים֙ נִרְא֣וּ בָאָ֔רֶץ
עֵ֥ת הַזָּמִ֖יר הִגִּ֑יעַ
וְק֥וֹל הַתּ֖וֹר נִשְׁמַ֥ע בְּאַרְצֵֽנוּ׃

13 הַתְּאֵנָה֙ חָנְטָ֣ה פַגֶּ֔יהָ
וְהַגְּפָנִ֣ים ׀ סְמָדַ֖ר נָ֣תְנוּ רֵ֑יחַ
ק֥וּמִי לָ֛ךְ רַעְיָתִ֥י יָפָתִ֖י
וּלְכִי־לָֽךְ׃

2 8 *The voice of my love: listen!*
bounding over the mountains
toward me, across the hills.

9 *My love is a gazelle, a wild stag.*
There he stands on the other side
of our wall, gazing
between the stones.

10 *And he calls to me:*
Hurry, my love, my friend,
and come away!

11 Look, winter is over,
the rains are done,
12 wildflowers spring up in the fields.
Now is the time of the nightingale.
In every meadow you hear
the song of the turtledove.

13 The fig tree has sweetened
its new green fruit
and the young budded vines smell spicy.
Hurry, my love, my friend
come away.

ב 14 יוֹנָתִ֞י בְּחַגְוֵ֣י הַסֶּ֗לַע
בְּסֵ֙תֶר֙ הַמַּדְרֵגָ֔ה
הַרְאִ֙ינִי֙ אֶת־מַרְאַ֔יִךְ
הַשְׁמִיעִ֖ינִי אֶת־קוֹלֵ֑ךְ
כִּי־קוֹלֵ֥ךְ עָרֵ֖ב
וּמַרְאֵ֥יךְ נָאוֶֽה׃

2 14 My dove in the clefts of the rock,
in the shadow of the cliff,
let me see you, all of you!
Let me hear your voice,
your delicious song.
I love to look at you.

ב

15 אֶֽחֱזוּ־לָנוּ שְׁוּעָלִים
שְׁוּעָלִים קְטַנִּים
מְחַבְּלִים כְּרָמִים
וּכְרָמֵינוּ סְמָדַר׃

2 15 **Catch us the foxes,**
the quick little foxes
that raid our vineyards
now, when the vines are in blossom.

ב

16 דוֹדִ֥י לִי֙ וַאֲנִ֣י ל֔וֹ
הָרֹעֶ֖ה בַּשּׁוֹשַׁנִּֽים׃

17 עַ֤ד שֶׁיָּפ֙וּחַ֙ הַיּ֔וֹם
וְנָ֖סוּ הַצְּלָלִ֑ים
סֹב֩ דְּמֵה־לְךָ֨ דוֹדִ֜י לִצְבִ֗י
א֛וֹ לְעֹ֥פֶר הָאַיָּלִ֖ים
עַל־הָ֥רֵי בָֽתֶר׃

2 16 *My beloved is mine and I am his.*
He feasts
in a field of lilies.

17 *Before day breathes,*
before the shadows of night are gone,
run away, my love!
Be like a gazelle, a wild stag
on the jagged mountains.

ג

1 עַל־מִשְׁכָּבִי֙ בַּלֵּיל֔וֹת
בִּקַּ֕שְׁתִּי אֵ֥ת שֶׁאָהֲבָ֖ה נַפְשִׁ֑י
בִּקַּשְׁתִּ֖יו וְלֹ֥א מְצָאתִֽיו׃

2 אָק֨וּמָה נָּ֜א וַאֲסוֹבְבָ֣ה בָעִ֗יר
בַּשְּׁוָקִים֙ וּבָ֣רְחֹב֔וֹת
אֲבַקְשָׁ֕ה אֵ֥ת שֶׁאָהֲבָ֖ה נַפְשִׁ֑י
בִּקַּשְׁתִּ֖יו וְלֹ֥א מְצָאתִֽיו׃

3 מְצָא֙וּנִי֙ הַשֹּׁ֣מְרִ֔ים
הַסֹּבְבִ֖ים בָּעִ֑יר
אֵ֛ת שֶׁאָהֲבָ֥ה נַפְשִׁ֖י רְאִיתֶֽם׃

4 כִּמְעַט֙ שֶׁעָבַ֣רְתִּי מֵהֶ֔ם
עַ֣ד שֶׁמָּצָ֔אתִי אֵ֥ת שֶׁאָהֲבָ֖ה נַפְשִׁ֑י
אֲחַזְתִּיו֙ וְלֹ֣א אַרְפֶּ֔נּוּ
עַד־שֶׁהֲבֵיאתִיו֙ אֶל־בֵּ֣ית אִמִּ֔י
וְאֶל־חֶ֖דֶר הוֹרָתִֽי׃

5 הִשְׁבַּ֨עְתִּי אֶתְכֶ֜ם בְּנ֤וֹת יְרוּשָׁלִַ֙ם֙
בִּצְבָא֔וֹת א֖וֹ בְּאַיְל֣וֹת הַשָּׂדֶ֑ה
אִם־תָּעִ֧ירוּ ׀ וְֽאִם־תְּעֽוֹרְר֛וּ אֶת־הָאַהֲבָ֖ה
עַ֥ד שֶׁתֶּחְפָּֽץ׃

3

1 *At night in my bed I longed*
for my only love.
I sought him, but did not find him.

2 *I must rise and go about the city,*
the narrow streets and squares, till I find
my only love.
I sought him everywhere
but I could not find him.

3 *Then the watchmen found me*
as they went about the city.
"Have you seen him? Have you seen
the one I love?"

4 *I had just passed them when I found*
my only love.
I held him, I would not let him go
until I brought him to my mother's house,
into my mother's room.

5 *Daughters of Jerusalem, swear to me*
by the gazelles, by the deer in the field,
that you will never awaken love
until it is ripe.

ג

6 מִ֣י זֹ֗את עֹלָה֙ מִן־הַמִּדְבָּ֔ר
כְּתִֽימֲר֖וֹת עָשָׁ֑ן
מְקֻטֶּ֤רֶת מֹר֙ וּלְבוֹנָ֔ה
מִכֹּ֖ל אַבְקַ֥ת רוֹכֵֽל׃

3 6 ***Who is that rising from the desert***
like a pillar of smoke,
more fragrant with myrrh and frankincense
than all the spices of the merchant!

ג

7 הִנֵּה מִטָּתוֹ שֶׁלִּשְׁלֹמֹה
שִׁשִּׁים גִּבֹּרִים סָבִיב לָהּ
מִגִּבֹּרֵי יִשְׂרָאֵל:
8 כֻּלָּם אֲחֻזֵי חֶרֶב מְלֻמְּדֵי מִלְחָמָה
אִישׁ חַרְבּוֹ עַל־יְרֵכוֹ
מִפַּחַד בַּלֵּילוֹת:

9 אַפִּרְיוֹן עָשָׂה לוֹ הַמֶּלֶךְ שְׁלֹמֹה
מֵעֲצֵי הַלְּבָנוֹן:
10 עַמּוּדָיו עָשָׂה כֶסֶף
רְפִידָתוֹ זָהָב
מֶרְכָּבוֹ אַרְגָּמָן
תּוֹכוֹ רָצוּף אַהֲבָה
מִבְּנוֹת יְרוּשָׁלָםִ:

11 צְאֶינָה ׀ וּרְאֶינָה בְּנוֹת צִיּוֹן
בַּמֶּלֶךְ שְׁלֹמֹה
בָּעֲטָרָה שֶׁעִטְּרָה־לּוֹ אִמּוֹ
בְּיוֹם חֲתֻנָּתוֹ
וּבְיוֹם שִׂמְחַת לִבּוֹ:

3 7 *Oh the splendors of King Solomon!*
The bravest of Israel surround his bed,
threescore warriors,
8 *each of them skilled in battle,*
each with his sword on his thigh
against the terror of night.

9 *King Solomon built a pavilion*
from the cedars of Lebanon.
10 *Its pillars he made of silver,*
cushions of gold,
couches of purple linen,
and the daughters of Jerusalem
paved it with love.

11 *Come out, O daughters of Zion,*
and gaze at Solomon the King!
See the crown his mother set on his head
on the day of his wedding,
the day of his heart's great joy.

ד

הִנָּךְ יָפָה רַעְיָתִי 1
הִנָּךְ יָפָה
עֵינַיִךְ יוֹנִים מִבַּעַד לְצַמָּתֵךְ

שַׂעְרֵךְ כְּעֵדֶר הָעִזִּים
שֶׁגָּלְשׁוּ מֵהַר גִּלְעָד׃

שִׁנַּיִךְ כְּעֵדֶר הַקְּצוּבוֹת 2
שֶׁעָלוּ מִן־הָרַחְצָה
שֶׁכֻּלָּם מַתְאִימוֹת
וְשַׁכֻּלָה אֵין בָּהֶם׃

כְּחוּט הַשָּׁנִי שִׂפְתֹתַיִךְ 3
וּמִדְבָּרֵךְ נָאוֶה

כְּפֶלַח הָרִמּוֹן רַקָּתֵךְ
מִבַּעַד לְצַמָּתֵךְ׃

כְּמִגְדַּל דָּוִיד צַוָּארֵךְ 4
בָּנוּי לְתַלְפִּיּוֹת
אֶלֶף הַמָּגֵן תָּלוּי עָלָיו
כֹּל שִׁלְטֵי הַגִּבֹּרִים׃

4

1 How beautiful you are, my love,
my friend! The doves of your eyes
looking out
from the thicket of your hair.

Your hair
like a flock of goats
bounding down Mount Gilead.

2 Your teeth white ewes,
all alike,
that come up fresh from the pond.

3 A crimson ribbon your lips—
how I listen for your voice!

The curve of your cheek
a pomegranate
in the thicket of your hair.

4 Your neck is a tower of David
raised in splendor,
a thousand bucklers hang upon it,
all the shields of the warriors.

ד

5 שְׁנֵי שָׁדַיִךְ כִּשְׁנֵי עֳפָרִים
תְּאוֹמֵי צְבִיָּה
הָרֹעִים בַּשּׁוֹשַׁנִּים׃

6 עַד שֶׁיָּפוּחַ הַיּוֹם
וְנָסוּ הַצְּלָלִים
אֵלֶךְ לִי אֶל־הַר הַמּוֹר
וְאֶל־גִּבְעַת הַלְּבוֹנָה׃

7 כֻּלָּךְ יָפָה רַעְיָתִי
וּמוּם אֵין בָּךְ׃

4 5 Your breasts are two fawns,
twins of a gazelle,
grazing in a field of lilies.

6 Before day breathes,
before the shadows of night are gone,
I will hurry to the mountain of myrrh,
the hill of frankincense.

7 You are all beautiful, my love,
my perfect one.

ד

8 אִתִּ֤י מִלְּבָנוֹן֙ כַּלָּ֔ה
אִתִּ֖י מִלְּבָנ֣וֹן תָּב֑וֹאִי
תָּשׁ֣וּרִי ׀ מֵרֹ֣אשׁ אֲמָנָ֗ה
מֵרֹ֤אשׁ שְׂנִיר֙ וְחֶרְמ֔וֹן
מִמְּעֹנ֣וֹת אֲרָי֔וֹת
מֵהַרְרֵ֖י נְמֵרִֽים׃

9 לִבַּבְתִּ֖נִי אֲחֹתִ֣י כַלָּ֑ה
לִבַּבְתִּ֙נִי֙ בְּאַחַ֣ת מֵעֵינַ֔יִךְ
בְּאַחַ֥ד עֲנָ֖ק מִצַּוְּרֹנָֽיִךְ׃

10 מַה־יָּפ֥וּ דֹדַ֖יִךְ
אֲחֹתִ֣י כַלָּ֑ה
מַה־טֹּ֤בוּ דֹדַ֙יִךְ֙ מִיַּ֔יִן
וְרֵ֥יחַ שְׁמָנַ֖יִךְ מִכָּל־בְּשָׂמִֽים׃

11 נֹ֛פֶת תִּטֹּ֥פְנָה שִׂפְתוֹתַ֖יִךְ כַּלָּ֑ה
דְּבַ֤שׁ וְחָלָב֙ תַּ֣חַת לְשׁוֹנֵ֔ךְ
וְרֵ֥יחַ שַׂלְמֹתַ֖יִךְ כְּרֵ֥יחַ לְבָנֽוֹן׃

4 8 Oh come with me, my bride,
come down with me from Lebanon.
Look down from the peak of Amana,
look down from Senir and Hermon,
from the mountains of the leopards,
the lions' dens.

9 You have ravished my heart,
my sister, my bride,
ravished me with one glance of your eyes,
one link of your necklace.

10 And oh, your sweet loving,
my sister, my bride.
The wine of your kisses, the spice
of your fragrant oils.

11 Your lips are honey, honey and milk
are under your tongue,
your clothes hold the scent of Lebanon.

ד

12 גַּ֣ן ׀ נָע֖וּל אֲחֹתִ֣י כַלָּ֑ה
גַּ֥ל נָע֖וּל מַעְיָ֥ן חָתֽוּם׃

13 שְׁלָחַ֙יִךְ֙ פַּרְדֵּ֣ס רִמּוֹנִ֔ים
עִ֖ם פְּרִ֣י מְגָדִ֑ים
כְּפָרִ֖ים עִם־נְרָדִֽים׃
14 נֵ֣רְדְּ ׀ וְכַרְכֹּ֗ם קָנֶה֙ וְקִנָּמ֔וֹן
עִ֖ם כָּל־עֲצֵ֣י לְבוֹנָ֑ה
מֹ֚ר וַאֲהָל֔וֹת
עִ֖ם כָּל־רָאשֵׁ֥י בְשָׂמִֽים׃

15 מַעְיַ֣ן גַּנִּ֔ים
בְּאֵ֖ר מַ֣יִם חַיִּ֑ים
וְנֹזְלִ֖ים מִן־לְבָנֽוֹן׃

4 12 An enclosed garden is my sister, my bride,
a hidden well, a sealed spring.

13 Your branches are an orchard
of pomegranate trees heavy with fruit,
flowering henna and spikenard,
14 spikenard and saffron, cane and cinnamon,
with every tree of frankincense,
myrrh and aloes,
all the rare spices.

15 You are a fountain in the garden,
a well of living waters
that stream from Lebanon.

ד 16 עוּרִי צָפוֹן וּבוֹאִי תֵימָן
הָפִיחִי גַנִּי יִזְּלוּ בְשָׂמָיו
יָבֹא דוֹדִי לְגַנּוֹ
וְיֹאכַל פְּרִי מְגָדָיו׃

ה 1 בָּאתִי לְגַנִּי אֲחֹתִי כַלָּה
אָרִיתִי מוֹרִי עִם־בְּשָׂמִי
אָכַלְתִּי יַעְרִי עִם־דִּבְשִׁי
שָׁתִיתִי יֵינִי עִם־חֲלָבִי

אִכְלוּ רֵעִים
שְׁתוּ וְשִׁכְרוּ דּוֹדִים׃

4 16 *Awake, north wind! O south wind, come,*
breathe upon my garden,
let its spices stream out.
Let my lover come into his garden
and taste its delicious fruit.

5 1 I have come into my garden,
my sister, my bride,
I have gathered my myrrh and my spices,
I have eaten from the honeycomb,
I have drunk the milk and the wine.

Feast, friends, and drink
till you are drunk with love!

ה

2 אֲנִ֥י יְשֵׁנָ֖ה וְלִבִּ֣י עֵ֑ר
קֹ֣ול ׀ דֹּודִ֣י דֹופֵ֗ק

פִּתְחִי־לִ֞י אֲחֹתִ֤י רַעְיָתִי֙
יֹונָתִ֣י תַמָּתִ֔י
שֶׁרֹּאשִׁי֙ נִמְלָא־טָ֔ל
קְוֻּצֹּותַ֖י רְסִ֥יסֵי לָֽיְלָה׃

3 פָּשַׁ֙טְתִּי֙ אֶת־כֻּתָּנְתִּ֔י
אֵיכָ֖כָה אֶלְבָּשֶׁ֑נָּה
רָחַ֥צְתִּי אֶת־רַגְלַ֖י
אֵיכָ֥כָה אֲטַנְּפֵֽם׃

4 דֹּודִ֗י שָׁלַ֤ח יָדֹו֙ מִן־הַחֹ֔ר
וּמֵעַ֖י הָמ֥וּ עָלָֽיו׃

5 קַ֥מְתִּֽי אֲנִ֖י לִפְתֹּ֣חַ לְדֹודִ֑י
וְיָדַ֣י נָֽטְפוּ־מֹ֗ור
וְאֶצְבְּעֹתַי֙ מֹ֣ור עֹבֵ֔ר
עַ֖ל כַּפֹּ֥ות הַמַּנְעֽוּל׃

5 2 *I was asleep but my heart stayed awake.*
Listen!
my lover knocking:

"Open, my sister, my friend,
my dove, my perfect one!
My hair is wet, drenched
with the dew of night."

3 *"But I have taken off my clothes,*
how can I dress again?
I have bathed my feet,
must I dirty them?"

4 *My love reached in for the latch*
and my heart
beat wild.

5 *I rose to open to my love,*
my fingers wet with myrrh,
sweet flowing myrrh
on the doorbolt.

ה

6 פָּתַחְתִּי אֲנִי לְדוֹדִי
וְדוֹדִי חָמַק עָבָר
נַפְשִׁי יָצְאָה בְדַבְּרוֹ

בִּקַּשְׁתִּיהוּ וְלֹא מְצָאתִיהוּ
קְרָאתִיו וְלֹא עָנָנִי׃

7 מְצָאֻנִי הַשֹּׁמְרִים הַסֹּבְבִים בָּעִיר
הִכּוּנִי פְצָעוּנִי
נָשְׂאוּ אֶת־רְדִידִי מֵעָלַי
שֹׁמְרֵי הַחֹמוֹת׃

8 הִשְׁבַּעְתִּי אֶתְכֶם בְּנוֹת יְרוּשָׁלִָם
אִם־תִּמְצְאוּ אֶת־דּוֹדִי
מַה־תַּגִּידוּ לוֹ
שֶׁחוֹלַת אַהֲבָה אָנִי׃

5 6 *I opened to my love*
but he had slipped away.
How I wanted him when he spoke!

I sought him everywhere
but could not find him.
I called his name
but he did not answer.

7 *Then the watchmen found me*
as they went about the city.
They beat me, they bruised me,
they tore the shawl from my shoulders,
those watchmen of the walls.

8 *Swear to me, daughters of Jerusalem!*
If you find him now
you must tell him
I am in the fever of love.

ה

9 מַה־דּוֹדֵךְ מִדּוֹד
הַיָּפָה בַּנָּשִׁים
מַה־דּוֹדֵךְ מִדּוֹד
שֶׁכָּכָה הִשְׁבַּעְתָּנוּ׃

10 דּוֹדִי צַח וְאָדוֹם
דָּגוּל מֵרְבָבָה׃

11 רֹאשׁוֹ כֶּתֶם פָּז
קְוֻצּוֹתָיו תַּלְתַּלִּים
שְׁחֹרוֹת כָּעוֹרֵב׃

12 עֵינָיו כְּיוֹנִים עַל־אֲפִיקֵי מָיִם
רֹחֲצוֹת בֶּחָלָב
יֹשְׁבוֹת עַל־מִלֵּאת׃

13 לְחָיָו כַּעֲרוּגַת הַבֹּשֶׂם
מִגְדְּלוֹת מֶרְקָחִים
שִׂפְתוֹתָיו שׁוֹשַׁנִּים
נֹטְפוֹת מוֹר עֹבֵר׃

5 9 ***How is your lover different***
from any other, O beautiful woman?
Who is your lover
that we must swear to you?

10 *My beloved is milk and wine,*
he towers
above ten thousand.

11 *His head is burnished gold,*
the mane of his hair
black as the raven.

12 *His eyes like doves*
by the rivers
of milk and plenty.

13 *His cheeks a bed of spices,*
a treasure
of precious scents, his lips
red lilies wet with myrrh.

ה

14 יָדָיו֙ גְּלִילֵ֣י זָהָ֔ב
מְמֻלָּאִ֖ים בַּתַּרְשִׁ֑ישׁ
מֵעָיו֙ עֶ֣שֶׁת שֵׁ֔ן
מְעֻלֶּ֖פֶת סַפִּירִֽים׃
15 שׁוֹקָיו֙ עַמּ֣וּדֵי שֵׁ֔שׁ
מְיֻסָּדִ֖ים עַל־אַדְנֵי־פָ֑ז

מַרְאֵ֙הוּ֙ כַּלְּבָנ֔וֹן
בָּח֖וּר כָּאֲרָזִֽים׃

16 חִכּוֹ֙ מַֽמְתַקִּ֔ים וְכֻלּ֖וֹ מַחֲמַדִּ֑ים

זֶ֤ה דוֹדִי֙ וְזֶ֣ה רֵעִ֔י
בְּנ֖וֹת יְרוּשָׁלִָֽם׃

5 14 *His arm a golden scepter with gems of topaz,*
his loins the ivory of thrones
inlaid with sapphire,
15 *his thighs like marble pillars*
on pedestals of gold.

Tall as Mount Lebanon,
a man like a cedar!

16 *His mouth is sweet wine, he is all delight.*

This is my beloved
and this is my friend,
O daughters of Jerusalem.

ו

1 אָ֚נָה הָלַ֣ךְ דּוֹדֵ֔ךְ
הַיָּפָ֖ה בַּנָּשִׁ֑ים
אָ֚נָה פָּנָ֣ה דוֹדֵ֔ךְ
וּנְבַקְשֶׁ֖נּוּ עִמָּֽךְ׃

2 דּוֹדִי֙ יָרַ֣ד לְגַנּ֔וֹ
לַעֲרוּג֖וֹת הַבֹּ֑שֶׂם
לִרְעוֹת֙ בַּגַּנִּ֔ים וְלִלְקֹ֖ט שׁוֹשַׁנִּֽים׃

3 אֲנִ֤י לְדוֹדִי֙ וְדוֹדִ֣י לִ֔י
הָרֹעֶ֖ה בַּשּׁוֹשַׁנִּֽים׃

6 1 ***Where has your lover gone,***
O beautiful one?
Say where he is
and we will seek him with you.

2 *My love has gone down to*
his garden, to the beds of spices,
to graze and to gather lilies.

3 *My beloved is mine and I am his.*
He feasts
in a field of lilies.

ו

4 יָפָ֨ה אַ֤תְּ רַעְיָתִי֙ כְּתִרְצָ֔ה
נָאוָ֖ה כִּירוּשָׁלָ֑ם
אֲיֻמָּ֖ה כַּנִּדְגָּלֽוֹת׃

5 הָסֵ֤בִּי עֵינַ֙יִךְ֙ מִנֶּגְדִּ֔י
שֶׁ֥הֵ֖ם הִרְהִיבֻ֑נִי

שַׂעְרֵךְ֙ כְּעֵ֣דֶר הָֽעִזִּ֔ים
שֶׁגָּלְשׁ֖וּ מִן־הַגִּלְעָֽד׃

6 שִׁנַּ֙יִךְ֙ כְּעֵ֣דֶר הָֽרְחֵלִ֔ים
שֶׁעָל֖וּ מִן־הָֽרַחְצָ֑ה
שֶׁכֻּלָּם֙ מַתְאִימ֔וֹת
וְשַׁכֻּלָ֖ה אֵ֥ין בָּהֶֽם׃

7 כְּפֶ֤לַח הָֽרִמּוֹן֙ רַקָּתֵ֔ךְ
מִבַּ֖עַד לְצַמָּתֵֽךְ׃

6 4 You are beautiful, my love, as Tirzah,
majestic as Jerusalem,
daunting
as the stars in their courses.

5 Your eyes! Turn them away
for they dazzle me.

Your hair is like a flock of goats
bounding down Mount Gilead.

6 Your teeth white ewes,
all alike,
that come up fresh from the pond.

7 The curve of your cheek
a pomegranate
in your thicket of hair.

ו 8 שִׁשִּׁים הֵמָּה מְלָכוֹת
וּשְׁמֹנִים פִּילַגְשִׁים
וַעֲלָמוֹת אֵין מִסְפָּר׃

9 אַחַת הִיא יוֹנָתִי תַמָּתִי
אַחַת הִיא לְאִמָּהּ
בָּרָה הִיא לְיוֹלַדְתָּהּ

רָאוּהָ בָנוֹת וַיְאַשְּׁרוּהָ
מְלָכוֹת וּפִילַגְשִׁים וַיְהַלְלוּהָ׃

10 מִי־זֹאת הַנִּשְׁקָפָה כְּמוֹ־שָׁחַר
יָפָה כַלְּבָנָה
בָּרָה כַּחַמָּה
אֲיֻמָּה כַּנִּדְגָּלוֹת׃

6 8 Threescore are the queens,
fourscore the king's women,
and maidens, maidens without number.

9 One alone is my dove,
my perfect, my only one,
love of her mother, light
of her mother's eyes.

Every maiden calls her happy,
queens praise her,
and all the king's women:

10 ***"Who is that rising like the morning star,***
clear as the moon,
bright as the blazing sun,
daunting as the stars in their courses!"

ו

11 אֶל־גִּנַּת אֱגוֹז יָרַדְתִּי
לִרְאוֹת בְּאִבֵּי הַנָּחַל
לִרְאוֹת הֲפָרְחָה הַגֶּפֶן
הֵנֵצוּ הָרִמֹּנִים׃

12 לֹא יָדַעְתִּי נַפְשִׁי
שָׂמַתְנִי מַרְכְּבוֹת עַמִּי־נָדִיב׃

6 11 Then I went down to the walnut grove
to see the new green by the brook,
to see if the vine had budded,
if the pomegranate trees were in flower.

12 And oh! before I was aware,
she sat me in the most lavish of chariots.

ז

1 שׁוּבִי שׁוּבִי הַשּׁוּלַמִּית
שׁוּבִי שׁוּבִי וְנֶחֱזֶה־בָּךְ

מַה־תֶּחֱזוּ בַּשּׁוּלַמִּית
כִּמְחֹלַת הַמַּחֲנָיִם׃

2 מַה־יָּפוּ פְעָמַיִךְ בַּנְּעָלִים
בַּת־נָדִיב

חַמּוּקֵי יְרֵכַיִךְ כְּמוֹ חֲלָאִים
מַעֲשֵׂה יְדֵי אָמָּן׃

3 שָׁרְרֵךְ אַגַּן הַסַּהַר
אַל־יֶחְסַר הַמָּזֶג

בִּטְנֵךְ עֲרֵמַת חִטִּים
סוּגָה בַּשּׁוֹשַׁנִּים׃
4 שְׁנֵי שָׁדַיִךְ כִּשְׁנֵי עֳפָרִים
תָּאֳמֵי צְבִיָּה׃

7 1 *Again, O Shulamite,*
dance again,
that we may watch you dancing!

Why do you gaze at the Shulamite
as she whirls
down the rows of dancers?

2 How graceful your steps in those sandals,
O nobleman's daughter.

The gold of your thigh
shaped by a master craftsman.

3 Your navel is the moon's
bright drinking cup.
May it brim with wine!

Your belly is a mound of wheat
edged with lilies.
4 Your breasts are two fawns,
twins of a gazelle.

ז

5 צַוָּארֵךְ כְּמִגְדַּל הַשֵּׁן
עֵינַיִךְ בְּרֵכוֹת בְּחֶשְׁבּוֹן
עַל־שַׁעַר בַּת־רַבִּים
אַפֵּךְ כְּמִגְדַּל הַלְּבָנוֹן
צוֹפֶה פְּנֵי דַמָּשֶׂק׃

6 רֹאשֵׁךְ עָלַיִךְ כַּכַּרְמֶל
וְדַלַּת רֹאשֵׁךְ כָּאַרְגָּמָן
מֶלֶךְ אָסוּר בָּרְהָטִים׃

7 מַה־יָּפִית וּמַה־נָּעַמְתְּ
אַהֲבָה בַּתַּעֲנוּגִים׃

7 5 Your neck is a tower of ivory.
Your eyes are pools in Heshbon, at the gates
of that city of lords.
Your proud nose the tower of Lebanon
that looks toward Damascus.

6 Your head crowns you like Mount Carmel,
the hair of your head
like royal purple. A king
is caught in the thicket.

7 How wonderful you are, O Love,
how much sweeter
than all other pleasures!

ז

8 זֹאת קוֹמָתֵךְ דָּמְתָה לְתָמָר
וְשָׁדַיִךְ לְאַשְׁכֹּלוֹת׃

9 אָמַרְתִּי אֶעֱלֶה בְתָמָר
אֹחֲזָה בְּסַנְסִנָּיו

וְיִהְיוּ־נָא שָׁדַיִךְ כְּאֶשְׁכְּלוֹת הַגֶּפֶן
וְרֵיחַ אַפֵּךְ כַּתַּפּוּחִים׃
10 וְחִכֵּךְ כְּיֵין הַטּוֹב

הוֹלֵךְ לְדוֹדִי לְמֵישָׁרִים
דּוֹבֵב שִׂפְתֵי יְשֵׁנִים׃

11 אֲנִי לְדוֹדִי
וְעָלַי תְּשׁוּקָתוֹ׃

7 8 That day you seemed to me a tall palm tree
and your breasts
the clusters of its fruit.

9 I said in my heart,
Let me climb into that palm tree
and take hold of its branches.

And oh, may your breasts be like clusters
of grapes on a vine, the scent
of your breath like apricots,
10 your mouth good wine—

That pleases my lover, rousing him
even from sleep.

11 *I am my lover's,*
he longs for me,
only for me.

ז

12 לְכָ֤ה דוֹדִי֙ נֵצֵ֣א הַשָּׂדֶ֔ה
נָלִ֖ינָה בַּכְּפָרִֽים׃

13 נַשְׁכִּ֙ימָה֙ לַכְּרָמִ֔ים
נִרְאֶ֞ה אִם־פָּֽרְחָ֤ה הַגֶּ֙פֶן֙
פִּתַּ֣ח הַסְּמָדַ֔ר
הֵנֵ֖צוּ הָרִמּוֹנִ֑ים

שָׁ֛ם אֶתֵּ֥ן אֶת־דֹּדַ֖י לָֽךְ׃

14 הַֽדּוּדָאִ֣ים נָֽתְנוּ־רֵ֗יחַ
וְעַל־פְּתָחֵ֙ינוּ֙ כָּל־מְגָדִ֔ים
חֲדָשִׁ֖ים גַּם־יְשָׁנִ֑ים
דּוֹדִ֖י צָפַ֥נְתִּי לָֽךְ׃

7 12 *Come, my beloved,*
let us go out into the fields
and lie all night among the flowering henna.

13 *Let us go early to the vineyards*
to see if the vine has budded,
if the blossoms have opened
and the pomegranate is in flower.

There I will give you my love.

14 *The air is filled with the scent of mandrakes*
and at our doors
rare fruit of every kind, my love,
I have stored away for you.

ח

1 מִֽי יִתֶּנְךָ֙ כְּאָ֣ח לִ֔י
יוֹנֵ֖ק שְׁדֵ֣י אִמִּ֑י
אֶמְצָאֲךָ֤ בַחוּץ֙ אֶשָּׁקְךָ֔
גַּ֖ם לֹא־יָב֥וּזוּ לִֽי׃

2 אֶנְהָֽגֲךָ֔ אֲבִֽיאֲךָ֖ אֶל־בֵּ֣ית אִמִּ֑י
תְּלַמְּדֵ֑נִי
אַשְׁקְךָ֙ מִיַּ֣יִן הָרֶ֔קַח
מֵעֲסִ֖יס רִמֹּנִֽי׃

3 שְׂמֹאלוֹ֙ תַּ֣חַת רֹאשִׁ֔י
וִימִינ֖וֹ תְּחַבְּקֵֽנִי׃

4 הִשְׁבַּ֥עְתִּי אֶתְכֶ֖ם בְּנ֣וֹת יְרוּשָׁלִָ֑ם
מַה־תָּעִ֧ירוּ ׀ וּֽמַה־תְּעֹרְר֛וּ אֶת־הָאַהֲבָ֖ה
עַד־שֶׁתֶּחְפָּֽץ׃

8 1 *If only you were a brother*
who nursed at my mother's breast!
I would kiss you in the streets
and no one would scorn me.

2 *I would bring you to the house of my mother*
and she would teach me.
I would give you spiced wine to drink,
my pomegranate wine.

3 *His left hand beneath my head,*
his right arm
holding me close.

4 *Daughters of Jerusalem, swear to me*
that you will never awaken love
until it is ripe.

ח

5 מִ֣י זֹ֗את עֹלָה֙ מִן־הַמִּדְבָּ֔ר
מִתְרַפֶּ֖קֶת עַל־דּוֹדָ֑הּ

8 5 ***Who is that***
rising from the desert,
her head on her lover's shoulder!

ח

5 תַּ֤חַת הַתַּפּ֙וּחַ֙ עֽוֹרַרְתִּ֔יךָ
שָׁ֚מָּה חִבְּלַ֣תְךָ אִמֶּ֔ךָ
שָׁ֖מָּה חִבְּלָ֥ה יְלָדַֽתְךָ׃

6 שִׂימֵ֨נִי כַֽחוֹתָ֜ם עַל־לִבֶּ֗ךָ
כַּֽחוֹתָם֙ עַל־זְרוֹעֶ֔ךָ

כִּֽי־עַזָּ֤ה כַמָּ֙וֶת֙ אַהֲבָ֔ה
קָשָׁ֥ה כִשְׁא֖וֹל קִנְאָ֑ה
רְשָׁפֶ֕יהָ רִשְׁפֵּ֕י אֵ֖שׁ
שַׁלְהֶ֥בֶתְיָֽה׃

7 מַ֣יִם רַבִּ֗ים לֹ֤א יֽוּכְלוּ֙
לְכַבּ֣וֹת אֶת־הָ֣אַהֲבָ֔ה
וּנְהָר֖וֹת לֹ֣א יִשְׁטְפ֑וּהָ

אִם־יִתֵּ֨ן אִ֜ישׁ אֶת־כָּל־ה֤וֹן בֵּיתוֹ֙
בָּ֣אַהֲבָ֔ה
בּ֖וֹז יָב֥וּזוּ לֽוֹ׃

8 5 *There, beneath the apricot tree,*
your mother conceived you,
there you were born.
In that very place, I awakened you.

6 *Bind me as a seal upon your heart,*
a sign upon your arm,

for love is as fierce as death,
its jealousy bitter as the grave.
Even its sparks are a raging fire,
a devouring flame.

7 *Great seas cannot extinguish love,*
no river can sweep it away.

If a man tried to buy love
with all the wealth of his house,
he would be despised.

ח

8 אָחוֹת לָנוּ קְטַנָּה
וְשָׁדַיִם אֵין לָהּ
מַה־נַּעֲשֶׂה לַאֲחוֹתֵנוּ
בַּיּוֹם שֶׁיְּדֻבַּר־בָּהּ׃

9 אִם־חוֹמָה הִיא
נִבְנֶה עָלֶיהָ טִירַת כָּסֶף
וְאִם־דֶּלֶת הִיא
נָצוּר עָלֶיהָ לוּחַ אָרֶז׃

10 אֲנִי חוֹמָה
וְשָׁדַי כַּמִּגְדָּלוֹת
אָז הָיִיתִי בְעֵינָיו
כְּמוֹצְאֵת שָׁלוֹם׃

8 8 **We have a little sister**
and she has no breasts.
What shall we do for our sister
when suitors besiege her?

9 **If she is a wall, we will build**
a silver turret upon her.
If she is a door, we will bolt her
with beams of cedarwood.

10 *I am a wall*
and my breasts are towers.
But for my lover I am
a city of peace.

ח

11 כֶּרֶם הָיָה לִשְׁלֹמֹה
בְּבַעַל הָמוֹן
נָתַן אֶת־הַכֶּרֶם לַנֹּטְרִים
אִישׁ יָבִא בְּפִרְיוֹ אֶלֶף כָּסֶף׃

12 כַּרְמִי שֶׁלִּי לְפָנָי
הָאֶלֶף לְךָ שְׁלֹמֹה
וּמָאתַיִם לְנֹטְרִים אֶת־פִּרְיוֹ׃

8 11 King Solomon had a vineyard
on the Hill of Plenty.
He gave that vineyard to watchmen
and each would earn for its fruit
one thousand pieces of silver.

12 My vineyard is all my own.
Keep your thousand, Solomon! And pay
two hundred to those
who must guard the fruit.

ח

13 הַיּוֹשֶׁ֣בֶת בַּגַּנִּ֗ים
חֲבֵרִ֛ים מַקְשִׁיבִ֥ים לְקוֹלֵ֖ךְ
הַשְׁמִיעִֽנִי׃

14 בְּרַ֣ח ׀ דּוֹדִ֗י
וּֽדְמֵה־לְךָ֤ לִצְבִי֙ א֚וֹ לְעֹ֣פֶר הָֽאַיָּלִ֔ים
עַ֖ל הָרֵ֥י בְשָׂמִֽים׃

8 13 O woman in the garden,
all our friends listen for your voice.
Let me hear it now.

14 *Hurry, my love! Run away,*
my gazelle, my wild stag
on the hills of cinnamon.

Afterword

ROBERT ALTER

THE POETRY of the Song of Songs is an exquisite balance of ripe sensuality and delicacy of expression and feeling. In Chana Bloch's apt phrase in her introductory chapter, "In the Garden of Delights," its language is "at once voluptuous and reticent," and that is precisely the challenge for the translator. The older English renderings, beginning with the King James Version, do have their splendid moments, but they also often fudge the frank sensuality of the original, trading tresses for demure veils, as readers of this translation and commentary will discover. In the proliferation in our own age of new English versions of the Song and of the Bible as a whole, translators have had difficulties negotiating between the extremes of clunky sexual explicitness and the pastels of greeting-card poetry, which are equal if opposite violations of the original. The problem of conveying the Hebrew poet's candid yet beautifully tactful imagination of love is compounded by the sensuous concreteness and the harmonious compactness of the poet's language. The task of unpacking the meaning of the Hebrew into the bulkier syntactic and idiomatic receptacles of a modern Western language can easily lead to ambling paraphrase or shuffling prose approximations of the biblical poem. Chana and Ariel Bloch's translation, a rare conjunction of refined poetic resourcefulness and philological precision, brings us closer to the magical freshness of this ancient Hebrew love poetry than has any other English version.

Let me illustrate with three lines of verse from the first chapter (1:12–14). To indicate the difficulties of getting the Hebrew right and getting it into English poetry, let us first look at the two translations that have exerted the greatest influence in the English-speaking world, the King James Version (completed in 1611) and the Revised Standard Version (a modernization and correction of the KJV undertaken in the 1880's and further revised in 1901 and 1946–52).

> While the king sitteth at his table, my spikenard
> sendeth forth the smell thereof.

A bundle of myrrh is my well-beloved unto me;
he shall lie all night betwixt my breasts.
My beloved is unto me as a cluster of camphire
in the vineyards of En-gedi.

While the king was on his couch,
my nard gave forth its fragrance.
My beloved is to me a bag of myrrh
that lies between my breasts.
My beloved is to me a cluster of henna blossoms
in the vineyards of En-gedi.

Compare these two time-honored versions to the Bloch translation:

My king lay down beside me
and my fragrance
wakened the night.

All night between my breasts
my love is a cluster of myrrh,
a sheaf of henna blossoms
in the vineyards of Ein Gedi.

The King James Version evokes a dinner scene in which the female dining companion appears to have doused herself with an excess of perfume. The crucial Hebrew word here, *bi-msibbo,* refers to reclining either at a table or on a bed, and the KJV, in consonance with a certain disposition to dilute the sexuality of the poem, opts with patent improbability for the former meaning. The Revised Standard Version sensibly puts the king back in bed where he belongs, but fails to solve a number of other problems, beginning with the identity of the king and his relation to the female speaker whose body is fragrant with all outdoors. The "is unto me" of the KJV, a literal rendering of the single Hebrew syllable *li,* is pared down to "is to me" by the RSV, but that is still not quite English. The Hebrew idiom for the wafting of odors, *natan reyḥo,* is translated quite literally by the RSV as "gave forth its fragrance" and almost literally by the KJV as "sent forth its fragrance."

One should immediately note that the Bloch translation manages with almost a third fewer words than its two precedessors, thus conveying much of the lovely concision that is one of the hallmarks of biblical poetry. By identifying the male lover as "my king"—the Hebrew does literally say "the king"—this version makes clear that the royal designation is a lover's epithet and that the bed on which he lies is not a divan in a palace but in all likelihood one of those bucolic resting places to which the young couple repair for lovemaking. "Beside me" after "lay down" is not in the Hebrew but is unavoidably implied by the two middle lines. In both the KJV and the RSV, the lover, metaphorically miniaturized as a cluster of myrrh, merely "lies" between the Shulamite's breasts. But as Ariel Bloch rightly observes in his Commentary, the Hebrew *yalin* means "to spend the night." This denotation reinforces the suggestion of a whole night of intimate embraces and provides warrant in the Bloch translation for both the adverbial "all night" (instead of a verb, as in the Hebrew) and the little elaboration, "my fragrance / wakened the night," which solves the problem of English usage in the "sending" or "giving forth" of fragrance. Finally, the compactness and fluency of the Bloch version also owe something to its elimination of an unneeded repetition ("my love" once instead of "my beloved" twice) and its telescoping "nard" and "fragrance" into "my fragrance." The specificity of myrrh and henna is retained, but most of us would in any case not know just what sort of scent nard was. The remarkable compactness of the Hebrew original is largely the result of formal linguistic properties—pronouns and possessives, for example, are not independent words but are indicated merely by the conjugated forms of verbs and the declined form of nouns. Thus an English translation must adopt other strategies of concision, something that the Blochs do with great flair.

THE SONG OF SONGS is the great love poem of commingling—of different realms, different senses, and of the male and female bodies. The lines we have just considered offer a microcosm of this poetics of intertwined realms. The night of lovemaking, as I have suggested, probably takes place in one of the bucolic settings typical of the whole poem. But as the bodies join, inside and outside do as well. In his partner's metaphor, the lover is a sheaf of henna blossoms, but the specification that these henna blossoms are from the lush oasis of Ein Gedi creates an odd spatial displacement, leaving us a little unsure whether the blossoms are merely *from* Ein Gedi (the obviously intended meaning) or whether, metaphor exfoliating into literal landscape, that is where the lovers embrace. Elsewhere, there are abundant cross-overs from the luxuriance of the landscape to the luxuriance of the human body. Perhaps the most famous instance is the sequence from 4:1 through 5:1, which first represents the woman's body as a mountainous landscape teeming with animal life, then evokes the actual mountains of northern Israel and Lebanon from which the lover asks his beloved to come down with him, and finally once again represents the woman's body as landscape: this time, an enclosed bower ripe with fruit, moistened by a fresh-running spring that has its source in Lebanon, the water thus flowing underground from the literal landscape just mentioned to the figurative garden.

What is equally noteworthy in regard to the aim of commingling is the poet's ability to interweave the senses—implicitly in our specimen from the first chapter and quite elaborately throughout the poem. There is a clear hierarchy in the deployment of the five senses in the imagery of the poem. The primary sense for the experience of physical love is, of course, touch, but in keeping with the delicacy of expression of the Song, touch is never mentioned directly (if one excepts a rather general verb like "embrace" in 2:6), never made the explicit object of figurative elaboration. It is, however, constantly and powerfully implied, as in "All night between my breasts / my love is a cluster of myrrh," where the perfume metaphor focuses attention on the attribute of fragrance while the image of a sachet resting between breasts also beautifully suggests the intimate and pleasurable touch of flesh upon flesh. The other four senses are characteristically grouped in two pairs in the poem: sight and sound, taste and smell, although sight also appears by itself. Sight and sound have their place, but it is definitely a secondary place, because they are the senses experienced at a distance, and this is a poem of physical closeness that repeatedly creates an illusion of immediacy of sensory experience. Thus, it is when the young man is playing a game of lovers' hide-and-seek that he invokes sight and sound, weaving the two together in an elegant chiastic (seeing-hearing-hearing-seeing) structure:

> Let me see you, all of you!
> Let me hear your voice,
> your delicious song.
> I love to look at you. (2:14)

The first time sight is mentioned in the poem (1:6), it is in a negative imperative, expressing an impulse to fend off a hostile judgment by the mere—and necessarily distant—ocular observer: "Do not see me only as dark." Elsewhere, sight is prominent in the spectacular set pieces, like the vision of the royal pavilion (3:7–11) or the description of the performing Shulamite: "dance again, / that we may watch you dancing!" (7:1). These two examples, it should be noted, are both eminently public moments, not occasions of intimate union. The one fleeting instance in which sight is a vehicle of intimacy is the exchange of lovers' glances in 4:9: "You have . . . / ravished me with one glance of your eyes, / one link of your necklace."

Again and again, however, it is taste and smell that predominate, almost always implying or associated with the pleasures of touching. The poem begins with an image of taste—"Your sweet loving / is better than wine"—immediately followed by one of smell—"You are fragrant, / you are myrrh and aloes." And whether by conscious design or rightness of poetic intuition, the concluding image of the poem is a little cloud of fragrance: "Run away, / my gazelle, my wild stag / on the hills of cinnamon." In a coordinate movement of symmetry between beginning and end, the young woman's first self-representation is of the body as landscape, the "vineyard" of 1:6, and in the final cross-over between nature and body like those we have noted, she who has just likened herself to a vineyard is last seen by her lover (8:13) sitting in a garden.

The experience of fusion conveyed through the immediate senses of taste and smell is reinforced by an interfusion of sound in the closely clustered alliteration associated with this imagery. Thus, the first half of the first line of the poem ("Kiss me, make me drunk with your kisses!") sounds something like this in the Hebrew: *yiššaQEni minneŠIqot PIhu* (uppercase letters indicate the accented syllable). The *sh* phoneme (transliterated here as *š*) is then picked up three times in the next verse in the words that mean literally "oil" and "your name," *ŠEmen* and *šimK̄A*. Verse 4:11, a verse that again moves from taste to smell, begins with a tiny explosion of *n*'s and *f*'s (transliterated as *p̄*) and *t*'s: *NOp̄et tiṬṬOP̄nah śip̄toTAYik̄*—"Your lips are honey, honey and milk / are under your tongue, / your clothes hold the scent of Lebanon."

The predominant order in this pairing of the senses is first taste, then smell. This sequence would appear to run counter to a prevailing pattern of biblical poetry, in which there is a movement of rising intensity from the first half of the line to the second in utterances that are more or less semantically parallel. Perhaps this small reversal of a general pattern reflects an impulse in the language of the poem to plunge into the immediacy of love's pleasures, for which tasting or drinking or eating is a primary metaphor, whereas fragrance is less a metaphor for the thing itself than a pleasurable secondary attribute associated with it. The small sequence of 4:10 is exemplary:

And oh, your sweet loving,
my sister, my bride.
The wine of your kisses, the spice
of your fragrant oils.

The speed of the English version here, achieved by eliminating verbs, is worth noting as a nice equivalent of the always economical Hebrew. The "oh, your sweet loving," instead of the conventional "how fair is your love," at once catches the rapturous excitement of the lover and justifies the omission of verbs. But what is crucial for conveying the sensuous concreteness of the poem is the decision to render the Hebrew *dodim* as "loving"—a decorous term, like the word it translates, but with a clear sexual implication, as it has in blues lyrics—instead of a term of emotional relationship, "love." If *dodim* did not have this physically concrete meaning, it could not be repeatedly associated as it is with delectable wine, with drinking, with the honeyed sweetness of the mouth (as in the verse following the one just cited), and thus by analogy, with the sweetness of the act of love. And if the term did not suggest the gratification of physical love, it would contribute far less effectively to the brilliant pun that joins the very end of 7:13 with the first word of the next verse: "There I will give you my love [*doday*]," a promise immediately followed by the scent of *duda'im,* mandrakes, plants presumed to be aphrodisiac.

The association of taste with the pleasures of love is subtly coordinated with the interweaving of natural landscape and body that we have noted. The triple function in the poem of the pomegranate vividly illustrates this coordination. The pomegranate first appears prominently, and perhaps to modern readers a little puzzlingly, in the head-to-breast description of the young woman in the opening verses of chapter 4: "The curve of your cheek / a pomegranate / in the thicket of your hair" (4:3). (As Ariel Bloch notes in his Commentary, the precise meaning of *raqqah* is uncertain, but the term clearly refers to some part of the face: cheek, temple, or forehead.) The literal meaning of the Hebrew is "a pomegranate slice," so the image evidently suggests the section of a delicately curving contour. The purplish red of the pomegranate's exposed fruit strikes one as the wrong color for any part of the girl's face, unless she were painfully blushing or smeared with rouge, both of which would seem to be out of character. Perhaps the poet is following a procedure evident elsewhere in the poem of concentrating on one aspect of likeness between the metaphor and its referent and excluding the associations of certain other aspects of the object involved in the metaphor. But if the pomegranate is adopted as an image for the cheek chiefly because of the pleasing curve, it has also been chosen because of the gustatory association with luscious, tangy fruit. There is, moreover, a metonymic as well as a metaphoric motivation for the image, since pomegranate trees, among other flora, are within hand's reach in the natural setting through which the young woman moves (again the cross-over between landscape and body is evident). Thus, her invitation in 7:13 to her lover to come out with her to make love in the vernal countryside:

Let us go early to the vineyards
to see if the vine has budded,
if the blossoms have opened
and the pomegranate is in flower.

There I will give you my love.

If the pomegranate in this actual landscape is just coming into flower, a few lines later, in an imagined indoor scene ("I would bring you to the house of my mother"), it reappears as fermented nectar in what is obviously a metaphor for the pleasures of love that the young woman proffers to her man: "I would give you spiced wine to drink, / my pomegranate wine" (8:2). The verb for giving drink, *'ašqeḵa,* as Ariel Bloch observes, puns on the verb for kissing, *yiššaqeni,* which is the very first Hebrew word of the whole poem, and so a circle is drawn between the kissing that is like drinking at the beginning and the drinking which is actually lovemaking here near the end.

To readers who particularly recall the extravagant imagery of artifact and architecture of the Song, the emphasis I have been placing on taste and smell, always ultimately leading back to touch, may seem one-sided, even if the figures based on artifice are less pervasive. But in the poetics of intertwinement manifested in the imagery of the poem, these seemingly opposed semantic fields actually overlap, run into each other. Let us consider a complete poetic unit, one of those public set-pieces to which I referred earlier, the evocation of the dancing Shulamite (7:1–7). Because the speaker invites us to follow with our eyes the rapid steps of the lovely dancer, this vertical description works from the feet upward, the reverse direction from that of the earlier vertical descriptions in the poem.

Again, O Shulamite,
dance again,
that we may watch you dancing!

Why do you gaze at the Shulamite
as she whirls
down the rows of dancers?

How graceful your steps in those sandals,
O nobleman's daughter.

The gold of your thigh
shaped by a master craftsman.

Your navel is the moon's
bright drinking cup.
May it brim with wine!

Your belly is a mound of wheat
edged with lilies.
Your breasts are two fawns,
twins of a gazelle.

Your neck is a tower of ivory.
Your eyes are pools in Heshbon, at the gates
of that city of lords.
Your proud nose the tower of Lebanon
that looks toward Damascus.

Your head crowns you like Mount Carmel,
the hair of your head
like royal purple. A king
is caught in the thicket.

How wonderful you are, O Love,
how much sweeter
than all other pleasures!

In the spectacle of the dance, it is of course the sense of sight that is invoked by the speaker to take in the beauty of the dancer, and the first-person plural at the beginning marks that beholding as the activity of a group, an actual audience. In the first moment of the description, there is a nice tension between the kinetic image of the graceful steps—the Bloch translation is quite precise here, for this is not the normal Hebrew word for "feet" but a term that suggests the rhythmic or pounding movement of footsteps—and the sculpturesque image of the thighs as beautifully crafted curves of gold. The immediately following metaphor for the navel, the moon's drinking cup, carries forward the reference to the semantic field of exquisite artifacts, but at the same time it associates the object of representation with two other realms of experience. First, it should be noted that the object in question is in all likelihood the navel, and not, as some self-consciously candid modern interpreters have rendered it, the vagina. A phonetically similar word occurring elsewhere in the Bible does mean navel; furthermore, it is utterly implausible to imagine the Shulamite dancing naked, her sex visible to the audience, and the poetic decorum of the Song precludes the direct naming of sexual organs, though the poet may well intimate *correspondences* between navel, or mouth, or door latch, and the woman's hidden parts.

The compact image of the drinking cup has two parts: *'aggan,* cup or bowl, and *sahar,* moon. One is not quite sure whether this is a moon-shaped drinking cup (perhaps a crescent design) or whether the moon itself is imagined as a celestial cup. In either case, the *sahar* component of the Hebrew construction points from art to nature. Even in the elaborate artifice suggested by the image, the natural world is inscribed on the woman's body. If the moon is seen as a cup and not the other way around, then she takes on an attribute of a moon goddess as the speaker looks at her bare midriff in the elastic movement of the dance. The drinking cup, moreover, is not just a pleasing shape but a receptacle brimming with wine. The term used here, *mazeg,* means literally "poured drink." Though it is not the standard word for wine—*yayin,* which occurs repeatedly elsewhere—it surely invites association with that predominant metaphoric usage in which drinking is a figuration of love's pleasures. Here, bodily proximity and the analogy of convexity make the sexual implication of the metaphor more explicit than elsewhere. In any case, through the most economical poetic means, the lovely shape of a glittering artifact is also identified with delectable wine, taste overlapping sight.

The images for belly and breast, wheat-mound and twin fawns, occur several times in previous passages. As metaphors drawn from flora and fauna, they hardly accord with the crafted gold and the drinking cup of the preceding lines. That lack of accord should by no means be thought of as a contradiction because the Song and biblical poetry in general, like many other poetic traditions, in no way assume consistency of imagery as an aesthetic norm. Such an assumption, we must remind ourselves, is a relatively modern Western literary convention. There is surely no universal poetic "logic" that would preclude a poet from speaking in one breath of shining goblets and in the next of fields edged with lilies.

The very recurrence of the image of wheat and fawns reflects another aspect of the figurative language of the Song. The metaphors are by and large drawn from what must have been a traditional stockpile of imagery for love poetry, in a fashion analogous to the inventive recycling of conventional images in the Renaissance sonnet from Petrarch down to the Elizabethans. Graceful orchestration of the traditional materials rather than novelty appears to have been the key aesthetic value, though there is also some pleasing interplay between familiar and novel images—as here, the familiar wheat-heap and gazelles are surrounded by the more unusual moon-goblet for the navel and the tower of ivory for the neck. This counterpoint is coordinated with the contrast between sight and the more intimate senses. That is, innovative imagery in the poem tends to be both literally and figuratively "spectacular": the desired body, beheld from a certain distance, is a splendid apparition, likened, in sometimes surprising comparisons, on a small scale to precious artifacts and on a large scale (or greater imagined distance) to grand architectural structures.

When, on the other hand, the poet evokes the fragrance and tactile beauty of the loved one, there is less of an impulse to strike off new metaphors like bright sparks, more of an inclination to rely on familiar sensuous figures: wine, honey and milk, perfumes, aromatic plants, and gentle animals. In the dance of the Shulamite, as the speaker's ascending gaze pauses on stomach and breasts, sight crosses over into the greater proximity of smell and implied touch in the image of the field surrounded by lilies with its (presumably) sun-warmed mound of wheat. Elsewhere in the Song, fawns as figures for breasts graze among lilies, so the associative path here from lily-edged wheat-mound to the twin gazelles is marked by poetic precedent. The image of fawns for breasts is not quite visual, since no precise similarity of shape could be implied. Rather, the similitude suggested is gracefulness, gentleness, perhaps an invitation to caress. It is as close as the Song will come to a tactile image.

The emphasis on twins, here and elsewhere in the poem, sets up a special resonance in the evocation of love's union. The breasts are of course compared to twin gazelles because they are perfectly matched. But the poem also reaches out toward a gratifying fantasy that the perfectly matched lovers might be twins. That, rather than any conjectured Egyptian precedent, is why he addresses her as "my sister, my bride." The fantasy becomes explicit at 8:1, where the Shulamite says:

> If only you were a brother
> who nursed at my mother's breast!
> I would kiss you in the streets
> and no one would scorn me.

A mere fraternal bond would be sufficient to legitimate the public kisses, but the young woman's imaging of brotherhood as nursing at her mother's breast could suggest twinship: the two infants nursing from the two breasts, and the nursing transmuted into kissing (remember "honey and milk / are under your tongue"), which in turn becomes lovemaking, over which the nurturing or guiding mother actually presides:

> I would bring you to the house of my mother
> and she would teach me.
> I would give you spiced wine to drink,
> my pomegranate wine.

The antithesis of this perfect consummation of union, for which fraternal incest serves as a surprisingly beautiful metaphor—shared life-source, shared nurturance, transmuted into the lovers' shared pleasuring—is the representation of the woman separated from her lover, desperately seeking him through the streets, in Chapters 3 and 5.

In the toe-to-head description of the Shulamite, as the lover's gaze moves up from breasts to neck and head, the figurative language pulls back from such suggestions of intimate closeness to an imposing view as though seen from an overlook. This sense of spacious topographic distance is effectively conveyed by the cluster of place-names: the eyes as "pools in Heshbon," the nose "the tower of Lebanon / that looks toward Damascus" (note how the visual perspective is carried well beyond the Israelite horizon), the head like Mount Carmel. But the intercutting we have been following between the spectacular distance of sight and the closeness of the other senses is manifested again in the last image of the sequence. The "royal purple" (*'argaman*) of the hair, no longer part of the complex of landscape and architectural images, suddenly turns into an alluring trap to catch a king. (The crucial Hebrew verb here implies something like "imprisoned" or "fettered.") The king in question is clearly not a hypothetical figure in a hyperbole but the lover himself, who uses the same designation that the woman used for him earlier. The encompassing of beauty from a distance with the eye is suddenly transformed into tactile entanglement. The Shulamite's loveliness, as the expression goes, is captivating, and in the final metaphor the captivation is carried out, the lover happily entangled by her luxuriant hair, presaging other interlacings.

In consonance with this contented captivity, the description of the Shulamite is then rounded off with a verse that stresses delicately but clearly the gratification of the senses: "How wonderful you are, O Love, / how much sweeter / than all other pleasures!" This is a precise counterpart from the male point of view to the summarizing line at the end of the woman's vertical description of her lover: "His mouth is sweet wine [literally 'his palate is sweets'], he is all delight" (5:16). The direct address to the abstract noun "love," *'ahabah,* is unusual, and the Blochs, taking a cue from love poetry of the English Renaissance, capitalize the word, treating it as a personification. (To me it seems plausible that Love here is a tender epithet for the young woman herself; since the noun is feminine in Hebrew, there is no grammatical change from the second person feminine singular that has governed the entire address to the dancing Shulamite. The word, however, is problematic. There is no precedent for using the abstract "love" as a term of endearment, but, in the alternate reading, there is also no precedent for apostrophes to abstract terms.) In any case, the use of the abstract noun at the end of this vividly concrete description conveys a sense that the woman is virtually an embodiment of love's beauty, a beauty that is in turn a kind of visual promise of love's pleasure. *Na'amt*—the verb rendered here adjectivally as "sweeter"—is a term that refers to things that please the ear or palate, and *ta'anugim,* "pleasures," the last word of this unit in the Hebrew as in the English, is a word associated with gratification of the senses.

In all these ways, the figurative language of the Song creates an intricate root system that firmly anchors love in the experience of the body, and Chana and Ariel Bloch's English version faithfully and gracefully registers that essential dimension of the poem. The graceful aspect of the original needs to be stressed, for metaphoric representation, certainly as it is deployed here, is artful mediation: if the poet frankly imagines the body, male and female, as an alluring map of erogenous zones, the figurative language of the poem again and again translates that bodily reality into fresh springs, flowering gardens, highlands over which lithe animals bound, spices and wine, cunningly wrought artifacts, resplendent towers and citadels and gleaming pools. In more explicit erotic literature, the body in the act of love often seems to displace the rest of the world. In the Song, by contrast, the world is constantly embraced in the very process of imagining the body. The natural landscape, the cycle of the seasons, the beauty of the animal and floral realm, the profusion of goods afforded through trade, the inventive skill of the artisan, the grandeur of cities, are all joyfully affirmed as love is affirmed.

The experience of love is enacted through the body, and the Song celebrates the body as few other poems, ancient or modern, have done. But though love manifests itself in bodily impulse, it is also conceived here as an abiding force that transcends the body, a force that cannot be bribed, bought, extorted, deflected by public censure, or prompted to exert its power before it is ripe. In a poem that never mentions God's name, love provides access to a kind of divinity, linking the lovers with each other in a union that ultimately recalls the primal unity of infant and maternal breast and at the same time linking them with the teeming bounty and beauty of the whole world. It is finely appropriate, and perhaps even an indication of architectonic design in this sequence of lyrics, that one of the concluding poetic segments (8:5–7) should be an evocation of the power of love in the larger scheme of human life.

The poet begins here with one of those images of inseparable closeness, like the bundle of myrrh between the breasts and the nursing brother: "Bind me as a seal upon your heart, / a sign upon your arm." The language of this verse could be a daring adaptation of religious imagery, for it is reminiscent of the injunction in Deuteronomy 11:18 to bind God's words on heart and hand and as a frontlet between the eyes. But from the closeness of heart and arm, the poet's perspective suddenly leaps out to death and the underworld (*She'ol*) and the great seas or water, *mayim rabbim,* which in biblical poetry repeatedly hark back to the primordial waters that God divided and hedged in to create the world. Underlying the physicality of love in the Song is an implicit metaphysics of love, and thus the passage that starts with the simile of a seal to represent intimate, inseparable closeness goes on to imagine love on a cosmic scale, and then the futility of attempting to coerce this cosmic force with anything so paltry as wealth. The poet who revels in the pleasures of love is also ultimately concerned with its meaning.

For love is as fierce as death,
its jealousy bitter as the grave.
Even its sparks are a raging fire,
a devouring flame.

Great seas cannot extinguish love,
no river can sweep it away.

If a man tried to buy love
with all the wealth of his house,
he would be despised. (8:6–7)

COMMENTARY

Introductory Note

THE COMMENTARY is addressed to an audience of both specialists and general readers; thus it has been written insofar as possible without technical jargon. However, a minimum of essential grammatical terms—such as *semikut, pi'el,* and *hip̄'il*—had to be used; these terms will be familiar to those who know Hebrew grammar.

Because so much of the Song remains open to interpretation, it seemed only right to accord the place of honor in the entries to the Hebrew before offering our own interpretation. Each entry therefore begins with the Hebrew as it appears in the Masoretic Text, followed by a simplified phonetic transliteration and a straightforward prose translation. Our intention is to let the Masoretic Text speak as directly as possible to the reader who has no knowledge of Hebrew, and to facilitate the comparison of our English version of the Song with the biblical text. The literal translations may often seem awkward in English; they have been designed to highlight the stylistic and syntactic features of the Hebrew.

Although the past decades have seen tremendous strides in biblical exegesis, philology, and Semitic linguistics, the earlier commentators still repay study. Even when one is tempted to smile at an interpretation by Rashi or Ibn Ezra, or at a "wrong" translation in the Septuagint, the Vulgate, or the King James Version, one must acknowledge that all these sources offer valuable insights, although—or perhaps precisely because—their point of view is so different from our own.

Among recent studies, no scholar can do without the seminal works by Marvin Pope (the *Anchor Bible* edition of the Song) and Michael Fox (*The Song of Songs and the Ancient Egyptian Love Songs*). With its comprehensive survey of the exegetical literature, Pope's book is indispensable for an overview of interpretations in the course of two millennia. Fox's superb commentary is distinguished by its intellectual rigor and the originality of its solutions to difficult textual problems. We have also benefited from Marcia Falk's and Roland Murphy's books on the Song. Of studies published in Israel, the commentary of Amos Hakham was particularly illuminating. We are indebted to all these scholars, even where we reach substantially different conclusions.

Since commentaries on the Song are arranged by chapter and verse, references to such works are given without page numbers. Scholarly sources are cited by the author's last name; more complete information is found in the Bibliography.

Verse numbers of biblical citations in the Commentary refer to the Hebrew text; the reader should be aware that occasionally the numbering in English translations differs from that in the Hebrew by a verse or two.

All translations from biblical texts in this book are our own, unless otherwise specified.

1:1 שִׁיר הַשִּׁירִים אֲשֶׁר לִשְׁלֹמֹה *šir ha-širim 'ašer li-šelomoh* "The Song of Songs which is Solomon's." Not to be taken to imply authorship by Solomon; it may mean something like "dedicated to" or in some other way "associated with" the biblical king. See pp. 10–11, 22–23.

This, the title of the book, is usually considered a secondary addition. It is not part of the first lyric; compare Ps. 23, which begins "The Lord is my shepherd," not "A Psalm of David."

For the superlative sense of *šir ha-širim,* compare similar constructions such as Exod. 26:33 *qodeš ha-qodašim* "the holiest of the holy places," and Eccles. 1:2 *hab̄el hab̄alim* "vanity of vanities."

אֲשֶׁר *'ašer* here is archaizing usage (for *še-*, see p. 24); this may have been intended to suggest the Hebrew of King Solomon's day.

1:2 יִשָּׁקֵנִי *yiššaqeni* evokes the phonetically similar *yašqeni* "O that he would let me drink," associated with "wine." The association between kissing and wine-drinking is more explicit in *'eššaqek̄a* "I would kiss you" and *'ašqek̄a* "I would give you to drink," 8:1–2. "Make me drunk" in the present translation attempts to capture the effect of this wordplay.

יִשָּׁקֵנִי מִנְּשִׁיקוֹת פִּיהוּ כִּי־טוֹבִים דֹּדֶיךָ מִיָּיִן *yiššaqeni mi(n)-nešiqot pihu, ki ṭob̄im dodeyk̄a mi(n)-yayin,* literally "O that he would kiss me with the kisses of his mouth, for your lovemaking is better than wine." The shift from the third to the second person typically occurs in direct addresses to persons of a higher social standing, as in Gen. 44:7 "Why does my lord speak [third person] such words as these? Far be it from your [second person] servants. . . ." The most plausible explanation is that the courtly, ceremonious tone of the Shulamite's address to her lover belongs to their fantasy world, in which he figures as her "king," her very own "Solomon," as it were; see comment on *ha-melek̄* in 1:4,12.

דֹּדֶיךָ *dodeyk̄a,* literally "your *dodim.*" The plural *dodim* is a comprehensive term for lovemaking, that is, kisses and caresses as well as intercourse. Compare Prov. 7:18, Ezek. 16:8, 23:17; in the Song see 1:4, 4:10, 5:1, 7:13. The word "love" in most translations is too general and evasive.

1:3 לְרֵיחַ שְׁמָנֶיךָ טוֹבִים *le-reaḥ šemaneyk̄a ṭob̄im,* literally "as regards scent, your oils are good." Unusual in Hebrew as in English, this syntax may have been deliberately chosen for the sake of chiasmus: (*A*) *ṭob̄im* "better," (*B*) *dodeyk̄a* "your lovemaking," (*C*) *mi(n)-yayin* "than wine," followed by (*C*) *le-reaḥ* "as regards scent," (*B*) *šemaneyḵa* "your oils," (*A*) *ṭoḇim* "good."

שֶׁמֶן תּוּרַק שְׁמֶךָ *šemen turaq šemeḵa*, literally "your name is *šemen turaq*." Enigmatic. The various interpretations proposed—"your name is oil poured out"/"Turaq oil," etc.—are problematic for grammatical or lexical reasons. All that can be said with certainty is that in the Bible a name often reflects a person's characteristic traits (compare 1 Sam. 25:25), and that the "oil" here, whatever its identity, is symbolic of the young man's sensual attractiveness.

The Peshitta has "oil of myrrh." We borrowed "myrrh and aloes" from 4:14 as a concrete referent for scent; compare 1:13 and Ps. 45:9.

עֲלָמוֹת *'alamot* "young women, girls." The word does not imply virginity, contra the interpretation of *'almah* in Isa. 7:14 as "virgin," based on the Septuagint's *parthenos*, which can mean "maiden" or "virgin."

עַל־כֵּן עֲלָמוֹת אֲהֵבוּךָ *'al ken 'alamot 'aheḇuḵa*, literally "therefore young women love you." While *'ahaḇ* "to love" in the Bible has a wide range of meanings, from spiritual to sexual—in the story of Amnon and Tamar it means "lust" (2 Sam. 13:4,15)—in the Song this verb most often refers to erotic love. Since the lover is described in purely sensual terms here (his kisses, the sweet scent of his oils), *'ahaḇ* probably refers to physical attraction.

1:4 **מָשְׁכֵנִי אַחֲרֶיךָ נָּרוּצָה** *mošḵeni 'aḥareyḵa naruṣah* "Take me by the hand [literally "pull/draw me after you"], let us run!"

הֱבִיאַנִי הַמֶּלֶךְ *heḇi'ani ha-meleḵ*, literally "the king has brought me." Here and in 1:12, "the king" is to be understood as the Shulamite's courtly epithet for her lover. It is by no means a reference to King Solomon as a rival for her love, as some have supposed (see p. 33). The explanatory paraphrase "my lover, my king" here is patterned after the chains of affectionate epithets in the Song, notably "my sister, my bride" in 4:10, or the longer chain in 5:2.

חֲדָרָיו *ḥadarav* "into his chambers." The king's "chambers" are best explained in terms of the lovers' vocabulary of make-believe. Since most of their erotic encounters take place out of doors, this word may designate the sheltered or hidden places in the woods or vineyards where they meet (see below, on the king's "couch," "our bed," and especially "our houses," 1:12,16,17). Note also the expression *ḥeder be-ḥeder,* literally "a chamber within a chamber, an inner chamber," a metaphor for a secret hiding place, 1 Kings 20:30, 22:25; 2 Kings 9:2.

נָגִילָה וְנִשְׂמְחָה בָּךְ *nagilah ve-niśmeḥah bak̄,* literally "let us exult and rejoice in you." This clause with its paired verbs recalls the formulaic expression of festivity and joy in Ps. 118:24 *nagilah ve-niśmeḥah bo* "let us exult and rejoice in it," and similarly Isa. 25:9.

נַזְכִּירָה דֹדֶיךָ מִיַּיִן *nazkirah dodeyk̄a mi(n)-yayin,* literally "let us recount/proclaim/extol [compare Ps. 45:18] your lovemaking more than wine." The segment *dodeyk̄a mi(n)-yayin* "your lovemaking more than wine" is repeated here verbatim from 1:2 as a kind of refrain. This may explain the interpretively difficult "*your* lovemaking," where one would rather expect something like "our lovemaking" or simply "lovemaking" (as in Prov. 7:18, "Come, let us take our fill of lovemaking till morning").

Similarly, one might have expected "Let us exult and rejoice" rather than "exult and rejoice *in you*" in the preceding phrase. The final word *bak̄* may serve no other purpose than to allude to the formulaic expression of joy just quoted, *nagilah ve-niśmeḥah bo* "Let us exult and rejoice *in it.*"

These two difficult clauses have given rise to various explanations. For example, it has been suggested that in using "we" in her address to her lover, the Shulamite is projecting her own love for him onto other young women. This is plausible, given his attractiveness to women (1:3,4), but it is far more likely that *nagilah, niśmeḥah,* and *nazkirah* have as their subject just the two lovers, as in "Take me by the hand, let us run together" earlier in the same verse.

מֵישָׁרִים אֲהֵבוּךָ *meyšarim 'ahebuka,* literally "indeed/truly/rightly they love you." The emphatic force of the adverbial *meyšarim* is enhanced by its position before the verb, as also in Ps. 58:2, 75:3.

This refrain echoes the statement at the end of 1:3. Refrains in the Song often occur with some variation in the wording, as here.

1:5 שְׁחוֹרָה *šeḥorah,* literally "dark, black" and the related *šeḥarḥoret* in 1:6 refer to the Shulamite's sunburned skin.

שְׁחוֹרָה אֲנִי וְנָאוָה *šeḥorah 'ani ve-na'vah.* Translations vary between "black am I *and* beautiful" (Septuagint) and "I am very dark, *but* comely" (RSV). This reflects a genuine ambiguity inherent in the Hebrew, where the conjunctive *ve-* may be used either in its common meaning "and" or in an adversative sense, as in Prov. 11:22 "beautiful but [*ve-*] without sense." See also Song 3:1,2 and 5:6. Sunburned skin is associated with a lower social status, a fair complexion being the mark of those who could afford not to work outdoors. In ancient Egyptian and Greek art, the women are shown as having lighter skin than the men, probably because the women worked indoors. The Shulamite's need to account for her dark skin sounds apologetic; on the other hand, since her dark skin may have contributed to her singularity and attractiveness, she may be boasting, not apologizing.

בְּנוֹת יְרוּשָׁלָםִ *benot yerušalayim* "daughters of Jerusalem." A group of women addressed by the Shulamite throughout the Song, e.g., 2:7, 3:5, 3:11, 8:4, and elsewhere. Except where she engages in a dialogue with them (5:8–9, 6:1–2), the daughters need not be imagined as actually present; they may be a purely rhetorical audience for her declamatory statements.

אָהֳלֵי קֵדָר *'oholey qedar* "the tents of Kedar." Tents of nomadic Bedouins in the Middle East are typically woven from the wool of black goats. The comparison here may have been chosen because Kedar is proverbial in the Bible for opulence (Isa. 21:16, 60:7, Jer. 49:28–29, Ezek. 27:21), and because the name Kedar involves a wordplay on the root *qdr* "to be dark, black."

יְרִיעוֹת שְׁלֹמֹה *yeri'ot šelomoh.* "Solomon's curtains" are mentioned nowhere else in the Bible, and may well belong to the accoutrements of his royal splendor, a memory of which has been preserved in folklore; compare 3:7–11. *Yeri'ot* are specifically mentioned among the booty to be taken from the Kedar in Jer. 49:28–29. The word "tapestries" here is borrowed from Falk's and Jay's translations.

1:6 **אַל־תִּרְאוּנִי שֶׁאֲנִי שְׁחַרְחֹרֶת** *'al tir'uni še-'ani šeḥarḥoret,* literally "do not see *me* that *I* am dark." For the syntax and semantic nuance of this statement, compare Prov. 23:31 *'al tere' yayin ki yit'addam,* literally "do not see *wine* that *it* sparkles red," an admonition not to consider only one superficial aspect of wine, its color, while ignoring its intoxicating power. Hence "only" in our translation.

שֶׁשֱּׁזָפַתְנִי הַשָּׁמֶשׁ *še-šezap̄atni ha-šameš.* Outside the Song, the verb *šazap̄* ("look upon, catch sight of") occurs only in Job 20:9 and 28:7, both times with the eye as agent. When the *sun* is considered poetically the "eye" that looks down, the verb acquires the secondary meaning "to tan, sunburn." In the Song we may see the intermediary stage between these two meanings: *šazap̄* is used in the sense of "to sunburn," though the original meaning "to look upon" still reverberates. In Modern Hebrew, the verb no longer means "to look upon," only "to sunburn."

בְּנֵי אִמִּי *beney 'immi,* literally "my mother's sons," a term for full brothers, brothers of the same mother. It sometimes implies a sense of special closeness, as in Judg. 8:19, Gen. 43:29, Ps. 50:20, 69:9. This is also the point of the image in Song 8:1. Brothers of a different mother would have been called "my father's sons," as in 1 Chron. 28:4, a relationship that often implies distance and rivalry, for example, Joseph's half-brothers; see also Judg. 11:2.

כַּרְמִי שֶׁלִּי *karmi šelli,* literally "my vineyard, mine," with the independent possessive added for emphasis. Though the vineyard may be real, the emphatic tone with which the Shulamite speaks of "her own" vineyard suggests an additional metaphorical sense. "Vine" and "vineyard" evoke her sexuality in 6:11 and 7:13 (both Hebrew words, *gep̄en* and *kerem,* are grammatically feminine). "Not having guarded" her vineyard is usually taken to mean either loss of chastity or neglect of her beauty because of work outdoors. For the brothers in the role of guardians of their sister's honor elsewhere, see Gen. 34 and 2 Sam. 13.

1:7 שֶׁאָהֲבָה נַפְשִׁי *še-'ahab̄ah nap̄ši,* literally "the one whom my soul loves," an epithet used also in 3:1–4.

אֵיכָה *'eyk̄ah* "where?" is the Aramaic equivalent of older Hebrew *'eyp̄oh.* On the significance of Aramaic and Mishnaic elements for dating the Song, see pp. 23–25.

אֵיכָה תִרְעֶה אֵיכָה תַּרְבִּיץ *'eyk̄ah tir'eh 'eyk̄ah tarbiṣ* "Where do you/will you pasture?" Given the imperfect form of the verbs, the question may apply either to the young man's customary place of pasturing, or his whereabouts on that particular day. See also next note.

בַּצָּהֳרָיִם *ba-ṣohorayim.* Meaning "at noon" in a general sense, as in most translations. It may also mean "today at noon" if the definite article is understood in the sense of "this," as in 1 Sam. 24:18 *ha-yom* "this day, today," Gen. 2:23 *ha-pa'am* "this time," Num. 22:8 *ha-laylah* "this night, tonight."

שַׁלָּמָה *šallamah* "lest," i.e., "tell me, . . . lest. . . ." A hapax particle patterned after the Aramaic *di le-mah;* see Ezra 7:23. Also see Dan. 1:10 *'ašer lamah.* The older Hebrew particle for "lest" is *pen.*

עֹטְיָה *'oṭeyah* is obscure. The interpretation offered here follows the Septuagint, Peshitta, Symmachus, Vulgate, and Targum, all of which translate "one who goes astray, loses her way," reflecting a variant reading *ṭo'iyyah* or *ṭo'ayah.* Compare the Aramaic verb *ṭe'ā,* which is used with this meaning also in the Peshitta of Gen. 37:15, Exod. 23:4, Prov. 21:16.

Verses 1:7–8 may reflect a stock rhetorical theme. Shepherding in the Bible is not infrequently associated with getting lost or losing one's way, as when Joseph loses his way in search of his brothers who are pasturing the flock (Gen. 37:12–17). Conversely, notions of straying from the right path or being led astray are often couched in images of shepherding (as also in the metaphors of the good shepherd and the lost sheep in the New Testament). These associations find expression in the interplay of two phonetically similar verbs, *ra'ah* "to tend flocks, to graze," and *ta'ah* "to lose one's way, get lost, go astray" (or in the causative hip̄'il, "to lead astray"), as in Jer. 50:6 "My people have been lost sheep; their shepherds have led them astray," with the verbs *ra'ah* and *ta'ah* alternating in close proximity (*ro'eyhem hit'um*). In Gen. 37:15–16, Joseph, "roaming around, lost" (from *ta'ah*) asks a man in the field, "Where are they pasturing?" (from *ra'ah*). In 1:7–8 the verb *ra'ah* "to shepherd" occurs three times, which confirms the likelihood of the reading *ṭo'iyyah* "lose my way." This reading reflects both the interplay of the two verbal roots, and the rich literary association of pasturing sheep and losing one's way.

A radically different interpretation, "lest I be like one-who-wraps-herself-up by your companions' flocks" (Fox, Pope), is based on the story of Tamar, who veils her face so that Judah will think her a harlot (Gen. 38:14–15). The verb *'aṭah,* though not used in the Tamar story, does indeed mean "wrap/veil/cover oneself." However, verbs with this range of meanings normally do not occur in isolation, without some indication of what is being covered (say, a specific body part, or simply the "self," typically expressed through the reflexive hitpa'el), or the article of clothing that serves as a covering. Thus Tamar "covered herself with a veil, wrapping herself up, . . . covered her face," and similarly, Rebecca "took the veil and covered herself" (Gen. 24:65). See also 1 Sam. 28:14, Jer. 43:12, Lev. 13:45, Ezek. 24:17,22, Micah 3:7, Ps. 104:2 (where the light is God's "covering"). Lacking any of these specifications or any sign of reflexivity, *'oṭeyah* is not likely to mean "wraps herself up."

1:8 אִם־לֹא תֵדְעִי לָךְ *'im lo' tede'i lak̄* "If you do not know." This *l-* with suffix (the so-called "ethical dative") occurs in the Song more typically with verbs of motion, or in contexts encouraging motion, as in the immediately following *ṣe'i lak̄* "go" (here, in the tracks of), and in 2:13, 17; 4:6; 8:14. See also Gen. 12:1.

הַיָּפָה בַּנָּשִׁים *ha-yap̄ah ba-našim,* literally "the beautiful one [feminine] among women," a way of expressing superlativity. The motif of excellence among lesser examples occurs again in 1:9, 2:2–3, 6:8–9.

1:9 לְסֻסָתִי ... דִּמִּיתִיךְ *le-susati . . . dimmitik̄.* This verse has usually been understood as expressing an act of comparison, as in RSV "I compare you, my love, to a mare," likewise Septuagint, Vulgate, KJV, JPS, NEB, Gordis, Pope, Fox, Murphy, and others. But this particular verb (*dimmah,* pi'el) also has another sense, "to think someone to be, imagine, conjure up a mental image," thus, Ps. 50:21 *dimmita heyot 'eheyeh k̄amok̄a* "You imagined me to be like yourself" (God speaking to the self-aggrandizing wicked man); Esther 4:13 *'al tedammi be-nap̄šek̄ le-himmaleṭ* "Do not imagine [literally in your soul] that you could escape." Here the lover is recalling his dreamlike wish or fantasy about the Shulamite; compare the chariot image in 6:12, and see pages 14–15 on *dimmah.*

The verb *dimmitik̄* should not be rendered in the present tense, as in the RSV and other translations. Indeed, all occurrences of *dimmah* in the perfect tense refer to the past, Judg. 20:5, Num. 33:56, Isa. 14:24, Ps. 48:10.

The placement of *le-* (*le-susati*) follows the pattern "to think X to be *le*-Y." See 1 Sam. 1:13 "Eli took her to be a drunken woman," *le-šikkorah;* Job 41:19 "He counts iron as straw," *le-teb̄en;* Job 35:2 "Do you think this to be justice?" *le-mišpaṭ;* Gen. 38:15 "He thought her to be a prostitute," *le-zonah.*

סֻסָתִי *susati* "my mare." Traditional Christian and Jewish exegesis devised various evasive strategies to explain away the potentially offensive association of a beloved woman with a mare. Horses are often associated in the Old Testament texts with worldly riches and high living, sinful pagan ways of life, and occasionally with lustfulness. See Deut. 17:16–17, Isa. 2:7–8, Jer. 5:8, Ezek. 23:20. One way to get rid of the troublesome mare was to replace it with a *cavalry* of horses, as in the Vulgate "to my cavalry . . . I likened you," or KJV "I have compared thee, O my love, to a company of horses," or NEB "to Pharaoh's chariot-horses." And thus, purged of all flesh and blood, the mare—now a cavalry—was made fit to enter heaven. But the noun *susah* is neither a collective (contra Rashi, who paraphrases the word with *qeb̄uṣat susim* "a group of horses"), nor a plural.

A different interpretive strategy, likewise going back to the Middle Ages, is to explain the possessive *-i* of *susati* by identifying it with the archaic *-i* in such cases as Isa. 1:21 *mele'ati mišpaṭ* "full of justice," Deut. 33:16 *šok̄ni seneh* "the dweller in the thornbush," or Ps. 114:8 *ha-hop̄ki ha-ṣur* "he who changes the rock." (For this so-called "suffix of connection," see GKC, 252ff. and WO, 127–28). Thus "my mare" became "a mare."

This interpretation, which has found its way into most modern translations (Christian Ginsburg is a notable exception) is based on a false analogy. As the suffix of connection, the *-i* in phrases such as those just mentioned is without semantic value, as is easily recognizable in variant versions of the same text, e.g., Ps. 113:7–8 *meqimi, le-hošib̄i,* and 1 Sam. 2:8 *meqim, le-hošib̄*. In contrast, the *-i* of *le-susati* makes perfect sense if read as a fully functional "my" in 1:9. This interpretive strategy was never applied to 2:14 *yonati* "my dove," despite the similar syntax: compare "my dove in the crannies of the rock" with "my mare among the chariots of Pharaoh." But since the dove is a symbol of purity and peace, the possessive "my dove" was no problem for the pious exegetes. Ironically, it was the allegorists who preserved the correct reading, "my mare," by making the people of Israel, the Church, or the faithful soul the object of the comparison, with God as the rider. In our reading, it is the young man who is the potential rider.

The comparison of a beautiful woman to a horse is well known in Greek poetry. Alcman compares Hagesichora to "a sturdy thundering horse, a champion" (Higham and Bowra, poem no. 114), and Theocritus writes of Helen: "As some . . . Thracian steed [adorns] the chariot it draws, so rosy Helen adorns Lacedaemon" (Gow, vol. 1, 143).

In Anacreon the image is given a distinctly erotic turn: "Thracian filly, . . . I could fit you deftly with a bridle / and, holding the reins, could steer you past the end posts of our course, /. . . you lack a rider with a practiced hand at horsemanship" (Bing and Cohen, 92). A similar image is used in our day by the poet Garcia Lorca: "That night I galloped on the best of roads, mounted on a mare all mother-of-pearl, without bridle or stirrups" ("The Faithless Wife," from *Romancero Gitano*).

בְּרִכְבֵי פַרְעֹה *be-rik̄bey p̄ar'oh* "among Pharaoh's chariots." Not referring to chariots in the possession of Pharaoh, but rather to the kind imported by King Solomon *from* Egypt; compare 1 Kings 10:28–29; see Bright, 217. For this type of semik̄ut-construction with the second word denoting point of origin, see 3:9 *'aṣey ha-leb̄anon* "cedar wood from Lebanon," 1 Chron. 29:4 *zehab̄ 'op̄ir* "gold from Ophir." For a discussion of the Solomonic images—horse, chariots, Pharaoh (as Solomon's trading partner), gold, and silver—see p. 10–11.

בְּ *be* in the sense of "among, in the midst of," as in 2:3,14,16. The noun *rek̄eb̄* (here in the pl., *rik̄bey p̄ar'oh*) can denote chariots, but may also be metonymic for chariot horses or simply riding horses (2 Sam. 8:4, 1 Chron. 18:4). In addition to the implied riding imagery, with its erotic overtones, this image may be understood in terms of the motif of excellence among lesser specimens, as in 1:8, 2:2–3, 6:8–9.

Commenting on 1:9, Pope refers to the ancient military stratagem, practiced by Thutmosis III in his campaign against Qadesh, of setting loose a mare in heat to distract the enemy's war horses. But a violent battle image is extremely unlikely in this lyric. The point here is the elegant *beauty* of the mare, not its unbridled ferocity; see 1:10–11. For genuine military imagery associated with the Shulamite, see the metaphors of "siege," "wall," and "towers" in 8:9–10. Compare also the "thousand bucklers" of 4:4.

רַעְיָתִי *ra'yati* "my friend," the lover's epithet for the Shulamite. She uses the corresponding masculine form *rea'* for him in 5:16 (*zeh re'i* "this is my friend"). The use of this term by both lovers highlights the mutuality and reciprocity of their relationship. Compare note on verse 7:11.

1:10 נָאווּ לְחָיַיִךְ *na'vu leḥayayik̄*, literally "beautiful are your cheeks!" This verse elaborates on the mare image in 1:9. Royal horses in antiquity were often decorated with ornaments. The Shulamite in her jewelry is as lovely as a royal mare with its trappings, tassles, fringes, and bridle.

Both in meaning and word order, this exclamation is the equivalent of the English "How beautiful/good are . . . !" Exclamatory constructions are more typically introduced by the particle *mah* "How!" as in Song 4:10, 7:2,7.

Leḥi "cheek" includes the entire area of the cheek, the side of the face, possibly also the cheekbone; compare Judg. 15:15, "jawbone."

בַּתֹּרִים *ba-torim,* literally "with/between the *torim.*" The word *tor* is unknown, but the root *twr* "to go around" suggests some circular ornament. For the understanding of the definite article in a demonstrative sense (literally "with those *torim*"), compare note 1:7 *ba-ṣohorayim.*

1:11 **תּוֹרֵי זָהָב ... עִם נְקֻדּוֹת הַכָּסֶף** *torey zahab̄ . . . ʿim nequddot ha-kasep̄,* literally "*torim* of gold . . . with dots/points of silver," probably refers to granulation, an ancient technique of jewelry decoration related to filigree. For a reference to the combination of these two metals in ornaments see Prov. 25:11 "apples of gold in a setting of silver." In the Song, gold and silver are emblematic of the splendors of King Solomon's reign; see 3:10, 8:11, and 1 Kings 10:21–22. Notice the intensification of the image: the simple *torim* of 1:10 are followed by golden ones in 1:11 (compare 2:1–2).

נַעֲשֶׂה־לָּךְ *naʿaśeh lak̄,* literally "we will make for you." The young man may be including others in his statement; alternatively, this line may be spoken by a group.

1:12 **עַד־שֶׁהַמֶּלֶךְ בִּמְסִבּוֹ** *ʿad še-ha-melek̄ bi-msibbo,* literally "while the king is in his reclining. . . ." On the epithet *ha-melek̄,* literally "the king," see note 1:4. The form *mesab̄* underlying *bi-msibbo* is understood here as the infinitive "to sit, recline, lie down," rather than as the noun "couch."

ʿAd še- expresses simultaneity; compare the use of *ʿad* in 2 Kings 9:22, 1 Sam. 14:19, Ps. 141:10. Elsewhere, *ʿad še-* means "before/until" as in Song 2:7,17; 3:4; 4:6. Possibly patterned after the Aramaic *ʿad di,* this conjunction is rare in biblical but common in Mishnaic Hebrew.

נִרְדִּי *nirdi* "my spikenard." Spikenard, a costly perfume extracted from the stems and leaves of a plant that grows in the Himalayas, mentioned again in 4:13–14 (compare Mark 14:3–6). On "night" in this translation see remark under *yalin* in note 1:13.

1:13 הַמֹּר *ha-mor* "myrrh," an aromatic resin from the stems and branches of a shrub that grows in Arabia, Abyssinia, and Somalia, which was used to perfume clothing, Ps. 45:9, and bedding, Prov. 7:17.

יָלִין *yalin* means to spend the night (root *lyn / lwn*).

הַכֹּפֶר *ha-kop̄er* "henna." A shrub with clusters of powerfully fragrant flowers whose scent resembles that of roses.

1:14 עֵין גֶּדִי *'eyn gedi.* Ein Gedi is a fertile oasis on the western shore of the Dead Sea. The association between the vineyard and female eroticism found throughout the Song (see note 1:6) is evoked here by the parallelism of "my breasts" and "the vineyards."

1:15 עֵינַיִךְ יוֹנִים *'eynayik̄ yonim* "your eyes are doves." The point of comparison may be the oval shape, possibly also the gentleness of doves. The *yonah* is the rock dove (*Columba livia*) which builds its nest "in the clefts of the rock" (2:14). One of the lover's epithets for the Shulamite is "my dove" (5:2). Notice that she too compares his eyes to doves in 5:12.

1:16 עַרְשֵׂנוּ רַעֲנָנָה *'arśenu ra'ananah,* literally "our bed is verdant." The adjective *ra'anan* is typically used in the Bible in reference to flourishing trees, young plants, fresh leaves, etc. (compare Ps. 92:15). Hence the statement is best seen as a metaphor for any spot of lush grass where the lovers lie down.

1:17 קֹרוֹת בָּתֵּינוּ *qorot bateynu,* literally "the beams of our houses." Since the two young lovers hardly own "houses," commentators taking the word literally are forced to devise ways of interpreting the plural as a singular, e.g. "our house," "our bower" (Pope, Fox, Ehrlich). The problem dissolves if "houses" is seen as a metaphor for places where the lovers meet. See note on 1:4, "the king's chambers."

The possessive "our" conveys not ownership but intimacy, something the two lovers share, as in 1:16 "our bed," 2:9 "our wall," 2:12 "our land." The same loving "possession" is reflected in the many "my"-bearing epithets by which they address each other.

אֲרָזִים *'arazim* "cedars" can denote the trees as well as the wood (for the latter, see 2 Sam. 7:7). The same double meaning is found in *'eṣim,* which is "trees" in 2:3, but "wood" in 3:9. Thus the statement could mean that the beams "are cedars" or "are made of cedar wood." Both readings make sense in the fantasy world of the lovers: they are either imagining the trees around their meeting place as "cedars," or imagining themselves in Solomon's luxurious buildings, known for their lavish cedar beams and paneling. See 1 Kings 7:2–3,7.

רַהִיטֵנוּ *rahiṭenu.* Meaning (as well as root and voweling) uncertain. Usually assumed to be related to the Syriac word for "rafter" (*rehṭā*) and taken as a collective noun for rafters, or strips running between ceiling beams.

בְּרוֹתִים *berotim* "fir trees," "pines," "cypresses," or "junipers" (compare Syriac *berūtā* "cypress"). On the divergent opinions about the identity of evergreens in the Bible, see Moldenke, 176.

2:1 חֲבַצֶּלֶת הַשָּׁרוֹן שׁוֹשַׁנַּת הָעֲמָקִים *ḥabaṣṣelet ha-šaron šošannat ha-'amaqim.* "I am the *ḥabaṣṣelet* . . . the *šošannah*. . . ." Neither the experts on Palestinian flora nor the commentators agree about the identity of these flowers. The *ḥabaṣṣelet* is variously translated as "rose" (KJV, RSV), "tulip" (Moldenke), "lily" (Feliks), "crocus" (Pope, Fox), or "wildflower" (Falk), and the *šošannah* as "lily" (KJV, RSV, JPS, Fox), "lotus" (Pope), "hyacinth" (Moldenke), or "narcissus" (Feliks, Falk). Since the identity of these flowers remains unknown, we have kept the familiar "rose" and "lily" because of their resonance in the tradition.

Ultimately, however, the botanical identity of these flowers may be less to the point than their symbolic value in the Bible. The same two flowers are singled out in prophetic visions about the restoration of Zion to her former glory: "The arid desert shall be glad, the wilderness shall rejoice and blossom like the *ḥabaṣṣelet* " (Isa. 35:1–2); "I [God] will be as the dew to Israel, he shall blossom as the *šošannah*" (Hosea 14:6–8). By connecting the *ḥabaṣṣelet* with the Sharon, the fertile coastal plain, Song 2:1 may be alluding to this passage in Isaiah, where the *ḥabaṣṣelet* is associated with "the majesty of Carmel and Sharon." In the Hosea text the *šošannah* is associated with the trees, fragrance, and wine of Lebanon.

Seen in this light, 2:1 is an expression of a young woman's proud awareness of her blossoming beauty. The Shulamite is not presenting herself—either modestly or coyly—as a common, ordinary flower of the field ("I am a mere flower of the plain," as Ginsburg and others would have it). Quite the contrary, she is identifying herself with the *ḥabaṣṣelet* and *šošannah,* two flowers that are the very epitome of blossoming in the symbolism of the Bible.

2:2 כְּשׁוֹשַׁנָּה בֵּין הַחוֹחִים *ke-šošannah beyn ha-ḥoḥim,* literally "like a *šošannah* among thistles." Confirms and reinforces the Shulamite's statement by expanding the *šošannah* image. This verse and the next introduce the motif of comparison: the lovers are unique, distinguished from all others. See 5:9–10, 6:8–9.

2:3 תַּפּוּחַ *tappuaḥ,* has usually been rendered "apple," but many botanists today are inclined to identify the *tappuaḥ* with the apricot (*Prunus armeniaca*), which is abundant in Palestine and most probably has been ever since biblical times. The common apple is not native to Palestine, having been introduced there comparatively recently. Moreover, its fruit in the wild state—before improvement by modern techniques of selection and cultivation—is small and acid, and not likely to be the subject of glowing praise (see Moldenke, 184–88). The apricot, on the other hand, is soft, golden, fleshy, and fragrant.

Notice that the form in the singular in 2:3 and in 8:5 refers to the tree (similarly, *te'enah* "fig tree," 2:13; *tamar* "palm tree" 7:9), but in the plural to the fruit, 2:5, 7:9. For the plural in a generic sense, compare *gannim* 4:15, *šošannim* "lilies" 2:16, 6:2.

בַּעֲצֵי הַיַּעַר *ba-'aṣey ha-ya'ar* "among the trees of the wood." The preposition *b-* alternates with the following *beyn* in the phrase "among the sons." The use of synonymous grammatical forms, prepositions, words, etc., as variants is one of the stylistic hallmarks of the Song. Compare *-hu* alternating with *-v* in 5:6.

חִמַּדְתִּי וְיָשַׁבְתִּי *ḥimmadti ve-yašabti,* literally "I delighted and I sat/lingered on." Meaning and syntax not entirely certain. The form of the verbs suggests a past tense, but the present is also possible; compare Exod. 21:5, "I love [*'ahabti*] my master," Gen. 29:5 *yada'nu* "we know." Normally *ḥamad* "to take delight in something, to covet" is in the qal, but here in the pi'el, possibly to denote continuity or a prolonged experience: "I took delight many times, repeatedly" (the "frequentative" pi'el, WO, 414).

The second verb, *yašab̄ti* "I sat," may relate to the first one as an infinitive, "I delighted to sit," as in Deut. 1:5 "undertook to explain," literally "undertook, explained," and Hosea 5:11 (according to Fox, Ginsburg, Gordis). Or *yašab̄* may have the meaning "to stay for a long time, linger on, tarry"; see Gen. 22:5, Num. 22:19. Translated freely: "I took delight many times, and stayed on and on."

בְּצִלּוֹ ... וּפִרְיוֹ ... *be-ṣillo . . . u-p̄iryo. . . .* Translating "that shade" and "the fruit" to preserve the delicate ambiguity of the suffix *-o,* which is lost in translations with "its" or "his" (the suffix can mean either in Hebrew). The image of the Shulamite sitting in the shade of the apricot tree savoring the fruit has obvious erotic implications, since her lover is identified with that tree. For the erotic import of the scene under the apricot tree, see also note 8:5.

2:4 בֵּית הַיָּיִן *beyt ha-yayin,* literally "house of wine." This could be a tavern or banquet hall (compare Esther 7:8), but it is more likely to be a metaphor for a place in the fields or orchards where the lovers meet to make love. "He brought me to the house of wine" recalls the scene in 1:4, "He brought me into his chambers," where lovemaking and wine are also associated.

וְדִגְלוֹ עָלַי אַהֲבָה *ve-diglo 'alay 'ahab̄ah,* literally "his banner over me [being] love," a circumstantial clause expressing simultaneity with the main action ("he brought me"). A poetic image of her delight in his exuberant demonstration of love; compare the image in Ps. 20:6, "Let us raise our banner [*nidgol*] in the name of our God," where the verb "to raise a banner" is derived from *degel* "banner, flag."

Scholars who resort to Akkadian *dgl* (*dagalu)* "to see," and by extension "to intend," have produced translations like "his intention/intent towards me was love" (Pope, Fox). But Hebrew *dgl* does not have this meaning. Nor is it likely that a language would borrow such a basic verb as "to see," or one of its nominal derivates, for which it has its own words (*ra'ah, hibbiṭ, mabbaṭ,* etc.). Rather, the semantic range of the various biblical words of this root follows a clear derivational progression: "banner, flag" → "to raise a banner" (see note on *nidgol,* just above) → "raise high, make conspicuous." The latter meaning is attested in the two passive formations of this root in the Song, *dagul* in 5:10 and probably *nidgalot* in 6:4,10.

2:5 סַמְּכוּנִי בָּאֲשִׁישׁוֹת רַפְּדוּנִי בַּתַּפּוּחִים *sammeḵuni ba-'ašišot rappeduni ba-tappuḥim,* approximately "prop me up, make my bed among [or "cover me with"] *'ašišot,* cushion me with/prop me up among apricots" (similarly Fox). The Shulamite dramatically proclaims her erotic hunger for her lover; apricots are "his" fruit, 2:3. *'Ašišot* is often translated as "raisins" and "raisin cakes" (compare 2 Sam. 6:19); according to Fox, one possible meaning is "inflorescence," i.e., blossoms. The word remains enigmatic.

The preposition *b-* may have an instrumental sense "with, by means of," as it is commonly translated. But it may also mean "among," as in 1:8, 2:3,16. For the roots *smk* and *rpd* with the meanings proposed here, see Judg. 4:18 *śemiḵah* "rug," "cover," or "blanket" (in the older spelling with *ś*); Job 17:13 "I spread [*rippadti*] my bed"; Job 41:22 (in English versions 41:30) "he spreads out [*yirpad*]." Also see Song 3:10, *rep̄idah* "cushions." For the image of spreading a bed as a prelude to an erotic encounter, see Prov. 7:16 "I have decked my couch with coverings."

For the use of the masculine plural in general requests addressing "everybody," compare Isa. 42:10 "sing [*širu,* masc. pl.] to the Lord a new song"; 1 Kings 1:2 "let a young maiden be sought [literally "let them seek," *yeḇaqqešu*]."

Translations like "sustain me with" and "refresh/comfort me with" (RSV, NEB, Pope) are on shaky ground. The English verbs "sustain," "comfort," and "strengthen" may refer to physical or spiritual support as well as to providing food, but this is not at all true of verbs of the root *smk* "prop up, help to walk straight," as in Ps. 3:6, 51:14, 145:14—and even less so of *rpd.* The semantic range of a linguistic expression in one language does not guarantee the same range in another.

חוֹלַת אַהֲבָה *ḥolat 'ahaḇah,* literally "sick with love," in this context meaning "faint from the intensity of erotic yearning." For *'ahaḇ* "to desire," see note 1:3.

2:6 שְׂמֹאלוֹ תַּחַת לְרֹאשִׁי וִימִינוֹ תְּחַבְּקֵנִי *śemo'lo taḥat le-ro'ši vi-ymino teḥabbeqeni,* literally "his left hand under my head and his right embracing me." A stylized representation of lovemaking. This refrain is repeated in 8:3. Compare a parallel from the Sumerian sacred marriage rite (Kramer, 105): "Your right hand you have placed on my vulva,/ Your left stroked my head." For an ancient Mesopotamian clay plaque showing lovers embracing on a bed in this posture, see Wolkstein and Kramer, 43. For *ḥabbeq* "to embrace" in a sexual sense, see Prov. 5:20. The phrase "holding me close" here is adopted from Jay's translation.

2:7 הִשְׁבַּעְתִּי אֶתְכֶם *hišba'ti 'etkem* "I hereby adjure you." With this oath formula, repeated in 3:5 and 8:4, the Shulamite imparts her own insight to her "audience," the daughters of Jerusalem, warning them against arousing love prematurely, before the time is right. The emphatic tone of this teaching with its repeated "never, never" is reminiscent of Wisdom literature; compare Prov. 31:2, where "do not" appears six times in a row. Underlying this statement is the belief that everything has its proper time of ripening, in human affairs as in nature; compare 2:11–13, 8:8–11.

The typical oath in the Bible is sworn in the name of God, e.g., Deut. 6:13; Josh. 9:18; 2 Chron. 15:14. Here the oath is reconfigured to suit the Song's landscape with its animal imagery of gazelles and deer in the fields. This is not an ironic reference to biblical religion but an artful remaking of a conventional usage.

The use of the perfect tense (here *hišba'ti*) in the sense of a present is common in oaths and other solemn assertions, e.g., Jer. 22:5 "I hereby swear [*nišba'ti*]"; Gen. 14:22 "I hereby lift [*harimoti*] my hand to the Lord in oath." See WO, 488.

Notice the masculine plural form *'etkem,* instead of the expected feminine *'etken* demanded by standard classical Hebrew; or 5:3 *'aṭannep̄em,* for expected *'aṭannep̄en;* similarly *ta'iru, te'oreru* in this verse; 5:8 *timṣe'u, taggidu,* etc. The gradual replacement of the feminine plural forms by the corresponding masculine forms is one of the indicators of the lateness of the Song. The special feminine plurals survive only vestigially, in the forms on *-nah,* 3:11.

אִם־תָּעִירוּ וְאִם־תְּעוֹרְרוּ *'im ta'iru ve-'im te'oreru,* literally "not/never to awaken and never to arouse," here applying to erotic arousal; compare 8:5. For *ha'ir* and *'orer* "to arouse, stir up, incite, excite," see Isa. 42:13 "stirs up [*ya'ir*] fury," Jer. 51:11 "stirred up [*he'ir*] the spirit," Job 3:8 "skilled to rouse up [*'orer*] Leviathan," Prov. 10:12 "hatred stirs up [*te'orer*] strife."

While usually meaning "if," the particle *'im* is regularly used with a negative sense in oaths, as in 2 Kings 5:16 *ḥay 'adonay . . . 'im 'eqqaḥ* "as the Lord lives, I will not take a thing," Gen. 14:22–23, 21:23, 2 Sam. 11:11, etc. The semantic shift from a conditional to a negative meaning may have come about as follows: "I swear, *if* I were to commit this crime (may such and such an evil come upon me)" → "I swear *not* to commit . . . ," with the negative consequence left unspoken.

2:8 **קוֹל דּוֹדִי הִנֵּה־זֶה בָּא מְדַלֵּג** *qol dodi hinneh zeh ba' medalleg,* literally "the voice/sound of my lover, here he/it comes, leaping." The syntax allows a rich variety of analyses. Grammatically, not only the lover, but his voice, or the sound of his footsteps, could be what is "coming near," "bounding," and "leaping." The latter reading is not as farfetched as it may seem. In the imagery of the Bible, a voice or sound—*qol* can mean either—may be treated almost as an independent animate agent, able to "cry out" (Gen. 4:10, Isa. 40:3,6), to "break the cedars of Lebanon" (Ps. 29:5), or "to follow" someone, as in "no doubt the sound of his master's footsteps will follow behind" (2 Kings 6:32). This sort of ambiguity was recognized in the traditional exegesis of Gen. 3:8, "They heard the sound of the Lord God walking in the garden" (*qol 'adonay 'elohim mithallek̄ ba-gan*), where either God, or his voice, or the sound of his walking, may be what is moving about. Thus the eagerly waiting Shulamite may be referring to either the lover's voice or the sound of his footsteps.

In a different analysis, *qol,* or the phrase *qol dodi,* can be viewed as a self-contained interjection, as in JPS "Hark! My beloved! There he comes. . . ."

The pi'els *medalleg, meqappeṣ* "leaping, bounding" are frequentative; compare 2:3.

2:9 **דּוֹמֶה דוֹדִי לִצְבִי אוֹ** *domeh dodi li-ṣeb̄i 'o* . . . , literally "my lover resembles a gazelle, or. . . ." The use of *domeh* "resembles" makes this a more explicit way of comparing than the usual juxtaposition of the two items as metaphor or simile, as in 4:1 "your eyes are doves" or 5:12 "his eyes are like doves." In this formal self-conscious statement of comparison, notice the use of "or" in the Hebrew with which the poet is calling attention to the very *act* of comparing. See also 2:17, 8:14; and compare the "or" in the formula of adjuration in 2:7 and elsewhere.

כָּתְלֵנוּ *kotlenu* "our wall." This and the following *ḥallonot* "windows" and *ḥarakkim* "gaps, crevices" are probably not to be taken literally, but rather as metaphors for, say, a rough stone wall outdoors with gaps between the stones. For the "house" metaphors and the meaning of "our," see note on "our houses," 1:17.

מַשְׁגִּיחַ מִן *mašgiaḥ min,* literally "peering from." The preposition as used here, in addition to its regular sense of marking the point of origin ("from"), implies a notion of direction, namely toward the speaker. The Shulamite is on one side of the "wall" and her lover on the other, so that his peering "comes" toward her from (*min*) the gaps in the wall. When windows, doors, holes, gaps, etc. are involved, *min* thus acquires a secondary sense of "through"; compare 4:1, 5:4. (Thus regularly in Arabic, "he entered through the window," literally "from").

2:10 עָנָה דוֹדִי וְאָמַר לִי *'anah dodi ve-'amar li,* literally "my lover responded and said to me." A conventionalized formula, occurring often elsewhere in the Bible. Originally used in a meaningful way to introduce the words of a respondent in a dialogue (as in Gen. 18:26–27 "the Lord said, . . . and Abraham responded"), this formula became a rhetorical stereotype used also outside of dialogues to introduce any spoken words, as in Deut. 26:4–5 "the priest shall take the basket from your hands . . . and you shall say before the Lord," literally "you shall answer and say. . . ." See also the beginning of many chapters in Job such as 4, 6, 8, 9, 11, 12, 15, 16, etc., and in the Aramaic of the Book of Daniel, 2:5,7,8,10.

קוּמִי לָךְ *qumi lak̄.* The lover, looking at the Shulamite from the other side of the "wall" (2:9), invites her to experience nature in its full bloom. Compare 7:11, where she is the initiator. *Qumi,* literally "arise, get up" could be intended in its primary, physical meaning, as in 5:5 *qamti* "I got up," or as an auxiliary to the main verb, "Come on!" as in, e.g., Gen. 27:19 *qum na' šeb̄ah* "Come on, sit down!" and with other verbs of motion in the imperative, Ps. 95:1 *lek̄u nerannenah* "Come now, let us sing!" (literally "go sing"). See note 1:8 on *lak̄.*

2:11 הַסְּתָו *ha-setav* "winter, rainy season." Spring begins when the rainy season ends in March or April. Variant consonantal spelling *styw.*

2:12 בָּאָרֶץ *ba-'areṣ,* literally "on the ground," with the preposition *ba-* (for the more common *'al*) denoting "on the surface of," as in Gen. 1:22, 6:17, 9:7, 31:54.

עֵת הַזָּמִיר *'et ha-zamir.* This can mean both "the time of pruning," and "the time of singing" (the root *zmr* has both senses). Some commentators see here a two-directional pun (Pope, Fox), the first meaning pointing backward to the spring (2:11) as the season of pruning, and the second pointing forward to the turtledove. (The second association has left its lexical imprint on Modern Hebrew, where *zamir* assumed the meaning "nightingale.")

תּוֹר *tor* "turtledove," a migratory songbird that returns early in April to Palestine (Jer. 8:7). While other songbirds are heard chiefly in the morning, the turtledove sings from dawn to sunset (Parmalee, 172).

בְּאַרְצֵנוּ *be-'arṣenu,* literally "in our land." The possessive "our" conveys intimacy; the phrase is best understood as referring to the immediate countryside with which the two lovers are familiar (compare 1:17, 2:9). Exegetes who misunderstand the preceding *ba-'areṣ* as "in the land" instead of "on the ground" consider *be-'arṣenu* an "unnecessary repetition," "prosaic and useless" (Pope and others). On the contrary, 2:12 exemplifies the way in which similar word forms may conceal subtle semantic differences.

2:13 **חָנְטָה** *ḥaneṭah.* Elsewhere *ḥanaṭ* "to sweeten, embalm, spice" (Ibn Ezra) occurs only in relation to embalming (Gen. 50:2,3,26), which involves the infusion of spices and aromatic plants. The fig tree and the vines are seen as actively involved in the processes of nature: making the figs sweet, giving off scent.

הַגְּפָנִים סְמָדַר נָתְנוּ רֵיחַ *ha-gep̄anim semadar natenu reaḥ* "the vines in [the state of] blossom give off scent" (and similarly 2:15). For the syntax, compare other statements denoting seasonal or agricultural phenomena, weather, etc.: Ezra 10:13 *ha-'et gešamim,* "it is the time of heavy rains," literally "the time is heavy rains"; Exod. 9:31 "the barley was in the ear and the flax was in bud," literally "was young ears, was bud." Notice the different syntax in 7:13, where *ha-semadar* functions like any regular definite noun in subject position: "if the blossoms [*semadar,* collective] opened."

Qumi lak̄ as in 2:10 is the correct reading for the consonantal spelling *qumi lky.*

2:14 **יוֹנָתִי** *yonati* "my dove." One of the lover's many affectionate epithets for the Shulamite (2:10,13; 4:1,10,12; 5:2; 6:9), "dove" in this particular instance is truly integral to the scene. In 2:9 the two are separated by a wall and he is attempting to catch a glimpse of her. Here the Shulamite is playfully hiding from him, like a dove in the rocky crevices, as he coaxes her out: "Let me see you, let me hear your voice." Compare 8:13: "All our friends listen for your voice."

בְּסֵתֶר *be-seter* "under the cover of . . . ," compare 1 Sam. 25:20. For the image of the dove hidden among rocks, see Jer. 48:28. For the present translation compare Ps. 91:1, where *be-seter* parallels *be-ṣel* "in the shadow of."

הַרְאִינִי אֶת־מַרְאַיִךְ *har'ini 'et mar'ayik̄,* literally "let me see your sights, views." The noun *mar'eh* "sight," denoting the image as received by the viewer (as in the German *Anblick*), is in the *plural* form, in the sense of something seen, broken into its constituent parts. Similar to Job 41:1 (41:9 in English versions) *mar'av,* literally "the sights of him," i.e., everything that is visible of him. The plural is meaningful and fully motivated: the lover wants to see the Shulamite from every side.

Standard English translations with "thy countenance," "your face," "your form" take the consonantal sequence of the Hebrew *mr'yk* for a *plene* spelling of the singular *mar'ek̄* (KJV, NEB, RSV, Pope, Fox, and some modern commentaries). But there is no need to depart from the traditional vocalization *mar'ayik̄,* which indicates the plural. Compare, for example, the corresponding feminine plural form *mar'ot* for "visions, sights" (in a dream or revelation) in Gen. 46:2, Ezek. 1:1, 8:3, 40:2, 43:3.

כִּי־קוֹלֵךְ עָרֵב *ki qolek̄ 'areb̄* "for your voice is delicious." Normally used in reference to sweet tastes and smells, *'areb̄* "delicious" is applied here synesthetically to the voice of the Shulamite.

מַרְאֵיךְ נָאוֶה *mar'eyk̄ na'veh,* literally "your sight is beautiful," meaning "you are lovely to look at." Here the consonantal sequence *mr'yk* can be read only as a singular (*plene* spelling), because of the agreement with the predicate *na'veh.* Translations that render the two words identically—e.g., RSV, "let me see your face . . . , your face is comely"—obliterate the semantic difference between the plural and singular forms.

2:15 אֶחֱזוּ־לָנוּ שׁוּעָלִים *'eḥezu lanu šu'alim,* literally "catch/grab us foxes." The concluding words explain the command: the foxes raid the vineyards right at the time when "our vineyards are in bloom" (*u-k̄era-menu semadar,* a circumstantial clause expressing temporal simultaneity, as in 2:4). The adjective "quick" in the present translation is adopted from Falk.

Though the literal meaning of this verse is unproblematic, everything else about it is enigmatic (speaker? relation to context? figurative meaning?). Since elsewhere the vineyards are symbolic of the Shulamite's blossoming womanhood, and the brothers are her guardians (1:6, 8:8), it seems likely that they are the speakers of 2:15.

This verse, perhaps originally a short folk song, calls to mind Judg. 21:20–22, where the Benjaminites seize wives for themselves from among the daughters of Shiloh, who are dancing in the vineyards. In Judges, as elsewhere in the Bible, the brothers (and fathers) are in a position of responsibility for the girls. Foxes in the vineyard appear in Theocritus' *Idylls,* I.48–50 and V.112.

2:16 **הָרֹעֶה בַּשּׁוֹשַׁנִּים** *ha-ro'eh ba-šošannim,* literally "the one who pastures among the lilies," the lover's epithet, as in 6:3. Like its English equivalent "to pasture," the Hebrew verb *ra'ah* can mean "to tend flocks," said of a shepherd, as well as "to graze, feed," said of the sheep, see Exod. 34:3. The image of the lover as shepherd (compare 1:7), when amplified by "grazing among the lilies," is an erotic double entendre, especially since lilies are mentioned in connection with the Shulamite's body, 4:5, 7:3, or her lover's lips, 5:13, and he is described as "gathering" lilies, 6:2.

2:17 **עַד שֶׁיָּפוּחַ הַיּוֹם וְנָסוּ הַצְּלָלִים** *'ad še-yap̄uaḥ ha-yom ve-nasu ha-ṣelalim,* literally "before the day breathes and the shadows flee," i.e., just before the break of dawn. For *yap̄uaḥ* (root *pwḥ*) "to breathe, blow," see discussion in note 4:16. Some commentators have associated the image of the "fleeing shadows" instead with late afternoon, before sunset, when the shadows lengthen. If that were the case, however, different verbs would probably have been used, as Fox convincingly argues. Compare Jer. 6:4 "the day turns away [*panah*], the shadows of the evening are about to decline [*yinnaṭu,* nip̄'al *naṭah*]," Ps. 102:12 "my days are like a declining [*naṭuy*] shadow," and Ps. 109:23. The last two quotations suggest firmly established collocations that would not be easily departed from.

סֹב דְּמֵה *sob̄ demeh,* literally "turn away, be like. . . ." For *sob̄* "to turn" in the sense of "to turn away from speaker," see 1 Sam. 22:17,18; 1 Kings 2:15. As daybreak approaches, the Shulamite urges her lover to hurry away, as in the aubade or alba of later tradition, where lovers part at dawn. Given this circumstance, it is unlikely that they are a married couple, as has sometimes been claimed.

עַל־הָרֵי בָתֶר *'al harey b̄ater.* The phrase "mountains of *beter*" is unclear. For a synopsis of interpretations see Fox, 116. If connected with *btr* "to cut, cleave, divide," the mountains could be "cleft" or "jagged."

3:1 בַּלֵּילוֹת *ba-leylot,* literally "in the nights," can mean "at night," as in 3:8, but also, and more likely in this particular context, "night after night," in a frequentative sense. Compare Ps. 16:7, 92:3, 134:1, where the contexts likewise suggest repeated activity.

3:2 בָּעִיר *ba-'ir* "in the city," i.e., Jerusalem, as always when "the city" is mentioned in the Bible; see Micah 6:9, Zeph. 3:1, and elsewhere (compare Latin "urbs" for Rome, "town" for London).

3:3 מְצָאוּנִי *meṣa'uni* "found me," in this case, "crossed my path" by chance. For this sense of the verb see Gen. 44:8, Num. 15:32, Prov. 25:16.

הַסֹּבְבִים בָּעִיר *ha-sob̄eb̄im ba-'ir,* literally "that make the rounds of the city," i.e., customarily, as the participle indicates. Compare Eccles. 1:6.

אֵת שֶׁאָהֲבָה נַפְשִׁי רְאִיתֶם *'et še'ahab̄ah nap̄ši re'item,* literally "the one I love have you seen?" The Shulamite quotes what she said to the watchmen without an introductory phrase such as "I asked them." The effect is a quicker pace, a heightened sense of drama and urgency, as in 5:2. The unusual word order, with the object phrase placed before the verb, serves the same purpose; see note on 1:4 "truly they love you." The repetition here of "Have you seen" is adopted from Wolkstein's translation to convey that urgency.

3:4 אֲחַזְתִּיו וְלֹא אַרְפֶּנּוּ עַד־שֶׁהֲבֵיאתִיו *'aḥaztiv ve-lo' 'arpennu 'ad še-hab̄e'tiv.* This could mean either "I clung to him without letting go, until I [actually] brought him," or alternatively "[next time] I won't let go until I have brought him." For the second alternative, with the perfect tense in the sense of a future perfect, compare 2 Sam. 17:13, Ezek. 34:21. However, the parallelism of the verbs in the perfect, *'aḥaztiv, hab̄e'tiv,* tilts the scales in favor of the first interpretation ("I clung, I brought"). Note a similar parallelism in 8:2, *'enhageḳa, 'ab̄i'aḳa* "I would lead you, I would bring you."

בֵּית אִמִּי *beyt 'immi* "my mother's house," also in 8:2. Compare Gen. 24:28 and Ruth 1:8. The mother's house is the place where matters pertaining to marriage may have been discussed. (See Campbell, 64–65; Meyers 1991.)

3:5 The adjuration is repeated verbatim from 2:7.

3:6 מִי זֹאת עֹלָה *mi zo't 'olah.* "Who is that rising" is a stylized formula of dramatization used also in Isa. 60:8, 63:1, Jer. 46:7, Job 38:2, always in the form "Who is that/Who are these." Spoken in the Song three times by the daughters of Jerusalem, the formula presents the Shulamite in terms of a supernatural phenomenon, a fantastic apparition that "rises" from the east; hence the desert (*midbar,* the East par excellence in the Bible, compare Judg. 11:22) and the morning star, 3:6, 6:10, 8:5. None of these three scenes is realistic; all are hyperboles, evoking images of the triumphant appearance of a majestic, numinous, even godlike figure.

It is worth noting in this connection that *'alah* "to rise," 3:6, 8:5, is also the verb commonly used for the rising dawn (Gen. 19:15, 32:25,27; Josh. 6:15; Judg. 19:25; Neh. 4:15). Finally, *nišqap̄* "to look forth," 6:10 (nip̄'al, but also hip̄'il elsewhere) is applied not only to simple mortals "looking forth" but also to towering mountains, abstract forces ominously looming from the sky, and even to God himself looking down onto the earth (Num. 21:20, 23:28; 1 Sam. 13:18; Jer. 6:1; Deut. 26:15; Ps. 14:2, and elsewhere). The astral imagery has been cited as a justification for the cultic theory (the latter is discussed on p. 34). But in the Song this imagery is much more appropriately explained as a poetic way of glorifying the Shulamite.

Contrary to what its words seem to suggest, the formula as used in the Song is purely rhetorical: no question is asked and there is no answer (compare Isa. 60:8). This formula proclaims the Shulamite's dramatic "entrance" onto the scene, as in 3:6 and 8:5.

כְּתִימֲרוֹת עָשָׁן *ke-timarot 'ašan,* literally "like pillars of smoke" (or "a pillar," if the plural is to be understood like that of *gannim* in 6:2). Perhaps in an attempt to make the image more realistic, some critics emend *ke-* "like" to *be-* "in," imagining the Shulamite in a cloud of dust or a sandstorm. But there is no need for an emendation: a Shulamite who appears on the horizon like the dawn or the morning star would surely have no difficulty emanating from the desert *like* (not just *in*) a pillar, even pillars, of smoke. There is no point in explaining the fantasy image of 3:6 in naturalistic terms; as with many other images in the Song, such an interpretation would be reductive.

מְקֻטֶּרֶת מֹר וּלְבוֹנָה *mequṭṭeret mor u-leḇonah,* literally "made fragrant with myrrh and frankincense." *Mequṭṭeret* is a passive participle from *qaṭṭer* "to burn incense"; see also *qiṭor* "thick smoke" and *qeṭoret* "incense." Frankincense is a balsamic resin obtained from the wood of various trees of the genus *Boswellia,* native to India, Somalia, and Southern Arabia.

For the semantics of this construction, compare phrases such as Ps. 104:2 *'oṭeh 'or* "clad in light," Ps. 107:10 *yošeḇey ḥošeḵ ve-ṣalmavet* "dwellers in darkness and gloom," 2 Sam. 6:14 *ḥagur 'ep̄od bad* "girded with a linen ephod," Exod. 27:17 *meḥuššaqim kesep̄* "banded with silver," expressing a range of meanings united by the basic notion "enveloped/clad in/surrounded by/intimately associated with."

מְקֻטֶּרֶת ... מִכֹּל אַבְקַת רוֹכֵל *mequṭṭeret . . . mi(n)-kol 'aḇkat rokel* is understood here, in a departure from the generally accepted translation, as "more fragrant than," literally "fragrant . . . more than," i.e., as a regular comparative phrase. Compare Judg. 14:18 *matoq mi(n)-deḇaš* "sweeter than honey," Ezek. 28:3 *ḥaḵam mi(n)-dani'el* "wiser than Daniel," Ps. 45:8, etc. In the combination *mi(n)-kol,* the sense is of an encompassing "more than any/all," as in Gen. 3:1 *'arum mi(n)-kol ḥayyat ha-śadeh* "more cunning than any wild creature," Gen. 34:19 *niḵbad mi(n)-kol* "more honored than all," 2 Kings 5:12 *ṭoḇ mi(n)-kol* "better than all."

The reference to "merchant" is an echo of the far-reaching Solomonic trade, the rich "traffic of the merchants" during his reign; see 1 Kings 10:15 (and pp. 10–11). Verse 3:6 is possibly also an allusion to the Queen of Sheba, who brought the king "a great quantity of spices," 1 Kings 10:10; see also Jer. 6:20, where frankincense is mentioned as coming from the land of Sheba.

3:7 **הִנֵּה מִטָּתוֹ שֶׁלִּשְׁלֹמֹה** *hinneh miṭṭato šel-li-šelomoh,* loosely "Here is Solomon's bed!" or "Now, look here at Solomon's bed!" When used in its undiminished force, as here, the presentational particle *hinneh* points dramatically to an object or person close at hand. Compare to Gen. 12:19, 31:51; Judg. 8:15, 1 Sam. 9:17, 18:17; 2 Sam. 9:6; 1 Kings 19:5.

The syntax of the phrase "Solomon's bed," literally "his bed which is to Solomon," *miṭṭato šel-li-šelomoh,* with the suffix *-o* "his" pointing forward to *šlomoh,* occurs nowhere else in the Bible, becoming standard only in Mishnaic and Modern Hebrew. Another sign of the Song's late date.

A note on our translation of 3:7 is called for. We have introduced a first line—"Oh the splendors of King Solomon!"—that has no equivalent in the Hebrew text, in order to make explicit what is unclear in most translations: (1) that 3:7 is not an answer to 3:6 but the beginning of a new, thematically self-contained unit, and (2) that 3:7 and 3:9 describe not one but two different items of luxury from Solomon's opulent court.

The allusion to the king's wedding in 3:11 and some of the other narrative tidbits of 3:7–11 have no basis in the biblical texts, and may well be reflexes of ancient orally transmitted Solomonic folklore such as that found in the Midrashic literature (compare Ginzberg, 1909–38, vol. 4, 125ff.). The royal wedding and the role of Solomon's mother in his coronation on that day provide the strongest support for this hypothesis: it is so unmistakably presented as a given, as assumed old information, that the notion of familiar, orally transmitted lore is almost inescapable. Material that is clearly Midrashic in nature certainly could have left its imprint on the Song, even though the Midrash itself was committed to writing only at a much later date.

Although most of the concrete details of 3:7–11 have their roots in extrabiblical folklore, the way they are described clearly calls to mind specific biblical texts. Notice above all the word order, as in literally "his bed, sixty warriors are around it," or "a pavilion Solomon made for himself, its pillars he made of . . . its cushions of . . . . its couches of . . . its interior paved with . . ." This is a word order typical of inventories, with the item that is the focus of attention named first (the "topic," sometimes with a pronominal referent pointing back to it in the body of the sentence). The language of the comparison text in 1 Kings 7:6–8 is characterized by a similar word order, literally "and the Hall of Pillars he made . . . and the Hall of the Throne he made . . . and a house he made for Pharaoh's daughter whom he had married." (See discussion of "its pillars," in note 3:10.) The second comparison text with an inventory of Solomon's possessions to be admired is Eccles. 2:4–8. Although no direct dependency is claimed here between any of these texts, their generic similarity does suggest some kinship.

The Shulamite is the most likely speaker of 3:7–11. This conclusion suggests itself because the unit ends in a direct address to the daughters of Jerusalem (3:11), as do five other units, all spoken by the Shulamite (2:7; 3:5; 5:8,16; 8:4). If the content bears any relation at all to the world of the two lovers, it is in association with their play-acting outdoors: Solomon as the Shulamite's "king," their royal "chambers," their leafy "bed," etc.

Much of the misinterpretation that has befallen 3:7–11 in the history of Song exegesis is rooted in the mistaken assumption that 3:6 and 3:7 are question and answer. This has yielded translations such as "What is that coming up from the wilderness . . . ? Behold, it is the litter of Solomon!" (RSV; compare NEB). Nothing in the text, however, suggests that the bed of 3:7 is moving. But once it was associated with "coming up" (3:6), the bed had to become ambulatory; thus, transformed into a "litter" with Solomon on board in a royal procession, it made its entry into a great many translations. The interpretation of *'appiryon* as "palanquin" or "chariot," etc. (see note 3:9) undoubtedly had a share in fostering this ambulatory image.

The theory of the ambulatory litter must be rejected, if only on linguistic grounds. In all of its occurrences in the Bible, the interrogative particle *mi* is used exclusively with animates, never with inanimates. No amount of linguistic speculation can change the "Who?" of this formula into a "What?" Nor does this particle ever mean anything other than "Who?" outside of the formula.

שִׁשִּׁים גִּבֹּרִים סָבִיב לָהּ *šiššim gibborim sab̄ib̄ lah,* literally "sixty warriors around it." For sixty as a typical number, compare 6:8. These warriors with their swords (3:8) surrounding the king's bed may be imagined inside a spacious royal bedchamber. Another narrative tidbit without a basis in the biblical texts, probably from folklore. For "surrounding" as an image of protection, see Ps. 125:2 "Jerusalem has mountains around it [*sab̄ib̄ lah*], and so the Lord is around [*sab̄ib̄*] his people."

מִגִּבֹּרֵי יִשְׂרָאֵל *mi(n)-gibborey yiśra'el.* Translations with parallel wording, as in RSV and other versions, "sixty mighty men of the mighty men of Israel," are grammatically unobjectionable, but a superlative reading of the second phrase seems more in line with the admiring tone of this entire section, "the bravest among. . . ." The use of a semik̄ut-construction in a superlative sense is especially common with words denoting an extreme degree or intense quality: Isa. 29:19 *'eb̄yoney 'adam* "the poorest [literally "the poor ones"] among men"; 2 Chron. 21:17 *qeṭon banav* "the smallest [literally "the small one"] of his sons"; Micah 7:4 *ṭob̄am* "the best [literally "the good one"] of them."

3:8 אֲחֻזֵי חֶרֶב מְלֻמְּדֵי מִלְחָמָה *'aḥuzey hereb̄ melummedey milḥamah,* literally "skilled with a sword, experienced in war." The passive participle *'aḥuz,* a hapax with the meaning "trained in, skilled," is probably modeled after the Aramaic cognate *'aḥīd,* used in the Peshitta of 1 Chron. 5:18 "experienced in war," which is synonymous with the present *melummedey milḥamah.* See BDB, 28.

מִפַּחַד בַּלֵּילוֹת *mi(n)-paḥad ba-leylot,* literally "because of the danger of the nights." Commentators who relate this to Solomon's wedding in 3:11 cite the widespread popular fear of supernatural dangers on a wedding night (Pope, Fox). On the other hand, a king, by the very nature of his position, would have to guard himself against usurpation and regicide. For *paḥad* used in the sense of "danger" (rather than the more usual meaning "fear"), see Isa. 24:17,18; Jer. 48:44, 49:5; Ps. 91:5; Prov. 3:25.

3:9 אַפִּרְיוֹן *'appiryon.* Hapax of uncertain meaning; a loan-word, probably from Persian or Greek. The Septuagint's *phoreion* "sedan chair," possibly based on no more than the phonetic similarity to the *'appiryon,* may itself have contributed to interpretation of the word as "litter" or "palanquin." It is thus understood in the Talmud and in many modern translations. However, the description of the *'appiryon* strongly suggests a *stationary* structure; see notes on its pillars and paved interior in 3:10. The *'appiryon* recalls the grandeur of the royal pavilion in Esther 1:6 with its marble pillars, beds (*miṭṭot,* pl. of *miṭṭah*) of gold and silver, and floor paved with precious stones.

A number of commentators have concluded that the context indicates a fixed structure—a palace or a throne room—rather than a portable litter. Ibn Ezra understood *'appiryon* as a "magnificent building," and the Zohar as a palace. Gerleman argued that the structure described in 3:9–10, with its "pillars" and "interior" suggests a building rather than a portable conveyance; other scholars have proposed the emendation *'appeden* ("palace," a biblical Aramaic loan-word from Persian; see Dan. 11:45); see summary in Pope, 441–2. Particularly suggestive in this regard is the reference in 1 Kings 7:8 to the palace that Solomon built for Pharoah's daughter, the most illustrious of his wives; this was constructed, it appears, with a lavish use of cedar and costly stones (7:7–9). If we are indeed dealing with a building rather than a portable structure, this palace would be a likely candidate.

עָשָׂה לוֹ *'aśah lo,* literally "he made for himself." The wording is close to Eccles. 2:4–8, with its detailed listing of the houses, vineyards, water pools, gold, silver, singers, etc. that Solomon acquired: "I built, I planted, I collected," with the verbs followed six times by *li-* "for myself" (*baniti li, naṭa'ti li, kanasti li*).

עֲצֵי הַלְּבָנוֹן *'aṣey ha-leḇanon* "Lebanon wood." The word for "trees," *'eṣim* (*'aṣey*), may also refer to the wood, compare Exod. 27:1 *'aṣey šiṭṭim* "acacia wood." Also see *'arazim* in Song 1:17. The plural form lends a concreteness to the Hebrew, suggesting, as it were, planks of wood in the hands of the craftsman.

3:10 **עַמּוּדָיו** *'ammudav* "its pillars." Typically the pillars associated with Solomon, described with evident admiration in the two books of Kings, are massive, astounding in height and circumference, supporting impressive buildings. Compare especially the description of the House of the Forest of Lebanon, with its rows of cedar pillars, and the Hall of Pillars, 1 Kings 7:2–6. Some measured twenty-three cubits in height, including their capitals, and twelve cubits in circumference; see 1 Kings 7:15–16. These pillars are mentioned also in 2 Kings 25:13–17 (compare Jer. 52:17–23) among the national treasures destroyed in the Babylonian onslaught of 587 BCE. They loomed large enough in the popular imagination to furnish a topographic metaphor: the rock cliffs near Timna in southern Israel are to this day called "the Pillars of Solomon." Given this association, the pillars admired in 3:10 are likely to be tall and massive, capable of supporting a building, not the slender poles of a traveling litter.

עָשָׂה כֶסֶף *'aśah ḵesep̄,* literally "[its pillars] he made silver," i.e., covered or simply decorated with silver. For a similar ornamentation of pillars see Exod. 27:17. As often in the biblical language for craftsmanship, *'aśah* "to make, work" applies here to the surface of the objects; compare the use of the corresponding noun *ma'aśeh* in the same sense in *ma'aśeh śeḇaḵah, ma'aseh šušan* "checker-work" (an ornamental network) and "lily-work," in 1 Kings 7:17,19.

רְפִידָתוֹ *repidato.* For an example of the root *rpd* in the sense of upholstery or bedding, compare Song 2:5; see also the related root *rbd* in "couch coverings," Prov. 7:16, 31:22. "Couches of gold and silver," described in Esther 1:6, are among the lavish furnishings in the court of Ahasuerus (Xerxes), another king of legendary wealth.

מֶרְכָּבוֹ *merkabo.* A generic term for anything to sit on, *merkab* is explained as *kol 'ašer yihyeh taḥtav* "whatever is under him" in Lev. 15:9–10.

תּוֹכוֹ רָצוּף אַהֲבָה מִבְּנוֹת יְרוּשָׁלָם *toko raṣup 'ahabah mi(n)-benot yerušalayim,* literally "its interior paved with love from [or "by"] the daughters of Jerusalem." Obscure. For different interpretations involving substantial emendations (from "love" to "stone," "ebony," and the like), see Gordis, Pope, Fox.

רָצוּף *raṣup* "paved." From *rṣp* "to join stones, inlay," which underlies the noun *riṣpah* "paved floor." Compare, for example, the *riṣpah* at King Ahasuerus' court in Esther 1:6, a splendid "mosaic pavement of porphyry, marble, mother-of-pearl, and colored stones" (Moore, *Esther*). For the syntax of *raṣup* "paved with," see the discussion of "perfumed with," 3:6.

מִבְּנוֹת יְרוּשָׁלָם Although problematic grammatically, the preposition *min* may be seen here to introduce the agent; compare Lev. 21:7 *'iššah gerušah me-'išah* "a woman divorced by [literally "from"] her husband."

3:11 צְאֶינָה וּרְאֶינָה *ṣe'eynah u-re'eynah* "come out and look!" Notice the archaizing usage with the verbs in the special feminine plural (*-nah*); see discussion under 2:7. The irregular form *ṣe'eynah,* instead of the grammatically expected *ṣe'nah* (with ' unpronounced), is used here to correspond phonetically with *re'eynah.*

עֲטָרָה *'aṭarah* "a king's crown, or wreath." Also a token of festivity and joy; see Esther 8:15.

שֶׁעִטְּרָה־לּוֹ אִמּוֹ *še-'iṭṭerah lo 'immo,* literally "which his mother set on him." Although the biblical account says nothing about Solomon's mother crowning him, she does figure prominently in the events preceding his investiture; see 1 Kings 1:11–31. In the Midrash, Bathsheba awakens Solomon on the day of the consecration of the Temple, when Pharaoh's daughter, his new bride, has kept him asleep (Ginzberg, vol. 4, 128–29). In the present verse, the "crowning" by his mother is part of Solomon's wedding ceremony. This narrative detail, too, may have its roots in the Solomonic legends.

Song 3:11 has a number of possible thematic connections with other parts of the Song: (1) King Solomon as the counterpart of the Shulamite's lover, who is called her "king," see 1:4,12; (2) the king as an object of admiration by the women of Jerusalem ("Come out and look at him!"), like the Shulamite's lover, 1:3; (3) the prominent role given to mother figures: King Solomon's mother at his wedding, and the Shulamite's mother as her teacher in matters of love, 8:2.

4:1 צַמָּתֵךְ *ṣammateḵ,* literally "your *ṣammah.*" Two radically different interpretations for the enigmatic *ṣammah* have been in circulation since the very beginning of Song exegesis: (1) "locks, tresses," "mass of hair," "braided hair," and (2) "veil." Although most English translations and commentaries have opted for the veil—RSV, JPS, NEB, Ginsburg, Gordis, Pope, Fox, Falk, Murphy, and others—there is considerable linguistic and textual evidence against this interpretation.

The word occurs twice more in the Song, 4:3, 6:7, and only once elsewhere in the Bible, in a passage that is crucial to the understanding of the word. In a harshly sarcastic address, the prophet Isaiah gloats over the downfall and humiliation of "the virgin Daughter of Babylon" (symbolizing the Babylonian empire), who will be defeated and forced to perform the most humiliating menial tasks. Here is the passage in the RSV:

> Take the millstone and grind meal, *put off* your veil [*galli ṣammateḵ*], *strip off* your robe [*ḥespi šoḇel*], *uncover* your legs [*galli šoq*], pass through the rivers. Your nakedness *shall be uncovered* [*tiggal 'ervateḵ*], and your shame shall be seen.
>
> (Isa. 47:2–3)

The first two italicized phrases are mistranslations of the Hebrew, while the last two are correct. The two verbs *galleh* and *ḥasap̄* mean "to reveal, expose, uncover, lay bare, show," *not* "to put off, strip off." For the alternating use of these two verbs in parallel verses, compare Jer. 49:10 "I have exposed [*ḥaśap̄ti*] Esau, I have uncovered [*gilliti*] his hiding places," and Jer. 13:22 (*niglu*), and 13:26 (*ḥaśap̄ti*). These verbs and others with the same semantic range are used in the Bible for notions of decorum, vulnerability, and inviolability, particularly of the human body. In this case, being forced to bare her thigh (*šoq*), underskirt (?) (*šob̄el*), and nakedness (*'ervah*) symbolizes the public humiliation of the Daughter of Babylon. For *galleh* compare also texts such as Lev. 20:11 and Deut. 27:20 with their euphemisms for genitals: *gillah 'ervat 'ab̄iv, gillah kenap̄ ab̄iv* "to uncover the nakedness" or "skirt" of one's father. From the domain of the human body these metaphors were extended to exposing the "nakedness" of countries (so Gen. 42:9–12), and "baring" the foundations of walls, fortresses, cities—a typical biblical image of military defeat and conquest (Ezek. 13:14, Micah 1:6). Also see Isa. 22:8 "they exposed the screen of Judah," where "screen" is a metaphor, like "shield, cover," etc., for a specific fortress overtaken by the Assyrians (see note in JPS). Here again, the verb is to "expose" (*galleh*), *not* "take away," as RSV.

In contrast, for taking off articles of clothing, headgear, finery, ornaments, jewelry, and the like, the Bible uses verbs other than those of the Isaiah passage—above all, *hesir*. In fact, this is precisely the verb one would expect for removing a veil; see Gen. 38:19 (*va-tasar ṣe'ip̄ah*), and the long list of items of women's luxury wear that the Lord will strip (*yasir*) from the bodies of the pampered daughters of Israel, Isa. 3:18–23. (Two other verbs of this semantic range, *pašaṭ* and *nasa' me-'al,* actually occur in the Song, 5:3,7.)

In keeping with the tone of the Isaiah passage, the *ṣammah* must refer to something that the Daughter of Babylon would be loath to expose (*galleh*) in public for reasons of decorum, along with her thigh, underskirt, and nakedness. In ancient Mesopotamian society, it was improper for a woman, especially one of the higher classes, to bare her head in public; conversely, a common harlot had to keep her head uncovered, and was not permitted to veil herself like other women (see Lerner, 134). While this information still does not tell us what the *ṣammah* really *is,* the weight of the evidence surely tilts the scales in favor of the traditional understanding of the word (e.g., Ibn Ezra) as relating to hair.

An additional argument in favor of this interpretation is based on the very form of the word. *Ṣammah* exhibits a relatively rare noun pattern: the doubled middle root-consonant preceded and followed by *a*, which is found in only a limited number of words, most relating to parts of the human body: *raqqah,* Judg. 4:21,22, 5:26, Song 4:3 and 6:7 "cheek/temple/forehead"; *dallah,* Isa. 38:12, Song 7:6, "thrums, tufts hanging down" (in a weaver's loom, or said of hair); *'ammah,* Deut. 3:11, "forearm"; *kappah* "palm of hand" (in the expression *kappat šoḥad* "an act of bribery"); and *gabbah* "eyebrow," the latter two being postbiblical back-formations from biblical plural forms in Lev. 14:9, Ezek. 1:18, and Isa. 33:15. This noun pattern appears to be very strongly (though not exclusively) associated with body parts.

In view of the well-known proclivity of the Semitic languages for associating specific formal patterns (*mišqalim*) with specific meanings, this particular association can hardly be accidental. *Raqqah* is associated with the head, and *dallah* (in the Song) with the hair, another factor supporting our identification of the *ṣammah*. Notice, too, the association of this particular noun pattern with paired parts of the body that are symmetrically opposed to each other—the arms, eyebrows, palms—and note further that this pattern is feminine, with *-ah,* just as the Hebrew words for "hand," "foot," "eye," etc., are all (unmarked) feminine. A final argument is that all the other nouns with the possessive "your" (*-ek̄, -ayik̄*) in this descriptive section, 4:1–5, are body parts, which would make "your veil" the sole exception.

There is no way to know how and when the Song's *ṣammah* first came to be understood as "veil," but it is an interpretation with a long history, attested already in the Septuagint and Symmachus. It is easy to understand why the reading "veil" established itself. The veil has long been a symbol of modesty: for example, Rebecca, meeting her future husband, Isaac, "took her veil [*ṣa'ip̄*] and covered herself" (Gen. 24:65). The image of a Shulamite whose face is modestly covered with a veil was in perfect harmony with the apologetic approach that governed much of traditional Jewish and Christian scholarship. Once well established in that tradition, the veil slipped undetected into most translations of the Song, including those that are entirely free of that bias—with the one noteworthy exception of the KJV, which has "thy locks."

מִבַּעַד לְ *mi(n)-ba'ad le-*, literally "from behind." This phrase has the same nuance "from the point of . . ." as expressed by *min-* in 2:9, 5:4. Rather than speaking of her eyes as simply the object of his observation (1:15 "your eyes are doves"), the young man describes them in 4:1 as actively looking out from behind her hair. Also compare the description of the eyes in 6:5.

Notice that the direction here is the reverse of 2:9, where his peering originates outside the wall and comes toward her (the observer/speaker), she being inside. Still, there is a consistency in the Song with a clear symbolic import in Mediterranean culture: *she* (or her eyes, forehead, etc.) is inside, and *he* outside some "barrier," such as her hair (4:1,3, 6:7), the wall (2:9), or the bolted door (5:2); she is concealed behind rock cliffs (2:14); she is *in* the garden (8:13), or is herself the locked garden (4:12).

שֶׁגָּלְשׁוּ *še-galešu.* The verb *galaš,* though a hapax, has been plausibly explained on the basis of its cognate in Ugaritic as relating to the streaming or surging of waters. Compare Greenfield (1969), 99 n. 36. (In Modern Hebrew the verb is commonly applied to gliding, sliding down mountains, also skiing, etc., as well as to spilling down, overflowing of liquids—meanings that most probably derive from the interpretation of this verse). The point of comparison is the movement of a flock of goats coming down the mountainside, suggesting heavy, thick, wavy hair in flowing motion. Contemporary readers remote from the landscape of the poet have sometimes found the similes in 4:1–2 odd or even comic, but sheep and goats were perfectly natural images for a biblical audience. The reference to hair picks up and elaborates *ṣammah* in the previous line, as with lily in 2:1–2, honey (*nop̄et/deb̄aš*) in 4:11 and spikenard in 4:13–14 (*neradim/nerd*)—another sign of conscious artistry.

4:2 **שִׁנַּיִךְ כְּעֵדֶר הַקְּצוּבוֹת** *šinnayik̄ ke-ʿeder ha-qeṣub̄ot* "your teeth are like a flock of ewes." Much of the language and imagery of this verse allows two readings: *qeṣub̄ot,* literally "those that are shorn," is (1) an epithet for *reḥelim* "ewes," as in the otherwise identical verse 6:6, or (2) "those that are similar in size, matching," with obvious relevance to both ewes and teeth. For these two interpretations, compare the root *qṣb* in 2 Kings 6:6, *va-yiqṣob̄* "he cut, sheared off," and the expression *qeṣeb̄ ʾeḥad* "the same form," 1 Kings 6:25, 7:37.

שֶׁעָלוּ מִן־הָרַחְצָה *se-ʿalu min ha-raḥṣah* "that have come up from the pond" (*raḥṣah,* literally "washing place"), hence the pure white of their wool.

שֶׁכֻּלָּם מַתְאִימוֹת *še-kullam matʾimot.* Here again the text allows two readings: (1) "all of whom bear twins," evoking a notion of fecundity and health of the animals. For *matʾimot* "twin-bearing" (hip̄ʿil from *teʾom* "twin"), see Jer. 4:31 *mab̄kirah* "one bearing her first child" (hip̄ʿil from *bek̄or* "first born"). Or (2) "all of whom are identical in shape," with relevance to both ewes and teeth (root *tʾm* "to be identical"); compare *qeṣub̄ot* in the sense "similar in size, matching."

וְשַׁכֻּלָה אֵין בָּהֶם *ve-šakkulah ’eyn bahem,* literally “and among whom there is none bereaved of offspring.” A *šakkulah* here is a ewe that has lost its lamb. Normally in a flock the lambs walk beside their mothers, so the place beside a *šakkulah* is empty. Here again, the image applies at the same time to the Shulamite’s teeth, none of which is missing. Note the wordplay of *še-kullam* and *šakkulah.*

4:3 וּמִדְבָּרֵךְ נָאוֶה *u-midbarek̄ na’veh,* literally “your *midbar* is lovely.” Derived from the verb *dabber* “to speak,” the problematical noun *midbar* can be interpreted as either (1) a poetic word for “speaking” (as in Ibn Ezra, Rashi) or even “voice,” or (2) “mouth,” as in most modern translations. Both interpretations are equally plausible linguistically: the word’s pattern can be associated with nouns of place, *miškan* “abode, place of dwelling,” *mip̄tan* “doorstep,” etc., hence conceivably (literally) “place of speech” → “mouth,” as well as with nouns denoting actions, abstract concepts, perceptions, e.g., *mišma‘* “that which is heard,” *mišpaṭ* “judging, justice,” *mib̄ḥar* “the choice, best of,” hence “speech, voice.” The following consideration favors the reading adopted here. It is hard to ignore the parallel between *u-midbarek̄ na’veh* in this verse and *u-mar’ek̄ na’veh* in 2:14, where the visual and the acoustic aspects are associated, literally “your voice is delicious and the sight of you [German *Anblick*] lovely.” This comparison seems to give preference to a reading of 4:3 such as “your lips are like a crimson ribbon [visual], and your voice/speaking [auditory] is . . .” over the somewhat redundant alternative “your lips/your mouth,” in which the “mouth” is treated as an object of visual beauty in addition to the lips.

כְּפֶלַח הָרִמּוֹן רַקָּתֵךְ *ke-p̄elaḥ ha-rimmon raqqatek̄,* literally “like a slice of pomegranate is your *raqqah.*” The word *raqqah* is uncertain; it is usually understood as referring to a part of the face or head: cheek, temple, or forehead. The point of the comparison is commonly assumed to be the color of the pomegranate; its smoothness to the touch and rounded contour may also be implied.

4:4 כְּמִגְדַּל דָּוִיד צַוָּארֵךְ בָּנוּי לְתַלְפִּיּוֹת *ke-migdal david ṣavva’rek̄ banuy le-talpiyyot,* literally “like the tower of David is your neck built *le-talpiyyot.*” The numerous, widely differing traditional interpretations of the enigmatic hapax *talpiyyot* are mostly based on pure speculation and dubious etymologies. In recent decades, a well-argued reading “built in courses” or “in terraces” has gained wide currency (see Pope,

466–68). The comparison in itself is plausible: a tower of David might have been built in rows, or courses, of stones, and a necklace of the Shulamite (1:10, 4:9) with its rows of beads could evoke the image of such a tower. But this interpretation conflicts with a feature of Hebrew syntax. Verbs of the general meaning to build, make, shape, craft are typically constructed with two objects and no preposition. Significant for the case at hand, this applies also when the resulting "product" consists of separate parts or segments: 1 Kings 6:36, literally "he built [*va-yiben*] the inner court three courses of hewn stones," where English has "with" or "in" three courses. Similarly Deut. 27:6, literally "whole stones you will build [*tibneh*] the altar"; 1 Kings 6:9, literally "he made the ceiling of the house [*va-yispon 'et ha-bayit*] beams"; Num. 11:8, literally "they made it [*ve-'aśu 'oto*] cakes," i.e., formed it into cakes; Num. 17:3, literally "they made them [*ve-'aśu 'otam*] hammered plates," i.e., converted them (the censers) into plates; Exod. 26:14, literally "you shall make [*ve-'aśita*] a covering for the tent tanned skins," i.e., from skins. The same is true of the corresponding passive construction: Ezek. 41:18, literally "it was made [*'aśuy*] cherubs and palm trees," i.e., it was composed of cherubs and palm trees (and compare the corresponding active in 1 Kings 6:29). Only exceptionally is a preposition used, and then it is not *le-* but *be-*, as in 1 Kings 6:15–16. Thus, it is precisely the preposition *le-* in *le-talpiyyot* that speaks against this particular reading and points in a different direction.

Like most of the earlier readings, "in courses" is based on the assumption that *talpiyyot* is a plural noun. But this approach may be too narrow. Hebrew has a handful of words ending on *-ot* and *-im* that are plurals in form only, having become functionally adverbials: Ps. 139:14 "I praise you, for I have been awesomely [*nora'ot*] made"; 1 Kings 8:13 "a place for you to dwell forever [*'olamim*]"; Song 1:4 "Truly/rightly [*meyšarim*] they love you." Now, adverbially used words are so commonly preceded by *le-* that this preposition can almost be considered a marker of this word class: Isa. 32:1, 42:3 *le-ṣedeq, le-mišpaṭ, le-'emet* "justly, righteously, faithfully"; Job 36:31, Neh. 5:18, and 2 Chron. 11:12 *le-makbir, le-harbeh* "in abundance, very much"; Joel 2:26 *le-hapli'* "wondrously"; Job 42:10 *le-mišneh* "twice as much"; Gen. 3:22 *le-'olam* "forever." And this applies also to the plural forms, Ps. 77:8, Eccles. 1:10 *le-'olamim* "forever"; Song 7:10 *le-meyšarim* "straight, directly, smoothly"; Ps. 140:12 *le-madḥepot* "in thrusts [?], speedily."

Even when the meaning of some of these words is uncertain, their adverbial function as such is usually not in doubt. This becomes especially evident in a case like 1 Sam. 15:32 "Agag went to him *ma'adan-not.*" This enigmatic word has been correctly understood as an adverb irrespective of the differing interpretations given to it: "with faltering step" (NEB), "cheerfully" (RSV), and "in chains" (Even-Shoshan, Segal). The same is true when a word shows slight fluctuations in meaning in different contexts; for example, the adverbial *meyšarim* in Song 1:4 as compared to 7:10. The approach followed here with respect to the problem phrase "built *le-talpiyyot*" is based on the conviction that its meaning cannot be deciphered via the etymology, root, or pattern of *talpiyyot,* as has been attempted throughout the tradition. But while the meaning of the word itself may forever remain obscure, the analysis adopted here—which focuses exclusively on the morphology (the preposition *le-* and the ending *-ot*) and syntax of this phrase—suggests a semantic range such as that covered by some of the *le-* adverbials listed above, perhaps "built wondrously, magnificently, to perfection," or the like.

In this understanding, the neck itself is the object of admiration, and it alone is compared with the tower, not the neck with its necklace (the necklace is evoked separately in the "bucklers" and "shields"; see next note). A tower of David "built magnificently, to perfection" in 4:4—whether real or imaginary, just as the one made of ivory in 7:5—symbolizes workmanship of the highest order, evoking a master architect. This would closely parallel 7:2, where the Shulamite's thighs are said to be "shaped by a master craftsman." Hence the unnamed early Jewish grammarians (*medaqdeqim,* mentioned by Ibn Ezra) who freely paraphrased *le-talpiyyot* "without equal" may well have been closest to the mark.

אֶלֶף הַמָּגֵן תָּלוּי עָלָיו *'elep̄ ha-magen taluy 'alav* "a thousand bucklers hang upon it." Warriors used to hang their bucklers, helmets, and other items of weaponry on towers and city walls for ornamental display, which "lent splendor" and "made perfect" the city's beauty, so Ezek. 27:10–11. The ornaments on the strands of the Shulamite's necklace evoke the image of the bucklers displayed on David's tower.

The reference to turrets and city walls in relation to the Shulamite (8:10) suggests a daunting, awesome beauty (*'ayummah,* 6:4,10). The "bucklers" around her neck accord with this image.

Literally "the thousand buckler hang," with the enumerated object in the collective singular, as is common especially with large round numbers (see e.g. Song 8:11). But the use of the definite article, as well as the construction with "hang" in the singular (*taluy*), instead of the expected plural (*teluyim*), is less usual and calls attention to itself. It suggests a reference to something well known, as if to say "those famous bucklers of which we have all heard," or perhaps "that group of one thousand strung up together," hence the singular construction. Since there is nothing in the Bible about a tower of David, nor about a thousand bucklers, this may be yet another indication of elements of popular folklore in the Song; see note 3:7 above. The figure "thousand" supports this conjecture.

כֹּל שִׁלְטֵי הַגִּבֹּרִים *kol šilṭey ha-gibborim* "all the shields of the warriors." In the passage just quoted from Ezek. 27:10–11, *šelaṭim* are mentioned among the weaponry displayed on city walls, along with shields and helmets, possibly denoting a special kind of shield, or else quiver, as probably in Jer. 51:11. The *šelaṭim* in 2 Chron. 23:9 are counted among King David's weaponry.

4:5 **תְּאוֹמֵי צְבִיָּה** *te'omey ṣebiyyah,* "twins of a gazelle," suggesting the identical shape of the breasts. Gazelles evoke grace and youthful liveliness.

הָרֹעִים בַּשּׁוֹשַׁנִּים *ha-ro'im ba-šošannim,* literally "that graze among the lilies." For the rich erotic associations of the image, see note 2:16.

4:6 **עַד שֶׁיָּפוּחַ הַיּוֹם** *'ad še-yapuaḥ ha-yom,* literally "before the day breathes." See note 2:17 for discussion.

הַר הַמּוֹר ... גִּבְעַת הַלְּבוֹנָה *har ha-mor . . . gib'at ha-lebonah* "the mountain of myrrh . . . the hill of frankincense." For the sensual association of these two spices with the Shulamite, see also Song 3:6, 4:14.

4:7 **כֻּלָּךְ יָפָה** *kullak yapah.* Hebrew *kullak* is far more concrete than implied in the English "you are wholly/entirely beautiful," and is better rendered freely as "your entirety is beautiful" or colloquially, "every inch of you is beautiful." Coming at the end of the lover's praise song to the Shulamite, this statement is paralleled by her concluding "he is all [*kullo*] delight" in 5:16.

וּמוּם אֵין בָּךְ *u-mum 'eyn bak,* literally "and there is no flaw in you." Our free translation, "my perfect one," is borrowed from Falk.

4:8 אִתִּי מִלְּבָנוֹן . . . תָּבוֹאִי *'itti mi(n) lebanon . . . tabo'i* "come with me from Lebanon." This and the other three mountains mentioned in this verse are symbols of inaccessibility and danger, and at the same time of majestic, primeval beauty. Much of the traditional misunderstanding of this verse is rooted in the insistence of many commentators on explaining it literally. But the Shulamite and her lover are *not* in the mountains of Lebanon, close to the dwellings of lions and leopards. This fantasy scene is not unlike the one in 8:5, where the two of them are "coming up" together from the wilderness. The verb *tabo'i,* in the imperfect, seems less a direct invitation (for which an imperative, *bo'i,* would be more appropriate) than a wishful thought, along the line of "Oh that you would come down with me . . ."; see the series of imperfects conjuring up a succession of wished-for, hypothetical events in 8:1–2. Moreover, this is yet another instance of the technique, so pervasive in the Song, of referring to the animal world (the mare, the gazelle, the dove, ewes, goats, the raven, etc.), in order to highlight some characteristic of the lovers, here evoking their freedom and vitality.

There is no compelling reason for the emendation of *'itti* "with me" of the Masoretic text to *'eti* "come!" as in Fox, Pope, and Falk.

כַּלָּה *kallah,* literally "bride," see note 4:9. The word order of the Hebrew, literally "With me from Lebanon, bride, with me from Lebanon come!"—*ABAC*—reflects a formal pattern that occurs frequently in the Song, 1:15, 4:1, 4:9, 5:9, 6:9, 7:1, sometimes with a variation in the repeating member (*A*), as in 4:10,12, 5:1, 6:1. For occurrences outside the Song, see Ps. 93:3, literally "the floods have lifted up, O Lord, the floods have lifted up their voice," or Ps. 67:4, literally "shall praise you nations, O Lord, shall praise you nations, all!" Characteristically, one member of the pattern—typically *B*—is an address or an epithet.

אֲמָנָה שְׂנִיר וְחֶרְמוֹן *'amanah śenir ve-ḥermon.* Amana, Senir, and Hermon, along with Mount Lebanon, are the northern mountains that figure prominently in the geography of the imagination of ancient Israel.

4:9 לִבַּבְתִּנִי *libbabtini* "you have ravished my heart," derived from the noun *leb* or *lebab* "heart." One of the functions of the pi'el verbal stem is to express the taking away, removal of something (compare English "to skin," "to bone"); Deut. 25:18 *zanneb* "to cut off at the rear," from *zanab* "tail"; Ps. 52:7 *šareš* "to uproot," from *šoreš* "root," see WO,

412. A different reading could be "you have heartened, encouraged, emboldened me," compare the pi'el *'ammeṣ* "to strengthen," Isa. 35:3. The translation "ravished" comes from the KJV.

אֲחֹתִי כַלָּה *'aḥoti k̄allah* "my sister, [my] bride." "Sister" suggests intimacy; for a metaphoric use of "brother" and "sister" elsewhere in the Bible, see Gen. 19:7; 2 Sam. 1:26; Job 30:29; and compare Job 17:14 and Prov. 7:4. See also note 8:1 below. In Egyptian love poetry, "sister" (and "brother") are used as terms of endearment (Fox, xii–xiii, 136). "Bride" is not to be taken literally as implying a wedding ceremony, though it may well convey a hope for marriage in the future. The combined epithet occurs again in 4:10,12, 5:1. The two components occur separately in "my sister" 5:2 and "bride" 4:8,11.

Be-'aḥaṭ is the correct reading for the spelling *be-'aḥad.*

עֲנָק *'anaq* "link, strand," "chain," or "pendant," or any other segment of a necklace; compare Prov. 1:9.

צַוְּרֹנָיִךְ *ṣavveronayik̄.* The meaning "necklace" is suggested by the derivation from the common word for "neck," *ṣavvar* (usually spelled *ṣavva'r,* e.g., 1:10, 4:4). The plural form suggests a necklace with more than a single strand, as is found in ancient Egypt (Fox, 136 and figs. 1–5). Compare the "thousand shields" of 4:4, which likewise suggest a more substantial necklace. The ending *-on,* though of many functions, occurs not infrequently with nouns denoting ornaments and cosmetics, as in Isa. 3:18,23 *śaharon* "crescent," *gilyon* "mirror," and Exod. 28:34 *pa'amon* "decorative bell."

4:10 **מַה־יָּפוּ . . . מַה־טֹּבוּ** *mah yap̄u . . . mah ṭob̄u,* literally, "how beautiful . . . how good are. . . ." A common biblical formula of admiration; see also Song 7:2,7. The young man's praise of the Shulamite as a lover corresponds to her praise of him, including the reference to wine and the fragrance of precious oils, 1:2–3.

4:11 **נֹפֶת תִּטֹּפְנָה שִׂפְתוֹתַיִךְ** *nop̄et tiṭṭop̄nah śip̄totayik̄,* literally "your lips drip honey," may allude to the Shulamite's sweet words in general or, more likely, specifically to her sweetness in seduction; compare Prov. 5:3, the only other occurrence of this specific phrase, *nop̄et tiṭṭop̄nah śip̄tey. . . .* The wetness of the young man's lips similarly enhances the erotic suggestiveness of the image in Song 5:13.

רֵיחַ לְבָנוֹן *reaḥ leb̄anon,* the "scent of Lebanon," could refer to the forest, or the wine, of that region, both of which are proverbial for their fragrance; see Hosea 14:7–8.

4:12 גַּן נָעוּל *gan na'ul* "a locked garden" symbolizes the Shulamite's sexuality, like the "hidden well" and "sealed spring": the garden is inaccessible to anyone but her lover, who alone is invited to enter, 4:16–5:1. For a similar use of water, well, cistern, see Prov. 5:15,18.

גַּל נָעוּל *gal na'ul.* Though of uncertain meaning, *gal* has been plausibly linked, via its root (*gll*), with the term "*gullot* of water," which in the context of Josh. 15:19 and Judg. 1:15 must refer to springs, water cisterns, or the like (Pope and others). Water has always been a precious commodity in the Middle East; sealing is one method employed in antiquity to keep a private source of water safe from use by strangers. On the custom of sealing water sources, see 2 Chron. 32: 2–4, and compare 2 Kings 20:20.

Fox opts for the variant reading *gan* (following Septuagint, Vulgate, Peshitta, and some Hebrew manuscripts), against the Masoretic Text's *gal.* But this position may be based on too narrow a view of the pattern involved, *ABAC,* which seems to allow for minor variations in the repeating (*A*), as in Song 4:10: (*A*) *mah yap̄u dodayik̄,* (*B*) *'aḥoti kallah,* (*A*) *mah ṭob̄u dodayik̄;* compare 6:1. (See also under note 4:8, above). Indeed, *gan–gal* may well be intended for its play of sound. With its rich water imagery alluding to woman's sexuality and fertility, Song 4:12 in fact calls to mind the language of Prov. 5:15, and also its sound play: "Drink water from your cistern, flowing water from your well," *borek̄a–be'erek̄a.*

4:13 שְׁלָחַיִךְ *selaḥayik̄* "your branches." A hapax of uncertain meaning, though the root *šlḥ* "to send, stretch out, extend" offers a clue. It is found several times in a characteristically biblical image: a richly flourishing tree/vine/cedar that spreads its boughs or roots over a large area, symbolizing a thriving person or nation, e.g., Isa. 16:8 "its branches [*šeluḥoteyha*] spread abroad and passed over the sea"; Ps. 80:12; and the vision of the tree in Dan. 4:7–9. And see also Jer. 17:8 "he is like a tree planted by water that sends out [*yešallaḥ*] its roots to the stream," and Ezek. 17:6.

Given the Song's wide use of tree and plant images in relation to the two lovers—the apricot and fig trees, the cedar and the date palm, the budding vines, the Shulamite's vineyard (1:6, 2:3, 7:6,8–9)—the common understanding of *šelaḥayik̄* as branches, boughs, or shoots seems more appropriate than the interpretations based on *šelaḥim* (*šelaḥin/ šalḥin*), Mishnaic for "irrigation channels," "irrigated land"; see Fox's "your watered fields," or Pope's "your groove."

שְׁלָחַיִךְ פַּרְדֵּס רִמּוֹנִים *šelaḥayik̄ pardes rimmonim* "your branches are an orchard of pomegranate trees." Apart from pomegranates and other delicious fruits, this fantasy orchard also contains an extravagant assortment of exotic spices. Of those mentioned in 4:13–14, only saffron and henna are known for certain to have grown in Palestine. Myrrh, cinnamon, and cane were probably imported, while spikenard, frankincense, and aloes were certainly luxury imports from distant lands, such as India, Arabia, Somalia, and even China (Feliks, 23–26). On the spices imported "from far away" compare Jer. 6:20 and note 3:6 above, "all the spices of the merchant."

פַּרְדֵּס *pardes* is a loan-word from Persian (and as such another indicator of the Song's lateness) originally meaning "enclosed park" or "pleasure ground," and is still used in that sense in Neh. 2:8. The notion of an enclosure would fit well with the metaphor of the locked garden, 4:12. It is only in the third century BCE that the word is attested with the primary meaning "orchard" in the *paradeisos* of Greek papyri (whence the English word "paradise"). See Ginsberg, 52.

4:15 **מַעְיַן גַּנִּים** *ma'yan gannim,* literally "a spring of gardens," with the plural in a generic sense, i.e., a spring such as is associated with gardens.

וְנֹזְלִים מִן־לְבָנוֹן *ve-nozelim min leb̄anon.* The syntax is uncertain. Most translators consider *nozelim* a plural noun, e.g., RSV "[a well of living water, and] flowing streams from Lebanon." This is plausible, since *nozelim* indeed occurs as a common poetic synonym for water, as in Isa. 44:3, Prov. 5:15, Ps. 78:16,44. On the other hand, *nozelim* could conceivably be an active participle with verbal function, "flowing" (*nazal* "to flow" as in Num. 24:7, Jer. 9:17, Job 36:28), paralleling *ḥayyim* "fresh," literally "living." Hence freely, reading against the liturgical accents: "a well of water, fresh and gushing from Lebanon." The word *nozelim* is indeed used in its verbal sense in Jer. 18:14, "waters . . . cold, flowing down," likewise in connection with

Lebanon, to epitomize water at its freshest. The "flowing" waters (4:15) would then parallel the dynamic and sensuous image of "streaming" (*nazal*) spices in 4:16. For a similar use of the participle as a verb in the Song, see 2:8 "bounding," 2:9 "gazing," 3:6 "rising," 5:2 "knocking."

4:16 הָפִיחִי *hap̄iḥi.* This difficult verb is often translated "to blow, breathe, exhale," on the basis of its use in the simple stem, 2:17, 4:6. But since the form in 4:16 is in the causative stem (root *pwḥ,* hip̄ʿil), a literal rendition might be closer to the mark: "to cause to breathe," perhaps with a secondary meaning "to bring to life." The association between breathing and bringing to life calls to mind the description of the creation of man in Gen. 2:7, "[God] breathed into his nostrils the breath of life, and the man became a living being." But the text most immediately relevant is Ezek. 37:9—"from the four corners come, O wind, and blow upon these slain that they may live!"—where the connection goes beyond the image to the basic level of phonetic similarity, *peḥi* "blow!" The root used in both the Genesis and Ezekiel texts is *npḥ* "to blow," phonetically and semantically a close cognate of *pwḥ.* In this interpretation, the Shulamite's garden in Song 4:16 is dormant and magically brought to life by the winds she summons. In its high drama, this verse with the Shulamite "commanding" the elements is also reminiscent of Isa. 5:6, "I will command the clouds."

גַנִּי ... גַנּוֹ *ganni . . . ganno.* "My garden" becomes "his garden," just as the Shulamite's "my vineyard" in 1:6 becomes the vineyard her lover calls his own in 8:12.

5:1 בָּאתִי ... אָרִיתִי ... *ba'ti . . . 'ariti . . .* "I have come, . . . I have gathered." The RSV has a present tense: "I come, I gather, I eat, I drink," apparently to imply *intended* actions (see similarly Robert's "je viens" in the sense of an imminent future, quoted in Pope). This interpretation must be rejected out of hand, if only on linguistic grounds. While the Hebrew "perfect" verb is indeed able to express a variety of temporal and aspectual nuances, its most typical role—especially in the Song—is to denote a narrative past, and a completed action (except for a limited number of well-definable uses, such as stative verbs, as in 4:10 *yap̄u,* or where the perfect is demanded by the syntactic structure, e.g., 2:17 *ve-nasu*). In this case, the perfect implies consummation.

מוֹרִי עִם־בְּשָׂמִי ... יַעְרִי עִם־דִּבְשִׁי *mori ʿim beśami . . . yaʿri ʿim dib̄ši,* literally "my myrrh with my spice, . . . my honeycomb with my honey." The preposition "with" (*ʿim*) implies a special semantic nuance that the regular connective "and" (*ve-*) cannot express: "Not only *a*, but *b*, too," or "*a* and, on top of it, *b*!" The same repeated *ʿim* occurs in the long list of rare spices that the lover finds in his magical garden, 4:13–14, where the tone is as exuberant: "henna, and spikenard too!" The same use of *ʿim* occurs in Josh. 11:21, "he wiped them out, as well as their cities" (*ʿim ʿareyhem*).

For *yaʿar* meaning "honeycomb" compare 1 Sam. 14:27 (*yaʿrat ha-deb̄aš*). *Beśami* is irregularly voweled, for the expected *bośmi.*

שִׁכְרוּ דּוֹדִים *šik̄ru dodim,* literally "get drunk on love." For *ravah dodim* "to drink one's fill of love," see Prov. 7:18. For the syntax *šak̄ar* + direct object, "to imbibe, get drunk on," see Isa. 29:9, 49:26.

In this reading, the sentence shows the favored address pattern of the Song: (*A*) "eat, (*B*) friends, (*A*) drink and get drunk (*C*) on love!," with the address form in the expected (*B*) slot. See note 4:8.

Interpreting rather differently, the Septuagint, Peshitta, Vulgate, Rashi, KJV, and others render *dodim* as a concrete plural noun in synonymous parallelism with "friends": "Eat, O friends, and drink: drink deeply, O lovers!" (RSV). One can see why this reading was preferred by those to whom the notion of getting drunk on love may have been too blatantly erotic. But it is an interpretation with a very low degree of plausibility. The word *dodim,* so well attested throughout the Bible in reference to lovemaking (see note 1:2)—including the expression just quoted, "to drink one's fill of *dodim*"—is not likely to have been used just this one time in a different meaning, especially in a text like the Song, which consistently associates erotic love with wine. If indeed there is an allusion to *dodim* as "lovers" here, it is only secondarily, in a delightful wordplay.

A self-contained epigram, this boisterous call to enjoy life's earthly pleasures may have been taken from a popular wine song (Segal, 1967). The words serve as an exuberant finale to this entire unit. They are thematically integral to the rest of the verse, and there is no compelling reason to assume that they are spoken by a different voice (Fox, Gerleman). Nor are the "friends" (*reʿim*) necessarily to be taken as referring to identifiable persons (say, the young man's companions of 1:7, 8:13). They may well be the proverbial friends or "comrades" rhetorically addressed in a wine song. Compare the analogous use of "young man!" in Eccles. 11:9, or the ubiquitous "my son!" in Proverbs.

5:2 אֲנִי יְשֵׁנָה וְלִבִּי עֵר *'ani yešenah ve-libbi 'er* "I was asleep but my heart was awake" fits the condition of the Shulamite who yearns for her lover at night; compare 3:1. The words suggest the kind of restless sleep in which the mind is not totally unconscious but stays alert in anxiety or expectation.

Many readers have taken this to be a dream. This is a possible interpretation, though 5:2–7 exhibits none of the typical features of dream narratives in the Bible, and the events narrated here seem realistic enough. The lyric may be read as a dream, a fantasy, or an actual event; the Song, characteristically, doesn't distinguish sharply between any of these.

קוֹל דּוֹדִי דוֹפֵק *qol dodi dop̄eq,* literally "the voice/sound of my lover, knocking." For a discussion of the multiple meanings and different syntactic ways to analyze this construction, see note 2:8.

פִּתְחִי־לִי *pitḥi li,* literally "Open to me." It is not uncommon for the verb "to open" to be used without a word for door, gate, etc. in unambiguous contexts, for example, in 2 Kings 15:16, literally "because they did not open to him," i.e., the gates of the city. Similarly Deut. 20:11, Isa. 22:22, and compare Isa. 45:8, Ps. 106:17. The erotic implications are therefore probably in the scene itself, not in the absence of the expected object noun "door," as is sometimes assumed (Pope, Fox).

Notice that the Shulamite quotes her lover's words without an introductory phrase, such as "he said to me," and does the same with her own words in the next verse. The effect is a quicker pace, a heightened sense of drama and urgency, as in 3:3. Contrast the more leisurely pace of 2:10.

קְוֻצּוֹתַי *qevuṣṣotay.* Occurring in the Bible only here and in 5:11 and usually translated "my locks." The word probably refers to thick, heavy hair; compare the related Midrashic *qavvaṣ* "bushy haired" (Pope).

רְסִיסֵי לָיְלָה *resisey laylah,* approximately "drops of night." Though *resis* is found nowhere else in this precise meaning, the word's connection with drops is plausibly suggested by its root *rss* "to moisten, sprinkle," Ezek. 46:14 (compare Arabic *ršš* "to spray, rain lightly"), as well as by the use of *resisim* for fragments, tiny bits, splinters, Amos 6:11. The word is likely a poetic synonym of "dew," *ṭal,* which is its parallel in this sentence. The dew falls copiously in the Near East during certain months; compare Judg. 6:38.

The motif of the frustrated lover begging admittance at the door of the beloved is a topos also of ancient Egyptian and Greek poetry. See Fox, 282–83, and the examples cited there.

5:4 שָׁלַח יָדוֹ מִן־הַחֹר *šalaḥ yado min ha-ḥor,* literally "stretched his hand through the hole," most likely the keyhole. A traditional door key in Near Eastern villages, commonly made of wood, was of considerable size, and the keyhole large enough for a man to put his hand through it and open an (unlocked) door from the outside by slipping the inside bolt (Pope). The word "latch" here is borrowed from the JPS and Falk's translation.

שָׁלַח יָד *šalaḥ yad* "to stretch out one's hand" is a standard biblical idiom; see Gen. 22:10, 1 Kings 13:4, Ezek. 10:7, Ps. 144:7. For a discussion of *min* "through" see notes 2:9, 4:1.

מֵעַי הָמוּ עָלָיו *me'ay hamu 'alav,* literally "my innards stirred for him." The inner organs, specifically the bowels, the heart, the "walls" of the heart, as well as the soul, are used metaphorically in poetic idioms, often with the verb *hamah* "to stir," to express emotions, intense excitement, love, desire, yearning, but also sorrow, regret, anxiety, as in Jer. 4:19, 31:19, Ps. 42:6; see also Ps. 40:9, Gen. 42:28. Our translation with the heart beating "wildly" borrows from Carmi, 175.

Notice the preposition *'al* (in *'alav*) to mark the object of the yearning, in contrast with *l-* in the same idiom in Jer. 31:19, *hamu me'ay lo* "my innards stirred for him." The preference for *'al* may be a peculiarity of the language of the Song; see also 7:11.

Some commentators have attempted to understand this verse as a euphemistic account of sexual intercourse. This is implausible in the context, since the Shulamite has yet to open the door (see Fox). Moreover, this approach is faulty, since it disregards the idiomatic nature—and hence inviolability—of these two phrases; since they are idioms, they cannot be understood by an analysis of their individual components.

5:5 מוֹר עֹבֵר *mor 'ober,* "liquid myrrh" (also 5:13) is probably the same as the oil of myrrh of Esther 2:12. If the Shulamite perfumed herself in anticipation of the young man's visit (see Ruth 3:3 and also Prov. 7:17, where the bed is perfumed), her speech in 5:3 is clearly a form of coquetry.

5:6 וְדוֹדִי *ve-dodi* "but my lover," with the adversative meaning of the conjunction *ve-* as in Song 3:1,2, and later in 5:6. See discussion in note 1:5.

חָמַק עָבָר *ḥamaq 'abar,* approximately "had slipped away, was gone." (Elsewhere *ḥamaq* occurs only in Jer. 31:21, in the hitpa'el "turn oneself, turn away"). Verbs of the general meaning "to pass, go away" in close sequence mark quick departure and total disappearance, as in Song 2:11, literally "has passed and is gone." See also Isa. 8:8, Dan. 11:10,40. The lover may have left abruptly because he was concerned about the watchmen making their rounds.

נַפְשִׁי יָצְאָה *napši yaṣe'ah,* literally "my soul went forth." Elsewhere an expression for dying; see Gen. 35:18, Ps. 146:4. Here it is a hyperbolical "I nearly died," expressing a deep emotional upsurge; compare 5:4.

בְדַבְּרוֹ *be-dabbero,* literally "as he spoke." The difficulty here is that the lover's speech occurs earlier, in 5:2. Various alternative readings and emendations have been proposed (Rashi, Ginsburg, Pope, Fox), but this appears to be the Shulamite's recollection of her feelings, an expression of regret about her delay (similarly Zakovitch, 1992).

5:7 הִכּוּנִי פְצָעוּנִי *hikkuni peṣa'uni* "they beat me, they wounded me." Whether this verse recounts an actual situation, a fantasy, or a dream, it reveals a tension between the conventional social mores and the behavior of the young lovers.

נָשְׂאוּ ... מֵעָלַי *naśe'u . . . me-'alay* "they took . . . from me," literally "they lifted from on top of me." For this less common use of the verb *naśa',* usually meaning "to lift, carry," compare Num. 16:15 "not even one ass have I taken [*naśa'ti*] from them."

The *redid,* a veil (Syriac *redīdā*) or shawl, or any other light article of clothing, is mentioned only once more, by Isaiah (3:23), in his list of the fashionable apparel worn by the wanton women of Jerusalem as they saunter about the city. Hence this would seem to suggest a stylish bit of finery rather than a basic article of clothing.

The translation offered here assumes a break after *me'alay* (in accord with the liturgical accents), with the words "the watchmen of the walls" following as an independent phrase. Far from being a superfluous addition, "tacked on" at the end of the utterance, this wording is a favored dramatizing device in many languages, often used in writing to imitate everyday spoken usage, as in English, "They haven't done a thing for the environment, those scientists!" A mark of excited speech, this syntax in 5:7 artfully captures the tone of exasperation in the words of the Shulamite as she relates the violent encounter. The nuance is lost in translations such as NEB: "The watchmen . . . struck me and wounded me; the watchmen on the walls took away my cloak." It is a sign of the subtly differentiated verbal artistry of the Song that this syntax is not used in the corresponding peaceful scene in 3:3.

5:8 הִשְׁבַּעְתִּי אֶתְכֶם *hišba'ti 'etkem,* literally "I hereby adjure you." Notice that the characteristic oath "never to awaken, never to arouse love" in the other three uses of the adjuration formula, 2:7, 3:5, 8:4, is conspicuously absent in 5:8; here the adjuration phrase is followed instead by a "real" request to the daughters of Jerusalem about what they should say to the lover if they find him. Song 5:8–9 involves an actual dialogue, with the Shulamite's "Swear to me" picked up by the daughters in their response, ". . . that we must swear to you?" The verb of adjuration loses much of its literal meaning here, and amounts to little more than an urgently solemn "I entreat you, please promise me!" We are dealing with a well-known phenomenon in language: the semantic "depletion" of originally emphatic expressions, specifically when used in a new context.

אִם־תִּמְצְאוּ אֶת־דּוֹדִי מַה־תַּגִּידוּ לוֹ שֶׁ *'im timṣe'u 'et dodi mah taggidu lo še. . . .* Literally, "If you find my lover, what will you tell him? That . . ." The question-answer format is purposeful, serving to emphasize the message "You must tell him, tell him nothing other than . . . !" and is similarly used in Hosea 9:14, "Give them, O Lord—What will you give them? Give them an aborting womb and dry breasts!" (Pope). The Song may in fact attempt to recapture here the actual broken speech of the exasperated Shulamite.

Notice that all four versions of the adjuration formula use the same particles, *'im* and *mah*. In 2:7, 3:5 and 8:4 they function as negations, while 5:8 uses them in their ordinary conditional and interrogative function.

5:9 מַה־דּוֹדֵךְ מִדּוֹד *mah dodek̄ mi(n)-dod,* literally "What is your lover from a lover?" A loose paraphrase would be something like "What's so special about your lover, what makes him different from others?" The positioning of this question suggests that it serves at least in part as a rhetorical invitation for the praise song to begin, 5:10–16. Compare the question in 7:1.

Though found nowhere else in the Bible, this specific question pattern—*mah* X *mi(n)* Y "How is this different from that?"—is a staple of talmudic and rabbinic usage, e.g., *mah yom mi(n)-yomayim* "How is this particular day different from others?" or *mah 'eloheyk̄em mi(n)-kol ha-'elohim* "How is your God different from all other gods?" (Rashi paraphrasing Song 5:9). For use of the preposition *mi(n)-* in the same sense but with the verb *šanah,* see *mah ništannah ha-laylah ha-zeh mi(n)-kol ha-leylot* "How is this night different from all other nights?," the well-known question in the Passover Haggadah. And see Esther 3:8 *dateyhem šonot mi(n)-kol 'am* "their laws are different from those of other nations."

Since the question of Song 5:9 is in the format *mah* X *mi(n)* Y? known from postbiblical Hebrew, this question is likely to have the "differentiating" meaning characteristic of that pattern rather than the comparative meaning commonly ascribed to it: "What/how is your lover better/above/more than any lover?" (KJV, RSV, NEB, Ginsburg, Gordis, Pope, Fox). In the latter reading, one would have expected an explicit predicate word (verb or adjective), as in the standard comparative structure of biblical Hebrew, e.g., Song 1:2 *ṭob̄im mi(n)-yayin* "better than wine," 4:10 *mah yap̄u . . . mah ṭob̄u mi(n)-yayin* "how much sweeter than wine," 5:10 *dagul me-reb̄ab̄ah* "more elevated than ten thousand." Since the question pattern under discussion is a syntactic hapax in the Bible, but a stylistic hallmark of postbiblical phraseology, its use in the Song is another indicator of late composition. Analyzed in this way, the Masoretic Text is surely not in need of an emendation because it makes no "grammatical sense," as claimed by Albright (quoted in Pope, 530).

שֶׁכָּכָה הִשְׁבַּעְתָּנוּ *še-kak̄ah hišba'tanu,* literally "that you make us swear in this way," more likely means simply "that you entreat us like that?" See note 5:8.

5:10 צַח וְאָדוֹם *ṣaḥ ve-'adom,* literally "white and red," but covering a broader spectrum, such as "radiant, shining," and "earth-colored, ruddy." Compare the idealized image of Jerusalem's princes in Lam. 4:7, "more radiant than milk, their bodies more ruddy than coral" (*ṣaḥḥu, 'ademu*). Since the image refers not only to the outward appearance of the lover, its broader symbolism is here suggested by a free rendition with "milk" and "wine," the pair of substances epitomizing "white" and "red" in the Bible. Milk and wine are associated with health, youthful strength, earthiness, and marvelous fertility, Gen. 49:11–12, Joel 4:18. In the Song, in addition, they evoke sweetness and intoxicating sensuality, in reference to both the young man and the Shulamite, 1:2; 4:10,11; 5:1,12; 7:10. Also compare Prov. 23:31, where the red sparkle of the wine is considered seductively attractive.

In the following passage the lover is presented in a mixture of images denoting, on the one hand, a sculptural or architectural solidity, and on the other, tenderness and sweetness. His statue-like image, the comparisons with precious metals, the movement from the "head of gold" down to the legs (5:15), call to mind the description of the idol in Dan. 2:31–33. The similarity extends to the very choice of terms; see note on *me'av,* 5:14. Both descriptions may owe something to the knowledge of Greek sculpture in Palestine (see p. 26). Also, the "rods of gold" and "marble pillars," 5:14,15, are reminiscent of Esther 1:6, where specific objects of accomplished craftsmanship at the court of King Ahasuerus are similarly described.

5:11 **כֶּתֶם פָּז** *ketem paz.* Two different types of gold, or poetic synonyms for the metal. The pairing of the two nouns means "pure gold," compare 2 Chron. 9:17, interpreting 1 Kings 10:18.

תַּלְתַּלִּים *taltallim* is a hapax. Whether meaning "fronds of a date palm" (Fox, based on Akkadian *taltallu*), or "hill upon hill," as in the Mishnaic interpretation of this verse, the word amplifies the notion of the young man's thick hair implied in the word *qevuṣṣot,* 5:2.

5:12 **עֵינָיו כְּיוֹנִים ...** *'eynav ke-yonim . . .* , literally "his eyes are like doves by streams of water, bathed in milk." A poetic fantasy. Doves indeed choose regions with abundant water, and "milk" may allude to the color of doves, or the whites of the lover's eyes, as has been suggested. But here again it is pointless to approach the images with a dogged literalism. Rather, the images of abundant waters and sensuous bathing in milk suggest lushness and a tranquil sensuality. In this understanding, the core of the image is the phrase *roḥaṣot be-ḥalab̄* "bathed/immersed/ awash in milk," a hyperbole of abundance similar to that of Job 29:6 "when my feet were bathed in butter," with the same verb *raḥaṣ be-*. For "milk" and "streams of water" in similar symbolic contexts elsewhere, compare Ps. 126:4, Joel 4:18, Judg. 5:25.

The enigmatic *mille't* occurs nowhere else, but the root suggests "plenty, fullness"; in this respect the image may be similar to that of the pools in 7:5.

5:13 כַּעֲרוּגַת הַבֹּשֶׂם *ka-ʿarugat ha-bośem* "like a bed of spices." The point of the simile is that the *scent* of the cheeks is like a bed of spices. There is no need to read "beds" (plural *ka-ʿarugot*) against the Masoretic Text, as do the Septuagint and most modern commentators. On the other hand, the plural form is fully justified in 6:2, which refers to "actual" spice beds in the lover's garden.

מִגְדְּלוֹת מֶרְקָחִים *migdelot merqaḥim,* literally "towers of perfumes, mixed spices, or ointments." A hyperbole for exquisite scent, bettering the preceding comparison—"a bed of . . . no, towers of!"—with the intensification expressed both in the shift from the singular to the plural and from the smaller to the larger. *Migdalot* "towers" are hyperbolic also for the Shulamite's breasts, 8:10. Again, there is no justification for revoweling the Masoretic Text to *megaddelot* (agentive piʿel) "that make grow," as correctly argued by Fox.

Spices were considered so precious that they were kept in storehouses along with other valuables; compare Hezekiah's "treasuries" (*'oṣarot*) for silver and gold, precious stones, spices, etc. in 2 Chron. 32:27.

שׁוֹשַׁנִּים *šošannim.* According to Ibn Ezra, the lilies are mentioned "for the smell, not the sight."

5:14 יָדָיו גְּלִילֵי זָהָב מְמֻלָּאִים בַּתַּרְשִׁישׁ *yadav geliley zahab̄ me-mulla'im ba-taršiš,* literally "his arms are rods of gold filled [i.e., studded, inlaid] with *taršiš,*" a precious stone of unknown nature, mentioned also Exod. 28:20, Dan. 10:6, and elsewhere. Normally *yad* "hand" can also be used in a broader sense for the upper as well as the lower arm.

מֵעָיו עֶשֶׁת שֵׁן *meʿav ʿešet šen,* literally "his belly a polished block of ivory." Unique use of *meʿayim,* elsewhere in the Bible exclusively denoting the inner organs, bowels, intestines, womb; see Gen. 15:4, Num.

5:22, Ezek. 3:3, Isa. 49:1, Jonah 2:1–2 (see note 5:4 above). The use of *me'ayim* in the sense of "belly" strongly points to the word's Aramaic cognate as the source for this meaning, especially since the present verse recalls the statue of the idol in Dan. 2:32, with "its belly [*me'ōhi*] made of bronze." The Song may have resorted to this term for the purpose of differentiation: the Shulamite's belly (7:2) is simply a *beṭen,* the common Hebrew word for this body part in humans and animals, with the comparison to a mound of wheat further suggesting softness. The youth's hard muscular belly, on the other hand, is referred to as *me'ayim,* a term that may have been borrowed from the technical vocabulary of sculpture.

עֶשֶׁת *'ešet,* a biblical hapax, but used in Mishnaic Hebrew in reference to a work of artistic craftsmanship, specifically a polished block or bar.

שֵׁן *šen* "ivory," not just stark white but also in rosy flesh tones, was treasured in ancient Israel as a rare and beautiful material. It was carved, covered with gold leaf, inlaid with semiprecious stones, and used for furniture, beds, and panels of palace walls, as in Amos 3:15, 6:4, 1 Kings 22:39, Ps. 45:9. Some of these decorative inlays have been found in an archaeological excavation at Samaria, the capital of the ancient northern kingdom of Israel. Solomon's luxury imports included ivory, and 1 Kings 10:18–22 singles out his "majestic ivory throne . . . overlaid with the finest gold." In Midrashic folklore, that throne in addition was "studded with beryls, inlaid with marble, and jeweled with emeralds, and rubies, and pearls, and all manner of gems" (Ginzberg, vol. 4, 157).

מְעֻלֶּפֶת סַפִּירִים *me'ullep̄et sappirim,* literally "covered with sapphires/lapis lazuli," i.e., adorned, inlaid with; see preceding note. For the root *'lp* see Gen. 38:14 *va-tit'allap̄* (hitpa'el) "she wrapped herself up," and compare the cognate Arabic root *ġlf* "to cover, wrap, envelop."

5:15 **מְיֻסָּדִים עַל־אַדְנֵי־פָז** *meyussadim 'al 'adney p̄az,* literally "set upon foundations of gold," i.e., the young man's feet/lower legs upon which his marble legs/thighs rest. Apart from providing a suitable closure to this account of the body parts which began with the head of gold (5:11), golden feet may also have been deliberately conceived as a contrast to feet of a baser material, such as those of iron and clay that spell the doom of the idol in Dan. 2:33–34. (This does not presuppose a connection between the accounts in Daniel and the Song, both of which may well go back to similar, yet independent, earlier sources).

מַרְאֵהוּ כַּלְּבָנוֹן *mar'ehu ka-leḇanon,* literally "the sight of him is like Lebanon." A hyperbole with Lebanon as the typical symbol of majesty evokes not just the mountain (Judg. 3:3), but also the towering cedar trees, lush vegetation, wine, and sweet fragrance associated with that region; see Isa. 35:2, 40:16, 60:13, Hos. 14:6, Nahum 1:4. Also see notes 2:3, 5:10.

בָּחוּר כָּאֲרָזִים *baḥur ka-'arazim,* literally "a young man like cedars," continues the preceding comparison. For the use of the plural in a generic sense to denote the species, compare Song 2:9, 4:15, 7:9. This translation understands *baḥur* as a noun (as in Deut. 32:25, Amos 2:11, Eccles. 11:9), but the interpretation as a passive participle "distinguished" is equally possible.

5:16 חִכּוֹ מַמְתַקִּים *ḥikko mamtaqqim,* literally "his palate is sweet wine," an allusion to his kisses (compare 7:10) or also sweet words, with the palate, *ḥeḵ,* as the organ of speech (compare Prov. 8:7, Job 31:30). For *mamtaqqim* "sweet wine," see Neh. 8:10. Here again, an image—"the palate as wine"—is applied to both lovers (5:16 and 7:10). Compare the image of the eyes as doves, 1:15, 4:1 and 5:12.

כֻּלּוֹ מַחֲמַדִּים *kullo maḥmaddim,* literally "his entirety is delight," a generalizing statement summing up the details of the praise song, paralleling the young man's words to the Shulamite at the end of his praise song, 4:7.

6:2 לִרְעוֹת בַּגַּנִּים *lir'ot ba-gannim,* literally "to pasture/graze in the gardens." For the garden metaphor and "pasturing," compare 2:16, 4:16, 6:3. For "gathering lilies," compare 5:1 "gathering myrrh and spices," with the same erotic meaning. The plural *gannim* probably does not refer to gardens but to a single garden or garden area, as the so-called plural of local extension; compare *panim* "face," *ṣavva'rim* "neck," *ma'amaqqim* "depth," *margelot* "area close to the feet," *miškanot* "dwelling place." See WO, 120.

6:4 יָפָה ... כְּתִרְצָה *yaḇah . . . ke-tirṣah* "beautiful as Tirzah." The purpose of the comparison with a renowned metropolis is to evoke the Shulamite's regal appearance and proud beauty. That the name Tirzah is associated via its root (*raṣah*) with notions such as "pleasant," "to please, favor" may have also been a factor.

Tirzah is yet another element in the rich allusive web that links the Song with the long bygone era when this ancient royal city, like Heshbon (7:5), was part of Solomon's vast empire. Its mention alongside Jerusalem—indeed, on a par with the revered city that is the "joy of all the earth," the "perfection of beauty" (Ps. 48:3, 50:2)—points to the glorious times before the breakup of that empire into a northern and southern kingdom in the tenth century BCE. Tirzah was the capital of the northern kingdom for a brief period, but by the time of the composition of the Song it was hardly more than a memory of a legendary royal city. Like all the references to Solomon and his glorious age, the reference to Tirzah should not be taken as an indicator of an early date of composition, as is sometimes done.

אֲיֻמָּה *'ayummah,* literally "terrifying," "awe-inspiring." The Shulamite's beauty is so intense, her appearance so majestic, as to strike awe in those who see her. This interpretation accords well with her cosmic attributes in 6:10. Alternatively, one may be dealing here with a semantic transition, such as found in many languages, from the literal sense, "frightful, horrible," to "extraordinary," "of unusual, exquisite quality"; compare English *terrific,* French *terrible.*

כַּנִּדְגָּלוֹת *ka-nidgalot,* see 6:10.

6:5 **הָסֵבִּי עֵינַיִךְ מִנֶּגְדִּי שֶׁהֵם הִרְהִיבֻנִי** *hasebbi 'eynayik̄ mi(n)-negdi še-hem hirhib̄uni,* literally "turn your eyes away from me, for they frighten me!" The free translation with "dazzle" is adopted here from the NEB. There is a gradual intensification in the way the Song speaks of the Shulamite's eyes: first simply "like doves," 1:15, 4:1, then as powerful enough to ravish the heart of her lover, 4:9, and finally even to elicit his fear, 6:5. Verse 6:5 breaks away from the conventional list, in which the eyes are merely described, or compared, and speaks of their effect on the young man. This breach of the convention is especially meaningful in chapter 6 with its hyperboles about the Shulamite's intimidating beauty.

6:8 **וּשְׁמֹנִים פִּילַגְשִׁים** *u-šemonim pilagšim,* literally "and eighty the concubines." Sixty and eighty are conventional round figures; see 3:7. Their juxtaposition is here possibly intended as a variation on the biblical "three-and-four" formula (e.g., Amos 1:3,6,9, 2:1), with the two figures representing multiples of three and four. Compare Greenfield (1965), 257.

Though the figures are far more modest than Solomon's "seven hundred royal wives" and "three hundred concubines" (1 Kings 11:3), the very mention of queens and concubines, and the court setting in 6:9, suggest another bit of extrabiblical Solomonic folklore, as in 3:7–11.

עֲלָמוֹת *'alamot,* "maidens," the same word as in 1:3. Simply young women, paralleling *banot* in 6:9, in contrast to the preceding two classes of women, which are associated with royalty.

6:9 **אַחַת הִיא יוֹנָתִי** *'aḥat hi' yonati,* literally "one she is, my dove," i.e., one of a kind, without equal. The Shulamite would stand out in any crowd, even among royalty. Compare the corresponding affirmation of the young man's uniqueness in 5:10.

אַחַת הִיא לְאִמָּהּ *'aḥat hi' le-'immah,* literally "one she is to her mother." A biblical idiomatic expression, involving a father or mother, to indicate a child's unique belovedness or preciousness; see Gen. 22:2, Prov. 4:3. For the use of the cardinal numeral "one" in the sense of "unique, one of a kind" (*yaḥid* elsewhere), compare 2 Sam. 7:23 *goy 'eḥad* "a unique nation on earth" (JPS).

This "listing" style, with the numeral characteristically in frontal position, followed by the subject, literally "Sixty they are, the queens, and eighty the concubines . . . One she is, my dove," is found in Prov. 30:24,29 "Four are the small of the earth" and later in the counting games of the Passover Haggadah, where various numerals are associated with specific entities.

בָּרָה הִיא לְיוֹלַדְתָּהּ *barah hi' le-yoladtah,* literally "clear/pure/without blemish she is to the one who bore her." Secondarily, the adjective evokes the notions "bright," "luminous," "full of light"; see its use with the sun in 6:10. For a similar association see Ps. 19:9, where *barah* is followed by "making the eyes light up" (*me'irat 'eynayim*).

רָאוּהָ בָנוֹת וַיְאַשְּׁרוּהָ . . . וַיְהַלְלוּהָ *ra'uha b̄anot va-ye'aššeruha . . . va-yehalleluha,* literally "women saw her and called her fortunate/happy/blessed . . . and praised her," compare to Gen. 30:13 *'iššeruni banot* "the daughters will call me happy." These two "speech act" verbs (see WO, 403) are used specifically to introduce a quotation of praise, see 6:10, and occur in the same order, and for the same purpose, in Prov. 31:28.

These are the only two occurrences of verbs with the *waw*-conversive in the Song. This deliberately archaizing usage is in keeping with the lofty tone of the passage. Compare *'ašer* in 1:1.

6:10 **מִי־זֹאת הַנִּשְׁקָפָה** *mi zo't ha-nišqap̄ah,* literally "who is that looking forth . . . ," a stylized formula; see note 3:6.

שָׁחַר *šaḥar* "dawn" or "morning star." Here most likely the latter, in parallelism with the astral bodies mentioned in the following. A beloved woman is compared to a star in the ancient Egyptian poem quoted on p. 15: "Behold her, like Sothis rising." Sothis is the star Sirius (Fox, pp. 52, 56).

כַּנִּדְגָּלוֹת *ka-nidgalot* "like the *nidgalot.*" Though *nidgalot* itself remains obscure, the word's morphology and its root (*dgl*) offer a clue. A passive participle (of the nip̄'al), the word has its closest formal parallel in the passive participle (qal) *dagul* in 5:10, "prominent, conspicuous, outstanding" ("towering above" in our free translation). Since it has the definite article, *nidgalot* is a nominalized plural adjective, literally "those who are prominent, conspicuous."

Examining the word in its context yields a further insight. Whenever "sun" and "moon" in the Bible are followed by a third term, that term is typically "stars," "the hosts of the heavens," or the like; see Gen. 37:9; Deut. 4:19, 17:3; 2 Kings 23:5; Jer. 8:2, 31:34; Ps. 148:3. Hence the word is best understood as an epithet for stars, or for a specific group of stars. This fits well with the two preceding words for the moon and the sun, which are epithets, *leb̄anah* "the white one" and *ḥammah* "the hot one." Analyzed in this way, the verse reveals a recognizable organizing principle: day-night-day-night (parallelism) or star-moon-sun-stars (chiasmus).

No similar argument based on contextual plausibility could be made in 6:4 for *nidgalot* as an epithet, say, for a group of cities distinguished by their elevated locations, as a parallel to Tirzah and Jerusalem. Observing that 6:4 lacks a fourth member, Goitein (1965) suggested that the phrase *ka-nidgalot* is integral only to 6:10, and secondary in 6:4. Though his approach differs from the one presented here, Goitein arrived at a similar conclusion concerning the meaning of *nidgalot,* proposing that this was a term of popular astronomy for especially brilliant stars of the first order of magnitude, for which the less technical term was *kok̄eb̄ey 'or* "stars of light," Ps. 148:3. The expression "daunting as the stars" reflects the awe the ancient Hebrews felt for these heavenly bodies, see Job 9:9, 38:31–33, Amos 5:8. The astral references in Song 6:10 must be understood as hyperboles of adulation, like the image of the Shulamite "rising" from the desert, 3:6. The free translation offered here ("the stars in their courses") borrows from Judg. 5:20.

Much of the fame of this enigmatic phrase, which occurs in the Bible only here and in 6:4, rests on fanciful translations of the type "like ranked phalanxes," "like bannered hosts," or "as an army with banners" (compare Septuagint, Ibn Ezra, KJV, RSV). But these readings cannot be upheld. Though they have the same root as *degel* "banner," the words *nidgalot* and *dagul* attest to the fact that by the time of the Song this root had developed new metaphorical meanings no longer associable with the literal "banner." See discussion in note 2:4.

6:11 At least some of the interpretive difficulties of 6:11–12 dissolve if the young man is understood as the speaker of both verses, rather than the Shulamite, as has generally been assumed (KJV, RSV, Pope, Fox, Murphy, and others). Although there is no grammatical way to tell the gender of the speaker in 6:11, the garden and fruit symbolism offers an important clue. Throughout the Song the garden is a symbol of the Shulamite and her sexuality: she is the "locked garden" (4:12), inaccessible to anyone but her lover; he alone is invited to the garden (4:16), and he alone enters it (5:1). He describes her as a "garden spring" (4:15) and addresses her as "the one who dwells in the gardens" (8:13). Only she is associated with both vines and pomegranates in erotic contexts (1:6, 4:13, 7:9,13, 8:2); the only fruit associated with him is the apricot. For all these reasons, it makes better sense to see the young man as the one "going down" to the garden in 6:11. This verse parallels 6:2, where the lover "has gone down to his garden."

The preceding argumentation is supported by a more general consideration. In the customary expression for sexual intercourse in the Bible, the male is the agent: "he came to her," never "she came to him." Correspondingly, in the Song it is always the man who comes to visit the woman, not the other way around: compare the two visits to the Shulamite, 2:8–14, 5:2–6, and the visits to the garden, 5:1, 6:2. Similarly, in the two parting scenes, 2:17 and 8:14, her request that he "run away" presupposes that he has come to visit her.

גִּנַּת אֱגוֹז *ginnat 'egoz,* literally "nut garden." For *ginnah* "garden" see Esther 1:5; 7:7,8. A biblical hapax, *'egoz* is the common term in postbiblical Hebrew for nuts, specifically walnuts (its close phonetic cognates suggest an old shared Mediterranean word; compare Arabic *jawz;* Ethiopic, Syriac, Persian *gawz;* Aramaic *goza, 'egoza;* Armenian *engoiz*). Here likely used as a collective noun for the trees rather than the fruit, paralleling the vine and the pomegranates in the following. Compare 2:3, *tappuaḥ.*

אִבֵּי הַנָּחַל *'ibbey ha-naḥal.* Based on Job 8:12 *be-'ibbo* "in its prime," the phrase is usually taken to refer to fresh young vegetation. *Naḥal* "valley, wadi," but also commonly "stream, torrent, brook," which would fit the water imagery associated with the Shulamite, 4:12,15.

6:12 Generally conceded to be the most difficult verse in the Song, 6:12 has received the widest range of interpretations imaginable and countless suggested emendations, and has at times been omitted as untranslatable (Segal, Falk). See Pope, 548ff. for an overview. The translation proposed here is based on the Masoretic Text, with a single crucial emendation at the end of the verse.

לֹא יָדַעְתִּי נַפְשִׁי *lo' yada'ti nap̄si,* literally "I did not know myself." A fixed idiom denoting the unexpectedness of the event described in the next clause, approximately meaning: "Before I knew myself [such and such happened]." For the connection between "not knowing" and the perception of suddenness, see also uses such as Isa. 47:11 "ruin shall come to you suddenly, and you will not know," Jer. 50:24 "I set a snare for you, and you were trapped unawares," literally "and you did not know" (Ginsburg).

But *lo' yada'ti nap̄ši* may be understood in a different way, namely as an expression of deep emotional agitation. Just as in the corresponding English phrase "I was beside myself with . . . ," the Hebrew expression marks only the intensity, not the nature, of the emotion; the latter is revealed by the context. (In Modern Hebrew literature, *lo' yada'ti nap̄ši* can indeed be followed by phrases such as "with grief/despair" as well as "with joy/delight." Compare also "my innards stirred for him," discussed in note 5:4.) In the one other occurrence of *lo' yada'ti nap̄ši* in the Bible, Job 9:21 "I do not know myself, I loathe my life," the context is one of despair. In 6:12, on the other hand, the context is clearly one of great joy, excitement, or amazement.

In either interpretation, *nep̄eš* "self," literally "soul," functions as an integral component of the idiom (marking reflexivity, as it does occasionally also in other contexts, e.g., Isa. 44:20, Prov. 22:5). Hence *nep̄eš* is not the subject of the following verb, as implied in translations of the type "my soul/fancy/desire has made/set/hurled me" (KJV and others).

שָׂמַתְנִי מַרְכְּבוֹת עַמִּי־נָדִיב *śamatni markeb̄ot 'ammi-nadib̄,* literally "she put/placed me in the chariots of *'ammi-nadib̄.*" We understand this as the young man's metaphorical description of his erotic encounter with the Shulamite.

A key to the enigma of *'ammi-nadib̄* may be found in a poetic expression that occurs in some of the most ancient texts in the Bible, "the nobles of the people." It manifests itself in this form, or with minor variations, in Num. 21:18 *nedib̄ey ha-'am,* Ps. 47:10 *nedib̄ey 'ammim* (with "people" in the plural), and Judg. 5:2,9, *be-hitnaddeb̄ 'am, ha-mitnaddeb̄im ba-'am,* referring to those who "behaved nobly among the people" (two forms of the root *ndb̄* followed by *'am* "people"). But most illuminating to the language and imagery of Song 6:12 are two parallel texts, Ps. 113:7–8, "He raises the poor from the dust, lifts up the needy from the ash heap, to seat them with nobles, with the nobles of His people" (*le-hošib̄i 'im nedib̄im, 'im nedib̄ey 'ammo*), and 1 Sam. 2:8, with identical wording but a modified ending, "He raises the poor . . . , lifts up the needy . . . , to seat them with nobles [*'im nedib̄im*], granting them a seat of honor."

The expression "the nobles of the people" contains the same two components that make up *'ammi-nadib̄,* though in reverse order. Hence, an emendation restoring the order would yield *nedib̄ 'ammi,* literally "the nobleman of my people," or in a superlative sense "the most noble of my people." Such an emendation would not be unique in the Bible. As Gordis (1933) has shown, the enigmatic Deut. 33:21 *sp̄wn vyt'* defies all interpretation, until the order is reversed to *vyt'sp̄wn* (a single word), which reads *va-yit'assep̄un* "and they gathered." This emendation, too, is supported by the context: thus restored, Deut. 33:21 reveals itself as semantically identical with Deut. 33:5 *be-hit'assep̄* "when (they) gathered." Two other cases of erroneous inversions are Jer. 17:3 and Ezek. 24:17 (Zakovitch, 117). The fact that *'m* stands orthographically for both "with" and "people" may have contributed to the error in Song 6:12. And so probably did the clause-final position of *nadib̄* "nobleman" in 7:2.

To "seat with the nobles" means, in a physical sense, to raise from the ground, to elevate someone to a higher location. But the image must also be understood in terms of its symbolism: to grace an individual by the gesture of letting him sit among the powerful. In Song 6:12 both associations come together: to be placed "in the chariot of the most noble of my people" evokes the notion of an "elevation," a grace granted by the Shulamite to her lover, in this case serving as a metaphor for the erotic act. The metaphor of the chariot performs a double role here: (1) a royal chariot is a place of great honor, as in the case of Joseph the viceroy, Gen. 41:43, and compare the expression in Isa. 22:18, "the chariots of your pride." Similarly, letting someone ride a horse, Esther 6:9,11, 1 Kings 1:33–38, or ride "the high places of the earth," Deut. 32:13, Isa. 58:14, Hab. 3:19. (2) In addition, in the context of Song 6:12, the "chariot" has a sexual connotation, evoking an image of riding, as in "my mare," 1:9. The Song in 6:12 thus uses for an erotic purpose a specific topos that is used elsewhere in the Bible in a nonerotic sense.

In this analysis, there is a thematic connection between two sets of verses: the anticipation of the erotic encounter in 4:16 "let my lover come into his garden" is followed by the fulfillment in 5:1 "I have come into my garden." Similarly, the anticipation of 6:11 "I went down to the walnut grove to see if . . ." is followed by the fulfillment in 6:12 "she sat me. . . ."

Finally, a few grammatical clarifications:

The plural "chariots" is the so-called plural of local extension; compare note 6:2 on *gannim.*

For the superlative sense of *nedib̄ ʻammi* "the most noble of my people" (instead of the literal "the nobleman of my people"), compare to similar semik̄ut-constructions listed in note 3:7, under *mi(n)-gibborey yiśra'el.* Taken in the superlative sense, the "chariot of the most noble of my people" implies something like "the most wonderful, most noble of chariots." The association of the Shulamite with nobility is all the more meaningful in the context of her epithet in 7:2.

The use of *śam* "to place something" without a preposition "in/on/at" is common in Hebrew: Gen. 28:11, Exod. 40:29, 1 Sam. 19:13. (The same applies to other verbs, as in Gen. 18:1 "to sit at" and elsewhere.)

7:1 Apart from the widespread assumption, accepted here, that verse 7:1 begins a scene involving a dance by the Shulamite, there is no consensus as to the identity of the other participants, the speakers involved in the verbal exchange, the physical setting, or indeed the meaning of the verse. The following is only one of several possible interpretations: two groups facing each other, possibly of the daughters of Jerusalem, are engaged in a dance (*meḥolat ha-maḥanayim,* see pp. 199-200), with the Shulamite, the object of everybody's attention, dancing between them. One group urges her on enthusiastically, while the other responds with a rhetorical question ("Why do you gaze at the Shulamite?"). This "elicits" the young man's praise of her in the next verse, just as the daughters' question in 5:9 "How is your lover different from any other?" elicits the Shulamite's praise of him in 5:10–16.

שׁוּבִי שׁוּבִי הַשּׁוּלַמִּית *šubi šubi ha-šulammit.* The wide variety of interpretations offered for the imperative *šubi* attest to the inherent difficulty of this usage. The translation offered here assumes that the verb *šub* is not used in its primary meaning, as reflected in translations of the type "Return, return, O Shulamite!" (KJV, RSV, JPS, Fox, and others), but in the special sense of "do again, do once more," or "go on doing!" When used with this meaning, the verb *šub* typically modifies another verb, as in Gen. 30:31 *'ašubah 'er'eh ṣo'nka* "I will again pasture your flock," literally "I will do again, I will pasture . . ."; Zech. 6:1 *va-'ašub va-'eśśa' 'eynay* "and once again I lifted my eyes," literally "and I did again, I lifted . . ."; Jer. 18:4 *ve-šab va-ya'aśehu* "[and the vessel he was making of clay was spoiled] and he reworked it [into another vessel]," literally "did again and made it into . . ." (also Jer. 36:28). Verbs other than *šub* are also used similarly, e.g., *yasap*: Gen. 25:1 *va-yosep va-yiqqaḥ 'iššah* "and took another wife," literally "did again, took a wife"; Job 20:9 *'ayin šezapattu ve-lo' tosip* "the eye glimpses him only once," literally "glimpses, and does not do again." (For more examples of this usage see WO, 656.)

Now, in situations where the activity referred to is evident from the context (the "scene"), a modifying verb of this class may be used *without* an accompanying content verb. Compare 1 Kings 18:33–34, where Elijah the prophet instructs his Baal-worshiping colleagues: "And he said, 'Fill four buckets with water, and pour it on the burnt offering, and on the wood.' And then he said [*šenu, va-yišnu . . . šallešu, va-yešallešu*] 'Do a second time'; and they did a second time. And he said 'Do a third time'; and they did a third time." In a context like this, there is no doubt as to the activity referred to by the verbs. Similarly, the spectators' urgently repeated *šubi, šubi* addressed to the dancing Shulamite can only be understood as a request such as "Go on, dance some more!" or simply "Encore, encore!" In both instances, the concrete situation obviates the need to spell out the request: it clearly refers to the activity being performed right there on the scene.

The same address pattern, *ABAC,* with a quadruple imperative and a strong dynamic rhythm, occurs in Judg. 5:12, where, similarly, it serves to "cheer on" the person addressed: *'uri, 'uri, deḇorah, 'uri, 'uri, dabberi šir,* literally "Awake, awake, Deborah, awake, awake, utter a song!" Here too, as in Song 7:1, the verb must not be understood in its primary literal meaning but as a call to action: "Come on, Deborah! Sing!" Compare note 2:10 on *qumi.*

Interpretations of *šuḇi* along the line of "Turn!" (Gordis, Murphy), "Leap!" (Pope), "Halt!" (Ehrlich), "Twist, whirl!" (Budde) are untenable, either requiring emendations, such as to *sobbi* to achieve "turn,"or to *šeḇi* to achieve a cognate of Arabic *wṯb* "to leap," or ascribing meanings to the Hebrew verb that it does not have.

The difficulty for commentators taking the imperative *šuḇ* to mean "Return!" is that they must explain why the Shulamite is being asked to come back, and from where. Despite differences in detail, the various explanations provided to account for her alleged departure (e.g., Ginsburg), or intention to leave (Hakham), are narrative "fillers" that have no basis in the text.

הַשּׁוּלַמִּית *ha-šulammit* "the Shulamite." Of uncertain meaning. Found in the Bible only in this verse, this word has been variously explained as (1) "the Shunammite," i.e., from the village Shunem in the Jezreel plain, Josh. 19:18; 2 Kings 4:8,12; and compare 1 Kings 1:3,15 (Septuagint, Budde, and others); (2) "the peaceable one," or "complete, perfect one," on the basis of different formations of the root *šlm* (Fox); (3) a formal blend of the name of the Mesopotamian war goddess Shulmānītu (Ishtar) and "Shunammite" (Albright); (4) a feminine name corresponding to the name Solomon (Rowley, Goodspeed). For surveys of the arguments, see Fox, 157; Pope, 596–600; Murphy, 181.

Despite their substantial differences, these four views agree that the word is derived from some base form by means of the ending *-i/-it* (masc./fem.), but disagree as to the identity of that base form. Now, one of the most common uses of *-i/-it* in the Semitic languages is to form adjectives from the names of places, tribes, cities, peoples, nations, etc., the so-called *nisbe*-formations, or "gentilics" (English words borrowed from Arabic and Hebrew ending on *-i,* like "Iraqi," "Israeli," and "Saudi" are of this origin). Such a formation indeed underlies "the Shunammite," though this is not likely to be the epithet intended in the Song. Apart from the formal discrepancy between "Shulamite" and "Shunammite," the association of the heroine of the Song with Shunem has little to recommend it. The Shulamite lives in "the city," as Jerusalem is called, a walled metropolis with streets and squares (3:2–3, 5:7), not in a distant village, as Fox has rightly observed.

This reasoning points in the direction of another view, one not discussed above. Medieval Jewish exegetes like Ibn Ezra understood the word as an epithet "the Jerusalemite [fem.]" derived from *šalem,* a poetic term for Jerusalem, and one of the city's ancient names. See Ps. 76:3, where *šalem* is in parallelism with Zion—"His tent is in Salem, His dwelling in Zion"—and probably also Gen. 14:18. (In both instances *šalem* is rendered "Salem," which became the name of a Puritan settlement in the United States). In this derivation, the *šulammit* retains the root of *šalem* (*šlm*), but adopts the vocalic sequence *u - a* contained in the fuller name *yerušalayim* "Jerusalem" (the *u* is long in both *šulammit* and *yerušalayim,* as reflected in the consonantal spellings with *waw,* that is, *šwlmyt* and *yrwšlm*). Such condensed morphology is not atypical in the formation of gentilics. For example, in Num. 26:39 *ha-šup̄ami* "the Shuphamite," a clan name, derives from *šep̄up̄am.* Here, too, the characteristic vowel sequence is maintained (it happens also to be *u - a*) despite the change in the consonantal makeup, *šp̄p̄m* → *šp̄m.*

In this interpretation, the woman in Song 7:1 is addressed by her epithet, "the Jerusalemite [fem.]." It is not uncommon in the Semitic languages for a person to be known not just by his or her name, but also by some gentilic term (of the type "Laban the Aramean"). Such a term may in fact become the major component of the form of address, as in the case of Mary Magdalene, who in Luke 8:2 is introduced as "Mary, called Magdalene" (from the town of Magdala; see Matt. 15:39).

This is not to rule out that *šulammit,* via its root *šlm,* may also allude to notions of peace, see Song 8:10 (*šalom*), or perfection, or to the name of Solomon (*šelomoh*), as assumed in views (2) and (4). Indeed this specific local epithet may have been chosen by the poet precisely for its echoes of *šalom* and *šelomoh.*

The article *ha-* of *ha-šulammit* fulfills the role of a vocative, hence literally "O Jerusalemite," or "O woman from Jerusalem," or the like. Compare 2 Sam. 14:4 *hoši'ah ha-melek̄* "help, O king!" and 2 Kings 6:26. It is only in Modern Hebrew that the word came to be a proper noun, Shulamit, in which status it no longer takes the article.

וְנֶחֱזֶה־בָּךְ *ve-neḥezeh bak̄,* literally "and we will watch you," with *ḥazah* perhaps implying specifically watching a scene, or even a "performance," to use a modern term. This may explain the choice of *ḥazah* here over the more common *ra'ah* in 3:11, 6:11 (in all three instances with *b-* introducing the object). Though both are verbs of seeing, *ḥazah* has a more specialized sense than *ra'ah,* as in *maḥazeh/ḥizzayon/ḥazut/ḥazon* "vision, theophany"; see Gen. 15:1, 2 Sam. 7:17, Isa. 21:2. (In Modern Hebrew, *ḥazah* underlies *maḥazeh* "theatrical performance," and its use in Song 7:1 may well have contributed to this noun's "secularization.")

מַה־תֶּחֱזוּ *mah teḥezu,* "Why do you [pl.] watch?" The plural may address the other group in this antiphonic exchange; alternatively, it may be the general, encompassing plural addressing "everybody," as in 2:5.

Though more typical in other interrogative functions, *mah* can be used in the sense of "why?" as in Exod. 14:15 *mah tiṣ'aq 'elay* "Why are you crying out to me?"; 2 Kings 7:3 *mah 'anaḥnu yošebim* "Why should we stay?"; 2 Kings 6:33 *mah 'oḥil* "Why should I wait?"

כִּמְחֹלַת הַמַּחֲנָיִם *ki-meḥolat ha-maḥanayim,* literally "as the dance of the two camps." Outside of Song 7:1, *maḥanayim* occurs only as the name of a specific location, in Gen. 32:3, 2 Sam. 2:8, and elsewhere. But an association of the dance with that place, say, a dance "à la Mahanayim," is out of the question because of the definite article (contra Murphy, 181). Rather, the dual form *maḥanayim* suggests a specific dance, such as one performed by two groups, or circles, or rows of dancers, as has been assumed by many commentators. The phrase itelf may well be a technical term for any dance characterized by two such formations.

Some translations assume the "camps" to be military, as in the RSV "a dance before two armies," and similarly KJV and Septuagint. But while a *maḥaneh* is often a military camp, it can also be simply a dwelling place of a tribe temporarily "settling down," or any group of people in a place at a given time, not necessarily soldiers; see Gen. 33:8, 50:9; Exod. 14:19,20; Lev. 17:3. Indeed, the "armies" of the Septuagint and the KJV have as little cause to appear in 7:1 as in 6:4 and 6:10.

Meḥolah is a variant of *maḥol* "dance." Similar doublets in nonanimate nouns are *magor/megorah* "terror," *ḥeleq/ḥelqah,* "portion, allotted territory," *ḥagor/ḥagorah* "loin covering, belt," *gil/gilah* "joy," *gan/gannah* (also *ginnah,* 6:11) "garden," *ya'ar/ya'rah* "honeycomb" (in 5:1 and 1 Sam. 14:27, respectively). These are far more common than is generally realized. For more examples, see WO, 106.

The interpretation adopted here is based on a widely accepted variant reading of Symmachus and various manuscripts, reflecting *bi-meḥolat ha-maḥanayim* "*in* the dance of the two camps." Attempts to make sense of the Masoretic Text's *ki-meḥolat* have yielded renditions such as "Why do you gaze upon the Shulamite as upon the dance of the two camps?" (Murphy), and "Why would you gaze . . . as if she were a camp-dancer?" (Fox). The second view requires either the acceptance of an exceptional "abbreviated form" *meḥolat* for the required *meḥolelet* (Hakham), or emendation of both the consonantal text and the vocalization, *ki-meḥolat ha-maḥanayim* → *ki-meḥolelet ha-maḥanim.* However, neither of these alternative interpretations can be entirely ruled out.

7:2 The dynamism of the scene, with the Shulamite described while she is dancing, as well as the order of the details, from feet to head, contrast with the order in the preceding three praise songs (4:1–5, 5:11–15, 6:5–7).

מַה־יָּפוּ פְעָמַיִךְ *mah yap̄u p̄e'amayik̄.* Commonly rendered "how graceful are your feet," KJV, RSV, NEB, JPS, Pope, Fox, Murphy, and others. But the plural of *pa'am* refers less typically to the feet as such (Ps. 58:11) than to their activity, as in the Septuagint and Vulgate, "your steps." The words *mah yap̄u*—literally "how beautiful!"—cover a range far beyond that of mere physical appearance, for instance, in 4:10, where they apply to the Shulamite's lovemaking. Moreover, the plural of *pa'am,* as well as of *regel* "foot," may pertain not just to the visual, but also the acoustic effect: Judg. 5:28 *maddua' 'eḥeru pa'amey markeb̄otav* "Why tarries the clatter of his chariots?" and Isa. 52:7 *mah na'vu 'al he-harim ragley meb̄asser* "How welcome on the mountain are the footsteps of the herald!" (JPS). Here in 7:2 the reference is to the graceful tapping sound of sandaled feet.

חַמּוּקֵי יְרֵכַיִךְ *ḥammuqey yerek̄ayik̄,* approximately "the turns/curves/rounds of your thighs." The root *ḥmq* (see 5:6) evokes notions of slippery smoothness.

כְּמוֹ חֲלָאִים מַעֲשֵׂה יְדֵי אָמָּן *kemo ḥala'im ma'asey yedey 'omman,* literally "like ornaments, the work of a craftsman's hands." The *ḥala'im* are ornaments of unknown identity. The singular *ḥali* parallels *nezem* "[ornamental] ring" in Prov. 25:12 and Hosea 2:15. For *'aśah* "to make, work" (here the noun *ma'aśeh*) specifically in relation to artistic craftsmanship, see 1:11, 3:9,10.

7:3 שָׁרְרֵךְ אַגַּן הַסַּהַר *šorerek̄ 'aggan ha-sahar,* literally "your navel is the bowl/basin/cup of the moon." Most commentators take the moon here as a metaphor for an idealized roundness, i.e., "Your navel is a rounded [i.e., moonlike] bowl" (RSV). Alternatively, the phrase "cup of the moon" may be understood in a possessive sense, as reflected in the present translation. The nature of the vessel called *'aggan* is uncertain. In Isa. 22:24, the *'aggan* is named along with other small vessels, indicating a cup or a bowl (rather than "basin," as elsewhere); the mention of wine in the following phrase also suggests a drinking vessel. In Akkadian *agannu* is a bowl.

The interpretation of *sahar,* a biblical hapax, as "moon" is supported by the cognates, Syriac *sahrā* "the moon" and Arabic *šahr* "month." The spelling with *s* (another indicator of lateness) replaces the earlier spelling with *ś* underlying Isa. 3:18 *śaharonim* "crescents." See the discussion in note 2:5 of *sammek̄uni.* The reference in Song 7:3 is most likely to the full moon, not a crescent or three-quarter moon, but see discussion in Pope, 618.

There is no compelling reason to support the assumption (Pope, Murphy) that the word *šorerek̄* is used here as a euphemism for the vulva. The related meaning "umbilical cord" occurs in Ezek. 16:4 and Prov. 3:8. And see the Arabic cognate *surr, surrah* "umbilical cord, navel." See pp. 41, 127.

אַל־יֶחְסַר הַמָּזֶג *'al yeḥsar ha-mazeg,* literally "may it never lack mixed wine." Wine was mixed with water and with other wines or spices; the Midrash relates the custom of mixing strong and weak wines so as to increase their intoxicating effect (Pope). For the underlying spirit of this verse, see Eccles. 9:8 *ve-šemen 'al ro'šek̄a 'al yeḥsar* "and may you never lack oil to anoint your head," quoted in its context on p. 12.

The root *mzg* is a biblical hapax, but see Aramaic *mezag* "to mix wine," *mizgā* "mixed wine, mixture," Arabic *mizāj* "mixture of liquids." The related Hebrew root is *msk̄* "to mix, pour," as in Ps. 75:9 *mesek̄* "wine mixed with spices [?]," similarly Prov. 23:30 and Isa. 65:11 *mimsak̄.*

בִּטְנֵךְ עֲרֵמַת חִטִּים *biṭnek̄ 'aremat ḥiṭṭim* "your belly is a mound of wheat." Insofar as *'aremah* applies to threshed and winnowed wheat (compare Ruth 3:2 and 3:7), the image suggests the softness of her belly, in contrast to the young man's belly which is literally "a polished block of ivory," see 5:14.

7:4 Compare 4:5.

7:5 צַוָּארֵךְ כְּמִגְדַּל הַשֵּׁן *ṣavva'rek̄ ke-migdal ha-šen* "your neck is like a tower of ivory." The comparison with a tower suggests a long neck, a quality praised in a woman also in Egyptian love poetry (Fox); compare 4:4. For a discussion of ivory as a precious material in the Bible, see note 5:14. The image suggests a tall, proudly erect Shulamite, who carries her head high. The reference to Mount Carmel (7:6) serves the same purpose. Compare also 7:8.

עֵינַיִךְ בְּרֵכוֹת בְּחֶשְׁבּוֹן *'eynayik̄ berek̄ot be-ḥešbon* "your eyes are pools in Heshbon." Heshbon figures prominently in the early history of Israel as the thriving capital of a once-powerful neighboring state (Num. 21:25–34). In the days of King Solomon, the city was part of the Israelite empire, together with Mahanayim, Gilead, and the "land of Sihon" between the Arnon and Jabbok rivers (May et al., 64). Heshbon was famous for its great fertility and rich vineyards; see Isa. 16:8–9. It was well supplied with water, and remains of a huge reservoir of excellent masonry have recently been excavated on the site (Pope). As an illustrious city of a glorious bygone era, Heshbon fulfills a role in the Song like that of Tirzah, evoking the Shulamite's great beauty and regal appearance; see note 6:4.

The association of eyes with abundant waters suggests a tranquil and lush sensuality; compare 5:12. It may furthermore have a basis in the fact that *'ayin* means both "eye" and "spring, water source."

עַל־שַׁעַר בַּת־רַבִּים *'al ša'ar bat rabbim* "at the gate of *bat rabbim.*" The enigmatic *bat rabbim* is understood here as a personifying epithet of the city of Heshbon.

The word *bat* "daughter" figures prominently in poetic epithets that personify cities and nations, as in Isa. 62:11 "Say to the Daughter of Zion: Behold, your salvation comes," where "Daughter of Zion" (*bat ṣiyyon*) symbolizes the nation of Israel. In Zech. 9:9, Micah 4:8, and Isa. 37:22, "Daughter of Zion," in poetic parallelism with its synonym "Daughter of Jerusalem" (*bat yerušalayim*), stands for the city of Jerusalem and, by extension, the people of Israel. In Jer. 8:20–23, 14:17, the epithet "Daughter of my people" (*bat 'ammi*) is used with the same meaning. In Isa. 47:1, "Daughter of Babylon" (*bat bab̄el*) and "Daughter of the Chaldeans" (*bat kaśdim*) personify the Babylonian empire; compare Ps. 137:8. The place called *gallim* (1 Sam. 25:44) is personified in the poetic address of the prophet, Isa. 10:30, "Cry out aloud, O Daughter of Gallim" (*bat gallim*).

In this reading, the phrase *bat rabbim* is taken to be in apposition with the name Heshbon, "in Heshbon, at the gate of *bat rabbim.*" For a similar apposition of name and epithet see Isa 10:32 (where the order is reversed): "He will shake his hand at the mount of the Daughter of Zion, the hill of Jerusalem." The plural *rabbim* functions here as a noun, meaning "important people," "the great and mighty," "the nobles." See Jer. 39:13 *rabbey melek̄ bab̄el* "the officials of the king of Babylon" (similarly Jer. 41:1); Isa. 53:12 *'aḥalleq lo ba-rabbim ve-'et 'aṣumim yeḥalleq šalal* "I will divide him a portion among the great, and he will share the spoil with the strong." For the corresponding singulars in the same meaning, see *rab̄* in Esther 1:8 *'al kol rab̄ beyto* "to every official of his household," and *rabbah* in Lam. 1:1 *rabbati ba-goyim* "the mighty one [fem.] among the nations."

Heshbon as a "daughter of nobles" would fit well with the dignified status which that legendary city held in national memory. Moreover, this epithet would be especially meaningful in view of the association the Song makes between Heshbon and the Shulamite, who is herself given the epithet "nobleman's daughter" (7:2). Since the epithet *bat rabbim* occurs only here in the Bible, it may be the poet's own creation, perhaps on the analogy of the many other city epithets where *bat* means "daughter of." For another likely poetic invention (Hill of Plenty) involving a place name in the Song, see 8:11.

אַפֵּךְ *'appek̄* "your nose." The comparison to a tower probably refers to the elegant straightness of the nose. The same idealization may have been a factor also in the reference to towers in the two descriptions of the neck, 4:4, 7:5. "Tower of Lebanon" may be a designation of the mountain itself, or of one of its peaks, or of an actual tower.

7:6 כַּכַּרְמֶל *ka-karmel* "like Mount Carmel." This mountain with its densely wooded summit is a common symbol of lush vegetation and majestic beauty in the Bible; see Jer. 50:19, Amos 1:2, Nahum 1:4, Isa. 33:9 and 35:2 (where it is mentioned together with the Sharon plain and Lebanon; see note 2:1).

וְדַלַּת רֹאשֵׁךְ *ve-dallat ro'šek̄*. Occurring elsewhere only in Isa. 38:12, in relation to threads, or thrums, hanging down in a weaver's loom, *dallah* in 7:6 is usually understood as referring to the Shulamite's long wavy hair.

אַרְגָּמָן *'argaman* "purple," as well as "purple thread and cloth" (see 3:10). Very dark hair has a sheen that may resemble blue-black or purple. The term "purple" is applied to hair in Anacreon and Lucian. The dye was derived from the murex shellfish and varied in color, including blue-black (Pope).

Fox observes here a two-directional ("Janus") pun: "Carmel" is the name of a mountain, and as such points back to Mount Lebanon in 7:5; at the same time it is phonetically close to the word *karmil* "crimson cloth," which evokes the following *'argaman* "purple cloth." *Karmil* occurs three times in the Bible (2 Chron. 2:6,13, 3:14), always alongside *'argaman* (or its variant *'argevan*), which supports the close association of these two words.

מֶלֶךְ אָסוּר בָּרְהָטִים *melek̄ 'asur ba-rehaṭim* "a king is bound/held captive/trapped in the *rehaṭim.*" The enigmatic *rehaṭim* is generally viewed as a metaphor for hair. He is her "king" (1:4), and is "held captive" by her long hair. For images of entrapment in Egyptian love poetry, see Fox, 160.

In Gen. 30:38,41 and Exod. 2:16, *rehaṭim* are "water troughs, conduits"; compare the Aramaic *rāhṭā* "watercourse, stream." The basic meaning seems to be something like "runners" (see also "rafter" 1:17), hence the possible metaphoric extension to long streaming hair. But this interpretation is highly uncertain.

7:7 **מַה־יָּפִית וּמַה־נָּעַמְתְּ אַהֲבָה בַּתַּעֲנוּגִים** *mah yap̄it u-mah na'amt 'ahab̄ah ba-ta'anugim,* literally "How splendid and how sweet you are, O Love, among [all] the delights!" This is another example of a type of statement frequent in the Song: "X is unique, better than all other specimens of its kind"; see 2:2–3, 4:10, 5:9–10, 6:8–9. The preposition *b-* in the sense of "among" marks the domain in which the statement applies; compare 1:8 *ha-yap̄ah ba-našim,* literally "the [most] beautiful among women," 2:3 *ke-tappuaḥ ba-'aṣey ha-ya'ar,* literally "like an apricot tree among the trees of the wood."

Having singled out for praise each of the Shulamite's body parts, the young man concludes this section with an enthusiastic paean addressed to Love itself. The shift from the specific and detailed (7:2–6) to the abstract and general (7:7) has its parallels in the two earlier praise songs, which likewise end with generalizing statements in 4:7 and 5:16. For the personification of another abstract concept, see Prov. 7:4 "Say to Wisdom, 'You are my sister,' and call Understanding your friend," Prov. 8:1 "Does not Wisdom call, does not Understanding raise her voice?" or Prov. 9:1 "Wisdom has built her house, has hewn her seven pillars."

Some commentators propose an alternative translation, "How beautiful you are, how pleasant, O love, delightful girl!" emending *ba-ta'anugim* to *bat ta'anugim,* "daughter of delights," and postulating *'ahab̄ah* "love" as a vocative addressed to the Shulamite. But an emendation is not necessary here. Nor is it at all likely that *'ahab̄ah* "love" was ever used in biblical Hebrew to address a beloved person as it is in contemporary English, for example, in "Kiss me, love."

7:8 **זֹאת קוֹמָתֵךְ דָּמְתָה לְתָמָר** *zo't qomatek̄ dametah le-tamar,* literally "this stature/height of yours was like/resembled a palm tree." The interpretive translation offered here for this verse is based on the conviction that the perfect form of the verb denotes a past tense, as it typically does in the Song (see note 5:1), not the present, as in most translations: "is like/resembles." If the present were intended, one would have expected a participle, the form most consistently used for this tense in the Song. Indeed, the participle of *damah* is used in 2:9, *domeh dodi* "my lover resembles." With the past tense the young man may be referring to an earlier point in time: when he saw the Shulamite—at a particular moment in the past—she seemed to him like a date palm bearing delectable fruit. This erotic fantasy about the Shulamite calls to mind the one about the mare in 1:9.

As Fox notes, the image of the palm tree suggests her initial inaccessibility. In this sense it resembles an image in Sappho: "Like the sweet-apple ripening to red on the topmost branch, /on the very tip of the topmost branch, and the apple-pickers have overlooked it— / no, they haven't overlooked it but they could not reach it" (Winkler, 183).

אַשְׁכְּלוֹת *'aškolot* "clusters." The *'eškol* usually refers to a cluster of grapes, but its association with henna blossoms in the Hebrew of 1:14 indicates that the term could be used in a broader sense. Here it applies to clusters of dates.

7:9 **אָמַרְתִּי** *'amarti,* literally "I said," in the sense of "I thought," as in Gen. 20:11, 44:28. A rhetorical device used often in the Bible to indicate the inner process of thought. Note also the related expressions of the type "I said in my heart," Eccles. 1:16, 2:1, 3:17,18, Isa. 14:13, 49:21.

בְתָמָר *be-tamar.* One would expect *ba-tamar;* the sense requires that "palm" here have the definite article.

אֹחֲזָה בְּסַנְסִנָּיו *'oḥazah be-sansinnav* "let me hold on to its *sansinnim.*" The exact meaning of *sansinnim* is uncertain. Possibly referring to the stringlike stalks of the palm tree that hold the fruit. One grasps these stalks to pick the fruit.

וְרֵיחַ אַפֵּךְ *ve-reaḥ 'appek̄,* literally "the scent of your nose." Since the nose is the organ associated with breathing and breath, as in the common expressions *nišmat 'appo, nišmat ruaḥ 'appo* "breath of his nose" (Gen. 2:7, 7:22; Isa. 2:22; 2 Sam. 22:16; Ps. 18:16), "nose" may be explained as a metonymy for "breath" here. See Isa. 52:7, where the literal "feet" is used in the sense of "steps."

7:10 **וְחִכֵּךְ כְּיֵין הַטּוֹב** *ve-ḥikkek̄ ke-yeyn ha-ṭob̄,* literally "and your palate like good wine." For the association of the lovers' palates with wine, see 5:16, and also 4:11, where the Shulamite's mouth is associated with sweetness.

הוֹלֵךְ לְדוֹדִי לְמֵישָׁרִים *holek̄ le-dodi le-meyšarim,* literally "going to my lover smoothly." Here the Shulamite playfully interrupts her lover, completing his sentence (see pp. 16–17). For *hlk̄* "go" in the sense of "flow" see Eccles. 1:7 and Joel 4:18 (3:18 in English versions), and especially Prov. 23:31, where the expression *yithallek̄ be-meyšarim* "flows smoothly" is said specifically of wine and its effect.

דּוֹבֵב שִׂפְתֵי יְשֵׁנִים *dob̄eb̄ śip̄tey yešenim.* Rashi, Ibn Ezra, and some modern commentators translate this enigmatic phrase along the lines of "[wine] that causes the lips of those that are asleep to speak or move." One possible way to understand this image is as a hyperbole: the wine is so powerful, and so irresistible, that it is capable even of arousing one from sleep. But the association of the root *dbb* with either "to speak" or "to move" is highly problematic, making the interpretation adopted here as conjectural as all others offered for this phrase.

7:11 **אֲנִי לְדוֹדִי וְעָלַי תְּשׁוּקָתוֹ** *'ani le-dodi ve-'alay tešuqato,* literally "I am my lover's and his desire is for me." The use of *tešuqah* "desire" calls attention to itself, since this particular word occurs at only two other points in the Bible—in decidedly negative contexts: Gen. 3:16 "your desire shall be for your husband [*'el 'išek̄ tešuqatek̄*] and he shall rule over you," and Gen. 4:7 "its [Sin's] desire is for you [*'eleyk̄a tešuqato*] yet you must master [literally, rule over] it." The resemblance between these three verses extends beyond the use of this particular word to a specific detail of syntax, namely that the prepositional phrase marking the object of desire occurs before *tešuqah* for emphasis; compare 1:4, 3:3.

In Genesis, man is expected to rule over woman, as well as over Sin (the use of the same verb—*mašal* "to rule"—in both verses makes the parallelism painfully obvious). Moreover, sexual desire is presented as entirely one-directional: woman desires man, and he has dominion over her.

In light of this patently similar wording, Song 7:11 reads almost like a deliberate reversal of Gen. 3:16, turning it upside down by making the *woman* the object of desire. And instead of the dominion of man over woman, the present verse speaks of a relationship of mutuality, expressed in a formula of reciprocal love like that in 2:16, 6:3. In the Song, sex is free of notions of control, dominion, hierarchy.

7:12 נָלִינָה בַּכְּפָרִים *nalinah ba-kep̄arim,* literally "let us pass the night among the henna bushes." Song 7:12–13 and 1:13–14 are similar in their sequence of associations: compare the sequence in 7:12–13 *nalinah* "to pass the night," *kep̄arim* "henna bushes" and *keramim* "vineyards" with that in 1:13–14 *yalin* "passing the night," *'eškol ha-kop̄er* "henna cluster" and *karmey 'eyn gedi* "vineyards of Ein Gedi" (Fox).

It has been suggested that the invitation in 7:12 allows two readings, "among the henna bushes" or "in the villages" (Fox, Murphy). For *kep̄arim* "villages" see 1 Chron. 27:25. But the tightly woven web of associated images in 7:12–13 and 1:13–14 supports only the reading "henna bushes."

7:13 נִרְאֶה אִם־פָּרְחָה הַגֶּפֶן ... הֵנֵצוּ הָרִמּוֹנִים *nir'eh 'im pareḥah ha-gep̄en . . . heneṣu ha-rimmonim,* literally "we will see if the vine is in bloom, . . . if the pomegranates have budded." Vines and pomegranates are associated with the Shulamite's sexuality throughout the Song, as in 1:6, 4:13, 7:9, 8:2. In the present verse this association is even more narrowly focused, and relates specifically to her readiness for a sexual encounter: in the place where the vines and pomegranates are in bloom, she promises, "There I will give you my love [*dodim*]." The wording, the scene, and the erotic association is much the same as in 6:11. In that case, it is the young man who goes down to the walnut grove in order to find out whether the vines and pomegranates are blooming, a visit that culminates in the sexual encounter of 6:12. In both instances erotic readiness is reflected in nature.

פִּתַּח הַסְּמָדַר *pittaḥ ha-semadar* "[if] the blossoms have opened." *Semadar,* occurring only in the Song, is a collective noun for buds or blossoms of the vine; compare 2:13,15. *Pittaḥ* (pi'el) is used here in an intransitive sense; compare Isa. 48:8 *lo' pitteḥah 'ozneka* "your ear has never opened up," Isa. 60:11 *pitteḥu še'arayik tamid* "your gates shall be open continually."

דּוֹדַי *doday,* literally "my lovemaking." The preceding verb "give" underlines the physical concreteness of *dodim;* compare note 1:2.

7:14 הַדּוּדָאִים *duda'im* "mandrakes." A native of the Mediterranean area, the mandrake plant, or mandragora (*Mandragora officinarum*) is found in most parts of Israel. It has large leaves, beautiful purple flowers, and juicy, golden fruits. Its odor is reportedly pungent and distinctive, and may have been considered pleasant or exciting (Pope). For the ancient belief in its aphrodisiac properties, see Gen. 30:14–16. The association of mandrakes with sex may rest in part on the fact that the sound of the word *duda'im* is similar to *dodim* "lovemaking." The poet plays with these sound associations in the present text, hence *doday* and *duda'im* in proximity (7:13–14), and *dodi* "my lover" in nearly every verse of this section (7:10,11,12,14).

נָתְנוּ־רֵיחַ *natenu reaḥ,* literally "have given off fragrance"; see 1:12, 2:13. Again, erotic readiness is mirrored by nature: "I will give you my love" (7:13) resembles "the mandrakes have given [their] fragrance" (7:14), with the use of the identical verb *natan* emphasizing the association.

עַל־פְּתָחֵינוּ *'al petaḥeynu* "at our doors." The "doors" belong to the "houses," or "chambers" in the outdoors where the two lovers meet; compare notes 1:4,17. The possessive "our" conveys loving intimacy, not ownership, as in 1:16 "our bed," 1:17 "our houses," "our rafters," 2:9 "our wall," 2:12 "our land." The phrase itself carries a special symbolism: in Hebrew, as in other languages, being "at the door" conveys immediate availability, closeness at hand, easy reach.

כָּל־מְגָדִים *kol megadim,* literally "all kinds of delicious things, delicacies." Outside the Song, this word occurs only in Deut. 33:13–16 (in the singular *meged*) with reference to the choicest bounties bestowed on mankind by nature. Since *megadim* was mentioned in 4:13,16 in association with fruit (*peri megadim*) and in the context of exotic spices, the reference in the present verse is probably to delicious rare fruit.

Kol, commonly just "all," may also mean "all kinds of," as in Gen. 2:9 *kol ʿeṣ neḥmad le-marʾeh,* implying "every kind of tree pleasant to look at."

חֲדָשִׁים גַּם־יְשָׁנִים *ḥadašim gam yešanim,* literally "both new and old." This particular expression, also used in relation to something valuable that is hidden, occurs in Matt. 13:52 in the parable of the householder who "brings out of his treasure things new and old." Such similarities of language and imagery may belong to a common stock of idiomatic expressions underlying the Old and New testaments.

The translation offered here presupposes this syntactic analysis (in simplified paraphrase, reflecting the Hebrew word order): "at our doors delicacies new and old I hid for you." This parsing of 8:14 seems more straightforward than the one suggested by the liturgical accents, which is syntactically rather problematical.

8:1 **מִי יִתֶּנְךָ כְּאָח לִי יוֹנֵק שְׁדֵי אִמִּי** *mi yittenḵa ke-ʾaḥ li yoneq šedey ʾimmi,* literally "if only you were like a brother to me, one who nursed at my mother's breasts." If the young man were her brother, she could kiss him freely in the street without being exposed to contempt or reprimand—or possibly even being taken for a harlot, like the woman in Prov. 7:13, who "caught hold of [a young man] and kissed him" in the street. These words should not be taken to imply that the Shulamite wishes for a brother-sister relation with her lover; rather, as Fox notes, a brother is someone to whom she could legitimately show her affection in public.

Mi yitten is commonly used to introduce a fervent wish, as in Jer. 9:1 "Oh that I were [*mi yitteneni*] in the desert at an encampment for wayfarers," or 2 Sam. 19:1 (18:33 in English versions) "Would that I had died instead of you!" (*mi yitten muti ʾani taḥteyḵa*).

The second phrase, *yoneq šedey ʾimmi,* is an expression of tenderness and intimacy: the Shulamite wants to be as close to her lover as if they were nursing together at their mother's breasts.

Ke- generally means "as, like," but in hypothetical, contrary-to-fact statements like this one, the particle may mean "as if," as in Gen. 27:12 "I shall seem to him as if I were someone who is mocking," *ki-metaʿteaʿ*; Ps. 126:1 "we were like those who dream," *ke-ḥolemim,* i.e., as if in a dream.

אֶמְצָאֲךָ ... אֶשָּׁקְךָ *'emṣa'aḵa . . . 'eššaqeḵa,* literally "I would find/meet you . . . I would kiss you." The logical relation is conditional-temporal: "If I were to meet you, or, when I met you, I would. . . ." For *maṣa'* used in the sense of incidentally crossing someone's path, see also 3:3, 5:8.

גַּם לֹא־יָבֻזוּ לִי *gam lo' yaḇuzu li* "yet no one would scorn/despise me," literally "they would not," with the masculine plural in the generalizing sense of "everybody." For *gam* in the adversative sense "yet," see Ps. 129:2 "Sorely have they afflicted me from my youth, yet they have not prevailed against me," *gam lo' yaḵelu li.*

8:2 אֶנְהָגְךָ אֲבִיאֲךָ *'enhageḵa 'aḇi'aḵa,* literally "I would guide you, I would bring you." Here and in 3:4 one may note a departure from the tradition, at least as reflected in Gen. 24:67, where it is the man (Isaac) who brings the woman (Rebecca) into his mother's tent. Compare note on 7:11.

For examples of the joining of verbs without an expected conjunction (called "asyndeton"), compare 2:11 *ḥalap̄ halaḵ,* literally "passed, was gone," 5:6 *ḥamaq 'aḇar,* literally "slipped away, was gone."

תְּלַמְּדֵנִי *telammedeni* can mean either "she will teach me," or "you [masc. sing.] will teach me"; either way the actual meaning remains uncertain. Since the word *telammedeni* does not itself constitute a complete line of verse, some commentators consider the Masoretic Text here corrupt, emending it to "and to the room of her who bore me," following the parallel in 3:4; this is supported by the variant readings in the Septuagint and Peshitta.

On the other hand, the unemended Masoretic Text in the reading "she will teach me" makes sense if the Shulamite were expecting her mother to instruct her in the art of love. Commenting on this verse, Landy (1983), 100, 250, sees the mother as participating in "the lovers' amorous education." Compare Ruth 3:1–5, where Naomi instructs her daughter-in-law to wash and anoint herself, and put on her best clothes, in preparation for her expected encounter with Boaz. This custom has ancient antecedents: the Sumerian goddess Inanna, at her mother's command, "bathed herself, anointed herself with goodly oil," before her meeting with Dumuzi; see Kramer (1969), 77.

אַשְׁקְךָ *'ašqeḵa* "I will give you to drink," compare *'eššaqeḵa* "I would kiss you," 8:1. The phonetic similarity between these two verbs points to the associative link between kissing and wine so prevalent in the Song; see also 1:2.

עֲסִיס רִמֹּנִי *'asis rimmoni,* literally "the juice of my pomegranate." *'Asis* is consistently used as a poetic term for wine and intoxicating juices in general, Isa. 49:26, Joel 1:5, 4:18 (3:18 in English versions), Amos 9:13.

8:3 See 2:6.

8:4 מַה־תָּעִירוּ וּמַה־תְּעֹרְרוּ *mah ta'iru u-mah te'oreru,* literally "never to . . . , and never to," as in 2:7 and 3:5, but here with *mah* instead of *'im* of the earlier adjurations. For *mah* as a negation see 1 Kings 12:16, Job 31:1, Prov. 31:2.

8:5 מִי זֹאת עֹלָה מִן־הַמִּדְבָּר *mi zo't 'olah . . .* "Who is that rising. . . ." See remarks in note 3:6.

מִתְרַפֶּקֶת עַל־דּוֹדָהּ *mitrappeqet 'al dodah,* literally "leaning on her lover." Though a biblical hapax, the root *rpq* occurs in a number of Semitic languages in words with meanings ranging from the noun "elbow" to the verb "to rest one's arm, lean on something."

תַּחַת הַתַּפּוּחַ עוֹרַרְתִּיךָ *tahat ha-tappuah 'orartika,* literally "under the apricot tree I awakened you," with "awaken" in the erotic sense, as in the adjurations 2:7, 3:5, 8:4. The erotic import is manifest in view of the implications of 2:3, where the Shulamite tells of sitting in the shade of the apricot tree and tasting its fruit. In the symbolism of 2:3, the apricot is of course *his* fruit. The speaker here is the young woman, as the Masoretic Text voweling clearly indicates.

שָׁמָּה חִבְּלַתְךָ אִמֶּךָ *šammah hibbelatka 'immeka,* literally "there your mother conceived you." *Hibbel* (pi'el) "conceive, get pregnant," as in Ps. 7:15 "He conceives evil [*yehabbel 'aven*], is pregnant with mischief, and gives birth to a lie."

שָׁמָּה חִבְּלָה יְלָדַתְךָ *šammah hibbelah yeladatka,* literally "there she conceived, gave birth to you," i.e., "conceived and gave birth," with the coordinate verbs joined asyndetically, as in 8:2, "I will lead you, bring you."

There can be little doubt that the conception and birth under the apricot tree must not be taken as realistic reportage, as in some commentaries. These details add a mythic dimension to the figure of the young man; the motif of a birth under a tree is found in many myths in antiquity (Pope, 663). But the association of birth and tree may have an additional explanation. In order to give birth to their fawns, hinds often return to their own birthplace under a tree (Feliks, quoted in Hakham, 16). Since the young lover in the Song is repeatedly compared to a gazelle (2:9,17, 8:14) this association would be especially evocative.

Many versions translate along the lines of "there your mother conceived you, there the one who bore you conceived," treating the last word of the sentence as if it were an epithet, "the one who gave birth to you," parallel to the preceding "your mother." In this understanding, only the conception takes place under the apricot tree, not the birth. But a reading with "the one who" would require a participial form *yoladteḵa,* a word that is typically spelled with a *waw* (*ywldtk*), as in Song 6:9, Jer. 50:12, Prov. 17:25, 23:25, whereas the word in the present verse unmistakably indicates a verb in the perfect, *yeladatḵa.* In an alternative approach, Fox (compare Grossberg, 488) suggests that the verb be understood as nominalized, literally "conceived [the] she-bore-you." But this admittedly attractive proposal is not without its own problems. Nominalizations of verbs do of course occur but, significant to the case at hand, they typically function attributively, as genitives or as relative clauses, and not as the subject of a verb. See also WO, 87, n. 13.

8:6 שִׂימֵנִי כַחוֹתָם עַל־לִבֶּךָ ... עַל־זְרוֹעֶךָ *śimeni ḵa-ḥotam ʿal libbeḵa . . . ʿal zeroʿeḵa,* literally "Set me as a seal upon your heart, . . . your arm." A seal on the heart and arm implies belonging, physical closeness, and intimacy. Seals or signets, made of metal or stone and often exquisitely engraved, were worn on the hand as a ring, higher up on the arm as an amulet, or on a cord around the neck, resting on the chest (Pope). A seal served as a form of identification, as in the story of Tamar and Judah (Gen. 38:18–26), and was numbered among a person's most precious possessions. Of deep symbolic significance, a seal stands for the owner's identity, honor, and fate; see Jer. 22:24, Hag. 2:23. For the weighty significance implied in placing an object of symbolic import on one's hand or heart, see Prov. 3:3, 6:21, 7:3, and Deut. 6:8, 11:18. (The verses in Deuteronomy furnish the biblical basis for the wearing of phylacteries.)

עַזָּה כַמָּוֶת *'azzah ḵa-mavet* "as strong/fierce as death." For *'az* used specifically in the sense of "fierce," see Deut. 28:50 *'az panim* "fierce of countenance," Judg. 14:18 *'az me-'ari* "more fierce than the lion" (rather than "more strong"; compare Prov. 30:30, where the lion is proverbial for ferocity, not strength).

קָשָׁה כִשְׁאוֹל *qašah ḵi-š'ol,* literally "hard/cruel as Sheol." Although Sheol is the personified netherworld in the biblical worldview (see Isa. 28:15,18, Ps. 89:49, Hab. 2:5), the word is often used simply as a synonym for "death."

קִנְאָה *qin'ah* "jealousy," as correctly noted by Fox (not "passion," as in many modern translators and commentators). What is meant here is not jealousy as an independent force, but the jealousy that is a by-product of love, the jealousy ignited by love. The real focus of this line, as of the ones that follow, is love. We have added the "its" in "its jealousy" to clarify the point.

רְשָׁפֶיהָ רִשְׁפֵּי אֵשׁ שַׁלְהֶבֶתְיָה *rešap̄eyha rišpey 'eš, šalheḇetyah,* literally "its sparks are sparks of fire, an enormous flame." The exact meaning of *rešep̄* is uncertain; in Job 5:7 the word has been widely understood as referring to sparks rising from a fire. Taking "spark" as a metaphor for something very small, we see in Song 8:6 an intensification by way of contrast. The image moves from the sparks to the flame: love is so powerful that even its tiny sparks burn like great fires.

It has long been debated whether or not *šalheḇetyah* contains the name of the God of Israel. While it is likely that *-yah* derives from "Yah," the short form of "Yahweh," this ending long ago lost its association with God's name, and became simply a suffix denoting intensity, as in Jer. 2:31 *ma'pelyah* "thick darkness," Ps. 118:5 *merḥaḇyah* "great relief." (For the semantic change involved, compare the expression 1 Sam. 14:15 *ḥerdat 'elohim* "a great terror," literally "God's terror," and similarly Gen. 35:5, 1 Sam. 11:7, and others.) The very spelling of *šalheḇetyah* as a single word supports this assessment, since the name "Yah" (God) is always spelled as a separate word, as in Ps. 115:18 *va-'anaḥnu neḇareḵ yah* "but we will bless the Lord," Exod. 15:2, 17:16, Ps. 68:19.

8:7 אִם־יִתֵּן אִישׁ ... בָּאַהֲבָה *'im yitten 'iš . . . ba-'ahaḇah,* literally "if a man gave [all the wealth of his house] for love," i.e., traded it, or tried/offered/intended to trade it, in exchange for love. The point of this aphorism is that love is beyond all material value, and cannot be bought for any price. Hence anyone attempting to buy love would be considered a fool. An alternate reading—the man who gives up everything for love is mocked by an uncomprehending world—seems less fitting in this context: the poet is praising the greatness of love, a cosmic force, not bemoaning the small-mindedness of human beings. The topos of comparison with mere earthly wealth continues in 8:11–12.

For the idiomatic expression "to give all the wealth of one's house" or "half of one's house" see 1 Kings 13:8 and Prov. 6:31. For the special sense of the preposition *b-* as used here, compare Gen. 29:18 *'e'ebodeka . . . be-raḥel* "I will serve you for [i.e., in order to obtain] Rachel."

בּוֹז יָבוּזוּ לוֹ *boz yabuzu lo* "he would be utterly scorned / despised" (the so-called absolute infinitive preceding the verb for strong affirmation; see WO, 586). One may perceive a closure here, formally echoing 8:1: "If only you were like . . . , no one would scorn me," "If a man gave . . . , he would be scorned." The formal similarity is more sharply profiled in Hebrew because of the presence of the verbs *yitten* and *būz* in both verses.

Despite the obvious differences in purpose and tone, this aphorism recalls the sayings in Matt. 13:44–46 and 16:26. In each case, something of material worth is weighed against a spiritual value such as love, the soul, the Kingdom of Heaven.

8:8–10 The great difficulty of this section is reflected in the widely differing interpretations given in the commentaries. There is hardly any consensus even on essential questions such as (1) the identity of the "little sister" (some commentators postulate a younger sister of the Shulamite); (2) the identity of the speakers in 8:8–9 (proposals include the brothers; a group of suitors; the brothers in 8:8, and the suitors in 8:9; the girls of Jerusalem; the young man; the Shulamite, quoting an earlier speech by her brothers); and, most crucially, (3) the meaning of the "wall" and "door" metaphors. For overviews of the various possibilities, see Pope and Fox.

8:8 The brothers are the most likely speakers in 8:8–9 (compare Pope, Fox, Falk). Responsibility of brothers for a sister is well established in the Bible, especially in matters pertaining to sexuality and marriage, as in the case of Rebecca, Gen. 24:29–60; Dinah, Gen. 34:6–17; and the daughters of Shiloh, Judg. 21:22. Song 1:6 clearly reflects the fraternal authority of the brothers over the Shulamite.

קְטַנָּה *qeṭannah* "little" does not refer to the Shulamite's size but to her sexual immaturity in her brothers' eyes. (In the language of the Mishnah, *qeṭannah* and *qaṭan* become the legal terms for minors, defined as "a girl up till twelve years and one day," and "a boy till thirteen and one day.")

וְשָׁדַיִם אֵין לָהּ *ve-šadayim 'eyn lah* "and she has no breasts." Well-formed breasts and pubic hair are indicators that a girl has reached sexual readiness, Ezek. 16:7–8 *'et dodim* "the age for lovemaking." (The same criteria apply in the Mishnah, see R. Biale, 206.) The brothers' statement about the Shulamite's having "no breasts" is as much a poetic hyperbole as her defiant counterassertion of having breasts "like towers."

בַּיּוֹם שֶׁיְּדֻבַּר־בָּהּ *ba-yom še-yedubbar bah,* literally "on the day when she will be spoken for/wooed," i.e., by prospective suitors. For an example of *dabber b-* used in this sense see 1 Sam. 25:39. Our free translation with the verb "besiege" borrows from the language and imagery of 8:9–10.

8:9 אִם־חוֹמָה הִיא ... וְאִם־דֶּלֶת הִיא ... *'im ḥomah hi' . . . ve-'im delet hi' . . . ,* literally "if she is a wall . . . and if she is a door. . . ." The question here is whether the "wall"/"door" metaphors are synonymous or antithetical. To commentators who see them as antithetical, the dualism has a sexual connotation—inaccessibility/accessibility—with the clear implication of a warning. Commentators who see the metaphors as synonymous, on the other hand, argue that no such contrast is intended, citing specific contexts in which *delet* unmistakably denotes the door as a structure rather than an opening.

The case for the antithetical reading is substantially stronger. In a familiar biblical pattern, *'im . . . ve-'im . . . ,* the second of the two coordinated conditional sentences spells out the negative consequence if the first condition is not fulfilled, as in Isa. 1:19–20, "If you are willing . . . you shall eat the good of the land; but if you refuse and rebel, you shall be devoured by the sword"; see also Deut. 20:11–1, etc. In this antithetical reading, the conjunctive *ve-* is the semantic equivalent of "but" (the adversative *ve-*, WO, 677); compare above 3:1,2, 5:6, and discussion in note 1:5. On the other hand, if these metaphors were indeed synonymous, one would have expected the two conditional sentences to be arranged in the opposite order, so that the verse would end on "turret of silver"—surely the more dramatic image—rather than on "panel of cedarwood." As Alter has shown (1985) 18ff., when parallelism occurs in biblical poetry, "the characteristic movement of meaning is one of heightening or intensification."

נִבְנֶה עָלֶיהָ טִירַת כָּסֶף *nibneh 'aleyha ṭirat kasep̄* "we will build a silver turret upon her." The meaning of *ṭirah* is uncertain, but the use in Ezek. 46:23 suggests some round formation of masonry. In a verse such as this, in which everything has a symbolic import, a *ṭirah* made of silver instead of stone surely adds a note of grandeur.

נָצוּר עָלֶיהָ לוּחַ אָרֶז *naṣur 'aleyha luaḥ 'arez,* literally "we will besiege her with a plank/panel of cedar," i.e., bolt her, or enclose her with it. Commentators trying to play down the harshness implied in this image tend to explain the board of cedar as primarily ornamental, like the silver turret. In a similar vein, others consider "silver" and "cedar" to be allusions to conciliatory gifts by the brothers (Hakham), or by suitors hoping to overcome the Shulamite's resistance (Gordis). But it is hard to ignore the contrast between these two materials. For although cedar wood was greatly prized for its strength and durability, silver was a far more precious material. It is therefore more plausible that these materials are named here for their difference, not for any possible similarity. Indeed, the contrast in value between silver and cedar is most likely intended to underline and enhance the "wall"/"door" antithesis.

A word on the language is called for. The most frequent use of the verb *ṣar* followed by the preposition *'al* occurs in contexts in which a siege is laid against a city, e.g., Jer. 37:5 *ha-ṣarim 'al yerušalayim* "those who were besieging Jerusalem," and 2 Kings 18:9 *va-yaṣar 'aleyha* "and he besieged it." If indeed a siege metaphor is implied in this verse, then the plank of cedar functions as the instrument with which the "siege" is carried out. In this regard, Isa. 29:3 provides a close analogue: *ve-ṣarti 'alayik̄ muṣṣab̄ va-haqimoti 'alayik̄ meṣurot* "I will besiege you [Jerusalem] with a *muṣṣab̄,* and I will raise siegeworks [*meṣurot*] against you," with the siege instrument as the direct object of the verb *ṣar,* as in the phrase at hand. (The identity of the term *muṣṣab̄* is unknown, but its syntactic parallelism with *meṣurot* "siegeworks" suggests a specific structure or instrument used in a siege.)

It is hard to ignore the antithesis between "building a silver turret" upon the Shulamite, which evokes notions of crowning, and the threatening siege metaphor in the second half of the verse. Notice in this connection the difference in the use of the preposition *'al.* With the verb *ṣar,* it has an adversarial sense, "laying a siege against" (*'al* with the meaning "against" occurs also with other verbs). But with *banah* "to build," *'al* has a simple locative sense, "we will build upon her" (as in 8:6 *'al libbeḵa, 'al zero'eḵa* "upon your heart, upon your arm").

8:10 אֲנִי חוֹמָה *'ani ḥomah* "I am a wall." Contrary to the common view (Pope, Ginsburg, and others), it is very unlikely that the Shulamite uses "wall" as a metaphor for chastity—no matter how her brothers intended that metaphor in the first place. A claim of chastity by the Shulamite would make little sense since the two lovers have spent the night together (1:13–14, and probably also 7:12–13), and have made love (5:1, 6:12, etc.); similarly Fox. A more plausible interpretation is to see the "wall" as related to another metaphor of the Song, the "locked garden," which symbolizes the Shulamite's sexuality: she is inaccessible to anyone but her lover. The common element of a wall and a locked garden is the sense of enclosure, of a concealed space behind a barrier. It evokes a sexuality that is hidden, even mysterious, and therefore all the more inviting. The lover has the key to the garden, as well as to the "door" in the wall. Viewed in this way, the "wall" activates a whole set of related images, such as the Shulamite as a dove concealed in the shadow of rocks (2:14), as a "hidden well" and "sealed spring" (4:12), as waiting behind the door at night (5:2–5), and as the mysterious "dweller in the gardens" (8:13).

כַּמִּגְדָּלוֹת *ka-migdalot,* literally "like towers," alludes both to the breasts and to towers or battlements on a wall. With this image the Shulamite sharply opposes her brothers' claim about her lack of physical maturity.

אָז הָיִיתִי בְעֵינָיו כְּמוֹצְאֵת שָׁלוֹם *'az hayiti ḇe-'eynav ke-moṣ'et šalom,* literally "so then I became in his eyes as one who finds peace." The phrase is so obscure that any interpretation is necessarily tentative. We presume an associative link between two images: the Shulamite under "siege" (8:9) and the besieged city that achieves peace, see Deut. 20:10–11. At the root of this association is the well-known symbolic connection between "city" and "woman" which manifests itself in various ways, such as in the typical feminine gender of the words for "city" in Hebrew and many other languages; the use of city epithets with "daughter" (see note 7:5); the obvious sexual connotations of conquering and entering a city. These associations may be combined in a hypothetical scenario: the victorious lover enters the gate of the city, which then becomes a city "that finds peace." (We owe this final image in our free translation to Robert Alter.)

In a different approach, several commentators understand the difficult idiom *moṣ'et šalom* as synonymous with *moṣ'et ḥen* "one who finds favor." However, because antithetical images dominate in 8:9, it seems more plausible to understand *šalom* in its regular meaning, "peace," and to see this concept as a deliberate contrast to the preceding expressions of war and siege, "we will besiege her," "breasts like towers/battlements" (see also Falk, 195).

The possessive pronoun "his" of "his eyes" has no explicit antecedent in the preceding verses. But since this is an exchange between the Shulamite and her brothers, who have just been discussing in her presence what to do when suitors ask for her hand (8:8), one can safely assume that her lover is uppermost in her mind, and that he is the one she refers to.

8:11–12 This Parable of the Vineyard implies that love outweighs the riches of this world; in this respect it resembles the spirit of 8:7. The young man, who is the speaker (as conclusively argued by Falk, and see also Fox), compares his lot to that of King Solomon and finds that he has the better deal—never mind the king's enormous wealth. Solomon owns a marvelously lucrative vineyard, but must share its profits with keepers who guard it and market its fruit. In contrast, the young man's "vineyard" is entirely his own, and that makes all the difference. The tone is sprightly with a touch of humor, a pleasant contrast to the weightiness of the preceding verses.

8:11 כֶּרֶם הָיָה לִשְׁלֹמֹה *kerem hayah li-šelomoh* "Solomon had a vineyard." The style is narrative, and the word order, beginning with an indefinite noun (literally "a vineyard was to Solomon") is like that in two other stories involving vineyards, the parable in Isa. 5:1 *kerem hayah li-ydidi* "my beloved had a vineyard," and the story of Naboth's vineyard in 1 Kings 21:1. Compare also the beginning of Job, *'iš hayah* "There was a man. . . ."

בְּבַעַל הָמוֹן *be-ḇa'al hamon* "in Baal Hamon." Even if Solomon did own a vineyard in a location called Baal Hamon (for possible identifications see Pope, 687), the historical existence of either the place or the vineyard is not relevant to the purpose of the parable. Read literally, *ba'al hamon* means "owner of great wealth" and thus may well be a playfully invented place name alluding to the king himself (compare *bat rabbim,* note 7:5), formed on the model of the many actual place names with *ba'al* as the first term, e.g., Josh. 11:17 *ba'al gad,* Num. 33:7 *ba'al ṣep̄on,* 2 Sam. 13:23 *ba'al ḥaṣor,* etc. For a similarly symbolic place name see Gen. 4:16 *'ereṣ nod,* literally "the Land of Wandering," the area of Cain's banishment; see Speiser, 31.

The meaning of *hamon* evokes the earlier *hon* "wealth" (8:7), and the phonetic similarity of the two words further enhances the association. A parallel is thus suggested between the wealthy king (*ba'al hamon*) who cannot fully enjoy his possessions but must keep a watchful eye over them, and the foolish man who thinks he can use his wealth (*hon*) to buy love.

נֹטְרִים *noṭerim* "watchmen/keepers," specifically of a vineyard (root *nṭr,* used also in 1:6, replacing earlier *nṣr*). The keepers and their specified wages are the one element that ties this parable to the reality of everyday life. In this regard, the keepers are the counterpart of the laborers in the New Testament parable of the vineyard in Matt. 20:1–16.

אִישׁ יָבִא בְּפִרְיוֹ אֶלֶף כָּסֶף *'iš yaḇi' be-p̄iryo 'elep̄ kasep̄,* literally "each would obtain/procure/bring for its fruit a thousand pieces of silver." Each keeper would sell the fruit of the plot in his charge and get a thousand pieces of silver for it, of which he would keep two hundred for his labor (8:12). A vineyard that brought in one thousand pieces of silver was proverbial for a rich vineyard, see Isa. 7:23; thus the one owned by Solomon must have been especially lucrative, since each of the keepers procured that sum.

8:12 **כַּרְמִי שֶׁלִּי לְפָנָי** *karmi šelli lep̄anay,* literally "my vineyard, mine, is before me." The independent emphatic possessive (*šelli* "my very own") is added to underline the contrast: Solomon must share his vineyard with others, whereas the young man has his vineyard all to himself. For the idiomatic use of "before me" in the sense of "right at hand, close by, within reach," sometimes also "in someone's care," see Gen. 47:6.

On the level of the metaphor, the "vineyard" represents the Shulamite's womanhood and, more specifically, her sexuality. This image provides a sense of closure: the vineyard she says she failed to guard earlier (1:6) is now in the care of her lover (8:12). Both lovers refer to the vineyard as theirs, *karmi šelli*—just as the "garden" she calls hers (4:16) is the one he calls "my garden" (5:1).

הָאֶלֶף לְךָ שְׁלֹמֹה *ha-'elep̄ lek̄a, šelomoh,* literally "the thousand be yours, Solomon!" i.e., the thousand pieces of silver you get from each keeper. Apart from the money, the statement may also allude to Solomon's thousand wives; see 1 Kings 11:3. This adds another implication to the phrase *ba'al hamon* (8:11), namely "husband of a multitude," since *ba'al* can mean both "owner" and "husband." The tone here is mocking: Have your thousand, great king, whatever they be!

לְנֹטְרִים *le-noṭerim,* but one variant reading has *la-noṭerim,* the vowelling one would expect, to indicate the definite article ("those who guard").

8:13 **הַיּוֹשֶׁבֶת בַּגַּנִּים** *ha-yošeb̄et ba-gannim,* literally "O the one who dwells [fem.] in the gardens." Probably meaning a woman associated with a garden, or gardens, with the plural *gannim* as in 4:15.

חֲבֵרִים מַקְשִׁיבִים לְקוֹלֵךְ הַשְׁמִיעִינִי *ḥab̄erim maqšib̄im le-qolek̄, hašmi'ini,* literally "companions/friends listen for your voice, let me hear [it]!" In the absence of any further identification, the indefiniteness of the noun "friends" is difficult; commentators have suggested various emendations of the Masoretic Text. In the present reading, the words are understood as one of the many hyperboles the lovers use in their enthusiasm for each other. Earlier, the Shulamite uses an indefinite *'alamot* "young women" in her emphatic assertion (1:3) "young women love you." In the same spirit, the young man is saying here in effect that *all* friends—his, hers, always!—listen for her voice. Interpreted in this light, *ḥab̄erim maqšib̄im* does not presuppose the actual presence of the friends at the scene, contrary to the many translations with "are listening."

The liturgical accents mark a break after *le-qolek̄* "your voice." An alternative though somewhat less natural parsing is to view this phrase as a fronted direct object of "let me hear," i.e., *le-qolek̄ hašmi'ini* (introduced by *le-,* as in Job 5:2). The meaning is the same in either case.

8:14 **בְּרַח דּוֹדִי וּדְמֵה־לְךָ לִצְבִי ... עַל הָרֵי בְשָׂמִים** *beraḥ dodi u-demeh le-ḵa li-ṣeḇi . . . ʿal harey ḇeśamim.* Literally "Run away, my love, and be like a gazelle . . . on the mountains of spices." Our free translation with "cinnamon" borrows from the NEB of 2:17, "the hills where cinnamon grows."

Coming at the end of the Song, this request by the Shulamite—"Run away"—has caused difficulties for many translators, who prefer to read "flee with me," or "flee to me," or "return," or "come into the open," or the like. All these readings are unacceptable, since *baraḥ* can only mean "to flee *away from*" someone, or something; nor is there any textual support for the suggestion that she asks him to run away with her. Rather, this final exchange between the two lovers, 8:13–14, evokes a familiar setting: the young man asking the Shulamite to let him hear her voice, as in 2:14, and she urging him to run away before sunrise so that he will not be caught, as in 2:17 (where *soḇ* "to turn" is likewise meant in the sense of "to turn away from speaker"). The Song thus ends with the motif of the lovers parting at dawn, as in the aubade of later traditions—an ending that looks forward in anticipation to another meeting.

Transliteration Table

THE TRANSCRIPTION represents the sounds as they are pronounced in Modern Hebrew, not the presumed original pronunciation. In specific cases, however, we depart from a purely phonetic representation in order to facilitate the recognition of the Hebrew forms and to enhance their grammatical transparency. For example, the transcription differentiates between ’ and ‘, *b̄* and *v*, *k̄* and *ḥ*, *ṭ* and *t*, *k* and *q*, *s* and *ś*, even though these sounds are no longer phonetically distinguished in Modern Hebrew. For the same reason, we reproduce the feminine ending *-ah,* even though the *h* is not pronounced. For the sake of simplicity, the doubling of consonants after the definite article and after the *waw*-conversive is not reproduced.

HEBREW LETTER	TRANSCRIPTION	PRONUNCIATION
א	’	glottal stop
בּ	*b*	*b*
ב	*b̄*	*v*
ג	*g*	*g* as in *garden*
ד	*d*	*d*
ה	*h*	*h*
ו	*v*	*v*
ז	*z*	*z*
ח	*ḥ*	German *ch* as in *doch*
ט	*ṭ*	*t*
י	*y*	*y* as in *young*
כּ	*k*	*k* as in *king*
כ	*k̄*	German *ch* as in *doch*
ל	*l*	*l* as in French, German, or Spanish

HEBREW LETTER	TRANSCRIPTION	PRONUNCIATION
מ/ם	*m*	*m*
נ/ן	*n*	*n*
ס	*s*	*s* as in *song*
ע	ʿ	glottal stop
פּ	*p*	*p*
פ/ף	*p̄*	*f*
צ/ץ	*ṣ*	*ts* as in *goats*
ק	*q*	*k* as in *king*
ר	*r*	French *r* as in *grand* (or rolled as in Spanish *oro*)
שׁ	*š*	*sh*
שׂ	*ś*	s as in *song*
ת	*t*	*t*

Abbreviations

AJSL	*American Journal of Semitic Languages and Literatures*
BA	*Biblical Archaeologist*
BDB	Brown, Driver, and Briggs, *Hebrew and English Lexicon of the Old Testament*
BCE	before the common era (B.C.)
BHK	*Biblia Hebraica* (Kittel et al., eds.)
BHS	*Biblia Hebraica Stuttgartensia* (Elliger and Rudolph, eds.)
BR	*Bible Review*
CBQ	*Catholic Bible Quarterly*
CE	common era (A.D.)
1 Chron.	First Book of Chronicles
2 Chron.	Second Book of Chronicles
Dan.	Daniel
Deut.	Deuteronomy
Eccles.	Ecclesiastes
Exod.	Exodus
Ezek.	Ezekiel
Gen.	Genesis
GKC	Gesenius' *Hebrew Grammar* (Kautzsch and Cowley, eds.)
Hab.	Habakkuk
Hag.	Haggai
HAR	*Hebrew Annual Review*
Isa.	Isaiah
JAOS	*Journal of the American Oriental Society*
JBL	*Journal of Biblical Literature*
Jer.	Jeremiah
Josh.	Joshua
JPS	Jewish Publication Society translation of the Old Testament
JSOT	*Journal for the Study of the Old Testament*
JSS	*Journal of Semitic Studies*

JTS	*Journal of Theological Studies*
Judg.	Judges
1 Kings	First Book of Kings
2 Kings	Second Book of Kings
KJV	King James Version (Authorized Version)
Lam.	Lamentations
Lev.	Leviticus
Matt.	Matthew
MT	Masoretic Text
NEB	New English Bible
Neh.	Nehemiah
NT	New Testament
Num.	Numbers
OT	Old Testament
Peshitta	Syriac version of the Bible
PMLA	*Proceedings of the Modern Language Association*
Prov.	Book of Proverbs
Ps.	Book of Psalms
RSV	Revised Standard Version of the Bible
1 Sam.	First Book of Samuel
2 Sam.	Second Book of Samuel
Septuagint	Greek version of the Old Testament
Song	Song of Songs
VT	*Vetus Testamentum*
Vulgate	Latin version of the Bible
WO	Waltke and O'Connor, *Introduction to Biblical Hebrew Syntax*
ZAW	*Zeitschrift für die alttestamentliche Wissenschaft*
Zech.	Zechariah
Zeph.	Zephaniah

Bibliography

I. Versions of the Bible

Biblia Hebraica. Ed. Rudolf Kittel et al. 7th ed. Stuttgart: Württembergische Bibelanstalt, 1951.

Biblia Hebraica Stuttgartensia. Ed. K. Elliger and W. Rudolph. 3rd rev. ed. Stuttgart: Deutsche Bibelgesellschaft, 1987.

Biblia Sacra Iuxta Latinam Vulgatam Versionem. Vol. 11. Rome: Typis Polyglottis Vaticanis, 1957.

The Holy Bible: Authorized King James Version. 1611. Reprint. New York: Oxford University Press, 1967.

The Holy Bible: Revised Standard Version. 1946–52. Reprint. New York: Oxford University Press, 1973.

The Holy Scriptures According to the Masoretic Text. 3 vols. Philadelphia: Jewish Publication Society, 1962–82.

The Jerusalem Bible. Garden City, N.Y.: Doubleday, 1966.

The New English Bible with the Apocrypha. New York: Oxford University Press, 1971.

Peshitta. The Old Testament in Syriac. Damascus: United Bible Societies, 1979.

The Revised English Bible. Oxford: Oxford University Press, 1992.

Septuaginta. Ed. Alfred Rahlfs. 1935. Reprint. 3rd ed. Stuttgart: Deutsche Bibelgesellschaft, 1979.

II. General Bibliography

Aharoni, Yohanan, and Michael Avi-Yonah. *The Macmillan Bible Atlas*. New York: Macmillan, 1968.

Albright, William Foxwell. "Archaic Survivals in the Text of Canticles." In *Hebrew and Semitic Studies Presented to Godfrey Rolles Driver*. Ed. D. Winton Thomas and W. D. McHardy. Pp. 1–7. Oxford: Clarendon Press, 1963.

———. *From the Stone Age to Christianity: Monotheism and the Historical Process*. Baltimore: The Johns Hopkins Press, 1940.

Alter, Robert. *The Art of Biblical Narrative*. New York: Basic Books, 1981.

———. *The Art of Biblical Poetry*. New York: Basic Books, 1985.

———. *The World of Biblical Literature.* New York: Basic Books, 1992.

Alter, Robert, and Frank Kermode, eds. *The Literary Guide to the Bible.* Cambridge: Harvard University Press, 1987.

Andersen, Francis I., and David Noel Freedman. *Hosea: A New Translation, with Introduction and Commentary.* Vol. 24 of *The Anchor Bible.* Garden City, N.Y.: Doubleday, 1980.

Aschkenasy, Nehama. *Eve's Journey: Feminine Images in Hebraic Literary Tradition.* Philadelphia: University of Pennsylvania Press, 1986.

Astell, Ann W. *The Song of Songs in the Middle Ages.* Ithaca, N.Y.: Cornell University Press, 1990.

Avi-Yonah, Michael. *The Holy Land from the Persian to the Arab Conquest (536 B.C.–A.D. 640): A Historical Geography.* Rev. ed. Grand Rapids: Baker Book House, 1977.

Baillet, M., J. T. Milik, and R. de Vaux. *Les 'Petites Grottes' de Qumran.* Oxford: Clarendon Press, 1962.

Bainton, Roland H. "The Bible in the Reformation." In *The Cambridge History of the Bible: The West from the Reformation to the Present Day.* Ed. S. L. Greenslade. Pp. 1–37. Cambridge: Cambridge University Press, 1963.

Bal, Mieke. *Death and Dissymmetry: The Politics of Coherence in the Book of Judges.* Chicago: University of Chicago Press, 1988.

———. *Lethal Love: Feminist Literary Readings of Biblical Love Stories.* Bloomington: Indiana University Press, 1987.

Barnard, Mary, trans. *Sappho: A New Translation.* Berkeley: University of California Press, 1958.

Barnstone, Willis. *The Poetics of Translation: History, Theory, Practice.* New Haven: Yale University Press, 1993.

———, trans. *The Song of Songs.* Athens: Kedros, 1970.

Barr, James. "Hebrew, Aramaic and Greek in the Hellenistic Age." In *The Hellenistic Age.* Vol. 2 of *The Cambridge History of Judaism.* Ed. W. D. Davies and Louis Finkelstein. Pp. 79–114. Cambridge: Cambridge University Press, 1989.

———. *Holy Scripture: Canon, Authority, Criticism.* Philadelphia: Westminster Press, 1983.

Bauer, Hans, and Pontus Leander. *Historische Grammatik der hebräischen Sprache.* Hildesheim: Georg Olms, 1965.

Bendavid, Abba. *Leshon Miqra u-Leshon Hakhamim* (Biblical Hebrew and Mishnaic Hebrew). Vol. 1. Tel Aviv: Dvir, 1967.

Bentzen, Aage. "Remarks on the Canonisation of the Song of Solomon." In *Studia Orientalia Ioanni Pedersen.* Pp. 41–47. Copenhagen: Munksgaard, 1953.

Bernard of Clairvaux. *On the Song of Songs.* 4 vols. Trans. Kilian Walsh and Irene Edmonds. In *The Works of Bernard of Clairvaux.* Cistercian

Fathers Series, nos. 4, 7, 31, 40. Spencer, Mass. / Kalamazoo, Mich.: Cistercian Publications, 1971–80.
Biale, David. *Eros and the Jews: From Biblical Israel to Contemporary America.* New York: Basic Books, 1992.
Biale, Rachel. *Women and Jewish Law: An Exploration of Women's Issues in Halakhic Sources.* New York: Schocken Books, 1984.
Bickerman, Elias J. "The Historical Foundations of Postbiblical Judaism." In vol. 1 of *The Jews: Their History, Culture, and Religion.* Ed. Louis Finkelstein. Pp. 70–114. 3rd ed. New York: Jewish Publication Society, 1960.
Bing, Peter, and Rip Cohen, trans. and eds. *Games of Venus: An Anthology of Greek and Roman Erotic Verse from Sappho to Ovid.* New York: Routledge, 1991.
Bird, Phyllis. "Images of Women in the Old Testament." In *Religion and Sexism: Images of Woman in the Jewish and Christian Traditions.* Ed. Rosemary Radford Ruether. Pp. 41–88. New York: Simon and Schuster, 1974.
Bloch, Ariel. "Questioning God's Omnipotence in the Bible: A Linguistic Case Study." In vol. 1 of *Semitic Studies in Honor of Wolf Leslau.* Ed. Alan S. Kaye. Pp. 174–88. Wiesbaden: Otto Harrassowitz, 1991.
Bloch, Chana. "Shakespeare's Sister." Review of *The Book of J,* by Harold Bloom and David Rosenberg. *Iowa Review* 21 (1991): 66–77.
Bloch, Joshua. "A Critical Examination of the Text of the Syriac Version of the Song of Songs." *AJSL* 38 (1921–22): 103–39.
Bloom, Harold, and David Rosenberg. *The Book of J.* New York: Grove Weidenfeld, 1990.
Bloom, Harold, ed. *The Song of Songs.* Modern Critical Interpretations. New York: Chelsea House, 1988.
Boyarin, Daniel. *Carnal Israel: Reading Sex in Talmudic Culture.* The New Historicism: Studies in Cultural Politics, no. 25. Berkeley: University of California Press, 1993.
Brenner, Athalya. "Aromatics and Perfumes in the Song of Songs." *JSOT* 25 (1983): 75–81.
———. *The Israelite Woman: Social Role and Literary Type in Biblical Narrative.* Sheffield: JSOT Press, 1985.
———. *The Song of Songs.* Old Testament Guides. Sheffield: JSOT Press, 1989.
———, ed. *The Song of Songs: A Feminist Reader.* Sheffield: Sheffield Academic Press, 1992.
Bright, John. *A History of Israel.* Philadelphia: Westminster Press, 1959.
Brockelmann, Carl. *Lexicon Syriacum.* 2nd ed. Halle: Max Niemeyer, 1928.
Brown, Francis, S. R. Driver, and Charles A. Briggs. *A Hebrew and English*

Lexicon of the Old Testament. 1907. Reprint. Oxford: Clarendon Press, 1952.

Brown, Peter. "Bodies and Minds: Sexuality and Renunciation in Early Christianity." In *Before Sexuality: The Construction of Erotic Experience in the Ancient Greek World.* Ed. David M. Halperin, John J. Winkler, and Froma Zeitlin. Princeton: Princeton University Press, 1990.

Bruns, Gerald L. "Midrash and Allegory: The Beginnings of Scriptural Interpretation." In *The Literary Guide to the Bible.* Ed. Robert Alter and Frank Kermode. Pp. 625–46. Cambridge: Harvard University Press, 1987.

Budde, Karl F. R. "Das Hohelied." In *Die fünf Megillot.* Ed. Karl Budde, Alfred Bertholet, and D. G. Wildeboer. Pp. 1–48. Kurzer Hand-Commentar zum Alten Testament. Freiburg: J. C. B. Mohr, 1898.

Campbell, Edward F. *Ruth: A New Translation, with Introduction, Notes, and Commentary.* Vol. 7 of *The Anchor Bible.* Garden City, N. Y.: Doubleday, 1975.

Carmi, T., ed. and trans. *The Penguin Book of Hebrew Verse.* Harmondsworth: Penguin Books, 1981.

Childs, Brevard S. *Biblical Theology in Crisis.* Pp. 186–99. Philadelphia: Westminster Press, 1970.

Cohen, Gerson D. "The Song of Songs and the Jewish Religious Mentality." Reprint. In *The Canon and Masorah of the Hebrew Bible: An Introductory Reader.* Ed. Sid Z. Leiman. New York: Ktav, 1974.

Cook, Albert. *The Root of The Thing: A Study of Job and the Song of Songs.* Bloomington: Indiana University Press, 1968.

Cooper, Jerrold S. "New Cuneiform Parallels to the Song of Songs." *JBL* 90 (1971): 157–62.

Daiches, David. *The King James Version of the English Bible.* Chicago: Chicago University Press, 1941.

Danby, Herbert, trans. *The Mishnah.* Oxford: Clarendon Press, 1933.

De Rougement, Denis. *Love in the Western World.* Trans. Montgomery Belgion. 1940. Rev. ed. New York: Pantheon Books, 1956.

Driver, Samuel R. *An Introduction to the Literature of the Old Testament.* 1913. Reprint. Cleveland: Meridian Books, 1956.

Ehrlich, Arnold B. *Randglossen zur hebräischen Bibel.* Vol. 7. 1914. Reprint. Hildesheim: Georg Olms, 1968.

Eilberg-Schwartz, Howard, ed. *People of the Body: Jews and Judaism from an Embodied Perspective.* Albany: State University of New York Press, 1992.

Eissfeldt, Otto. *The Old Testament: An Introduction.* Trans. Peter R. Ackroyd. New York: Harper and Row, 1965.

Epstein, Louis M. *Sex Laws and Customs in Judaism.* 1948. Reprint. New York: Ktav, 1967.

Even-Shoshan, Avraham. *Ha-Millon he-Hadash* (The New Lexicon). 3 vols. Jerusalem: Kiryat Sefer, 1982.

Exum, J. Cheryl. "A Literary and Structural Analysis of the Song of Songs." *ZAW* 85 (1973): 47–79.

Falk, Marcia. *The Song of Songs: A New Translation and Interpretation.* San Francisco: HarperCollins, 1990.

Fauna and Flora of the Bible. 2nd ed. New York: United Bible Societies, 1980.

Feliks, Yehuda. *Song of Songs: Nature, Epic and Allegory.* Jerusalem: Israel Society for Biblical Research, 1983.

Fisch, Harold. *Poetry with a Purpose: Biblical Poetics and Interpretation.* Bloomington: Indiana University Press, 1988.

Fishbane, Michael. *Text and Texture.* New York: Schocken Books, 1979.

Fishelov, David. "The Song of Songs: Hard and Soft, Dynamic and Static" (in Hebrew). In *'Iyyunim ba-Dimmuy ha-Po'eti* (Studies in Poetic Simile). Unpublished manuscript.

Fohrer, Georg. *Introduction to the Old Testament.* Trans. David Green. Nashville: Abingdon Press, 1968.

Fox, Michael V. *The Song of Songs and the Ancient Egyptian Love Songs.* Madison: University of Wisconsin Press, 1985.

Freedman, David Noel. "Psalm 113 and the Song of Hannah." *Eretz Israel* 14 (1978): 56–69.

Friedman, Richard Elliott. *Who Wrote the Bible?* New York: Harper and Row, 1987.

Frye, Northrop. *The Great Code: The Bible and Literature.* New York: Harcourt Brace Jovanovich, 1981.

———. *Words with Power.* New York: Harcourt Brace Jovanovich, 1990.

Fuchs, Esther. "The Literary Characterization of Mothers and Sexual Politics in the Hebrew Bible." In *Feminist Perspectives on Biblical Scholarship.* Ed. Adela Yarbro Collins. Pp. 117–36. Chico, Calif.: Scholars Press, 1985.

Gerleman, Gillis. "Die Wurzel *šlm.*" *ZAW* 85 (1973): 1–14.

———. *Ruth, Das Hohelied.* Vol. 18 of Biblischer Kommentar: Altes Testament. Neukirchen-Vluyn: Neukirchener Verlag, 1965.

Gesenius, Friedrich H. W. *Hebrew Grammar.* Ed. E. Kautzsch. Trans. and rev. A. E. Cowley. 2nd English ed., 1910. Reprint. Oxford: Clarendon Press, 1966.

Ginsberg, H. L. "Introduction to the Song of Songs" and "Introduction to Ecclesiastes." In *The Five Megilloth and Jonah.* Pp. 3–4, 52–56. Philadelphia: Jewish Publication Society, 1969.

Ginsburg, Christian D. *The Song of Songs and Coheleth: Translation and Commentary.* 1857. Reprint. New York: Ktav, 1970.

Ginzberg, Louis. "Allegorical Interpretation of Scripture." In his *On Jewish Law and Lore.* Pp. 127–50. Philadelphia: Jewish Publication Society, 1955.

———. *The Legends of the Jews.* 7 vols. Philadelphia: Jewish Publication Society, 1909–38.

Givón, Talmy. "The Drift from VSO to SVO in Biblical Hebrew: The Pragmatics of Tense-Aspect." In *Mechanisms of Syntactic Change.* Ed. Charles N. Li. Pp. 181–254. Austin: University of Texas Press, 1977.

Goitein, S. D. "*Ayumma Kannidgalot* (Song of Songs 6:10)." *JSS* 10 (1965): 220–21.

———. "Women as Creators of Biblical Genres." Trans. Michael Carasik. *Prooftexts* 8 (1988): 1–33.

Gollancz, Herman, trans. *The Targum to "The Song of Songs."* 1908. Reprint in *The Targum to the Five Megilloth.* Ed. Bernard Grossfeld. New York: Hermon Press, 1973.

Gollwitzer, Helmut. *Song of Love: A Biblical Understanding of Sex.* Trans. Keith Crim. Philadelphia: Fortress Press, 1979.

Good, Edwin. "Ezekiel's Ship: Some Extended Metaphors in the Old Testament." *Semitics* 1 (1970): 79–103.

Goodspeed, E. J. "The Shulammite." *AJSL* 50 (1933): 102–4.

Gordis, Robert. "Critical Notes on the Blessing of Moses (Deut. 33)." *JTS* 34 (1933): 390–91.

———. *Koheleth, The Man and His World: A Study of Ecclesiastes.* 1951. Reprint. New York: Schocken Books, 1968.

———. "The Root *dgl* in the Song of Songs." *JBL* 88 (1969): 203–4.

———. *The Song of Songs and Lamentations: A Study, Modern Translation and Commentary.* New York: Jewish Theological Seminary, 1954.

Gottwald, N. K. "Song of Songs." In vol. 4 of *The Interpreter's Dictionary of the Bible.* Pp. 420–26. Nashville: Abingdon Press, 1962.

Goulder, Michael D. *The Song of Fourteen Songs. Journal for the Study of the Old Testament.* Supplement Series no. 36. Sheffield: JSOT Press, 1986.

Gow, A. S. F., ed. and trans. *Theocritus.* 2 vols. Cambridge: Cambridge University Press, 1950.

Graves, Robert, trans. *The Song of Songs: Text and Commentary.* New York: Clarkson N. Potter, 1973.

Green, Arthur. "The Song of Songs in Early Jewish Mysticism." *Orim* 2 (1987): 49–63.

Green, Peter. *Alexander to Actium: The Historical Evolution of the Hellenistic Age.* Berkeley: University of California Press, 1990.

Greenberg, Moshe. *Ezekiel, 1–20: A New Translation, with Introduction and Commentary*. Vol. 22 of *The Anchor Bible*. Garden City, N.Y.: Doubleday, 1983.

———. "The Stabilization of the Text of the Hebrew Bible, Reviewed in the Light of the Biblical Materials from the Judean Desert." *JAOS* 76 (1956), 157–67.

Greenfield, Jonas C. "Amurrite, Ugaritic and Canaanite." In *Proceedings of the International Conference on Semitic Studies, 1965*. Pp. 92–101. Jerusalem: Israel Academy of Sciences and Humanities, 1969.

———. Review of *Hebrew and Semitic Studies presented to Godfrey Rolles Driver*, ed. D. Winton Thomas and W. D. McHardy. *JAOS* 85 (1965): 256–58.

Greenspahn, Frederick E. "Words that Occur in the Bible Only Once: How Hard Are They to Translate?" *BR* 1 (Feb. 1985): 28–30.

Greenstein, Edward L. "Theories of Modern Bible Translation." *Prooftexts* 3 (1983): 9–39.

Grossberg, Daniel. "Noun/Verb Parallelism: Syntactic or Asyntactic." *JBL* 99 (1980): 481–88.

Hadas, Moses. *Hellenistic Culture: Fusion and Diffusion*. New York: Columbia University Press, 1959.

Hakham, Amos. "Commentary on the Song of Songs" (in Hebrew). In *Hamesh Megillot* (The Five Scrolls). Ed. Aharon Mirsky, Feibel Meltzer, and Yehuda Kiel. Pp. 1–76. Jerusalem: Mossad Harav Kook, 1990.

Halperin, David M. *Before Pastoral: Theocritus and the Ancient Tradition of Bucolic Poetry*. New Haven: Yale University Press, 1983.

Hartman, Louis F., and Alexander A. Di Lella. *The Book of Daniel: A New Translation, with Introduction, Notes, and Commentary*. Vol. 23 of *The Anchor Bible*. Garden City, N.Y.: Doubleday, 1978.

Havelock, Christine M. *Hellenistic Art*. Greenwich, Conn.: New York Graphic Society, 1971.

Held, Moshe. "A Faithful Lover in an Old Babylonian Dialogue." *Journal of Cuneiform Studies* 15 (1961): 1–26.

Hengel, Martin. *Judaism and Hellenism: Studies in their Encounter in Palestine During the Early Hellenistic Period*. Trans. John Bowden. 2 vols. Philadelphia: Fortress Press, 1974.

———. *Jews, Greeks and Barbarians: Aspects of the Hellenization of Judaism in the Pre-Christian Period*. Trans. John Bowden. Philadelphia: Fortress Press, 1980.

Higham, T. F., and C. M. Bowra, eds. *The Oxford Book of Greek Verse in Translation*. Oxford: Clarendon Press, 1938.

Hirst, Michael, et el. *The Sistine Chapel: A Glorious Restoration*. New York: Harry N. Abrams, 1994.

Honeyman, A. M. "Two Contributions to Canaanite Toponymy." *JTS* 50 (1949): 50–52.

Hrushovsky, Benjamin. "Prosody, Hebrew." *Encyclopedia Judaica.* 1971 ed.

Hunt, Morton M. *The Natural History of Love.* New York: Knopf, 1959.

Hurvitz, A. "The Chronological Significance of 'Aramaisms' in Biblical Hebrew." *Israel Exploration Journal* 18 (1968): 234–40.

———. "Linguistic Criteria for Dating Problematic Biblical Texts." *Hebrew Abstracts* 14 (1973): 74–79.

Hyde, Walter Woodburn. "Greek Analogies to the Song of Songs." In *The Song of Songs: A Symposium.* Ed. W. H. Schoff. Pp. 31–42. Philadelphia: Commercial Museum, 1924.

Ibn Ezra, Abraham. "Commentary on the Song of Songs" (in Hebrew). In *Hamesh Megillot* (The Five Scrolls). The *Miqra'ot Gedolot* Commentary. Pp. 415–72. New York: Abraham Y. Friedman, n.d.

Jastrow, Morris. *The Song of Songs: A Collection of Love Lyrics of Ancient Palestine.* Philadelphia: J. B. Lippincott, 1921.

Jay, Peter, trans. *The Song of Songs.* Introduction by David Goldstein. London: Anvil Press Poetry, 1975.

John of the Cross. *The Poems of St. John of the Cross.* Trans. John Frederick Nims. 3rd ed. Chicago: University of Chicago Press, 1979.

John of the Cross. "The Spiritual Canticle." In *The Collected Works of St. John of the Cross.* Trans. Kieran Kavanaugh and Otilio Rodriguez. Pp. 393–565. New York: Doubleday, 1964.

Josipovici, Gabriel. *The Book of God: A Response to the Bible.* New Haven: Yale University Press, 1988.

Koehler, Ludwig, and Walter Baumgartner. *Hebräisches und aramäisches Lexikon zum Alten Testament.* 3rd ed. Leiden: E. J. Brill, 1967.

Kramer, Samuel Noah. *The Sacred Marriage Rite: Aspects of Faith, Myth, and Ritual in Ancient Sumer.* Bloomington: Indiana University Press, 1969.

Kristeva, Julia. "A Holy Madness: She and He." In her *Tales of Love.* Trans. Leon S. Roudiez. Pp. 83–100. New York: Columbia University Press, 1987.

Kugel, James L. *The Idea of Biblical Poetry: Parallelism and Its History.* New Haven: Yale University Press, 1981.

———. "On the Bible and Literary Criticism." *Prooftexts* 1 (1981): 217–36.

———. "On the Bible as Literature." *Prooftexts* 2 (1982): 323–32.

Landsberger, Franz. "Poetic Units Within the Song of Songs." *JBL* 73 (1954): 203–16.

Landy, Francis. "Beauty and the Enigma: An Enquiry into Some Interrelated Episodes in the Song of Songs." *JSOT* 17 (1980): 55–106.

———. *Paradoxes of Paradise: Identity and Difference in the Song of Songs.* Sheffield: Almond Press, 1983.

———. "The Song of Songs." In *The Literary Guide to the Bible.* Ed. Robert Alter and Frank Kermode. Pp. 305–19. Cambridge: Harvard University Press, 1987.

———. "The Song of Songs and the Garden of Eden." *JBL* 98 (1979), 513–28.

Lapson, Dvora. "Dance: Ancient Israel." *Encyclopedia Judaica.* 1971 ed.

Lehrman, S. M. "The Song of Songs: Introduction and Commentary." In *The Five Megilloth.* Ed. A. Cohen. Pp. 1–32. London: Soncino Press, 1946.

Leiman, Sid Z. *The Canon and Masorah of the Hebrew Bible: An Introductory Reader.* New York: Ktav, 1974.

———. *The Canonization of Hebrew Scripture: The Talmudic and Midrashic Evidence.* 1976. 2nd ed. New Haven: Transactions of the Connecticut Academy of Arts and Sciences, 1991.

Lerner, Gerda. *The Creation of Patriarchy.* New York: Oxford University Press, 1986.

Levine, Amy-Jill, ed. *"Women Like This": New Perspectives on Jewish Women in the Greco-Roman World.* Atlanta: Scholars Press, 1991.

Loewe, Raphael. "Apologetic Motifs in the Targum to the Song of Songs." In *Biblical Motifs: Origins and Transformations.* Ed. Alexander Altmann. Pp. 159–96. Cambridge: Harvard University Press, 1966.

Lord, Albert B. *The Singer of Tales.* Cambridge: Harvard University Press, 1960.

Luther, Martin. "Lectures on the Song of Songs: A Brief but Altogther Lucid Commentary." Trans. Ian Siggins. In vol. 15 of *Luther's Works.* Ed. Jaroslav Pelikan and Hilton C. Oswald. Pp. 189–264. St. Louis: Concordia, 1972.

Maccoby, Hyam. "Sex According to the Song of Songs." Review of *The Song of Songs,* by Marvin H. Pope. *Commentary* 67 (June 1979): 53–59.

Mandelkern, Solomon. *Veteris Testamenti Concordantiae Hebraicae atque Chaldaicae.* 2 vols. 2nd ed. 1937. Reprint. Graz: Akademische Druck- und Verlagsanstalt, 1955.

Margolis, Max L. "How the Song of Songs Entered the Canon." In *The Song of Songs: A Symposium.* Ed. Wilfred H. Schoff. Pp. 9–17. Philadelphia: Commercial Museum, 1924.

Matter, E. Ann. *The Voice of My Beloved: The Song of Songs in Western Medieval Christianity.* Philadelphia: University of Pennsylvania Press, 1990.

May, Herbert G., et al., eds. *Oxford Bible Atlas.* 2nd ed. London: Oxford University Press, 1974.

———. "Some Cosmic Connotations of *Mayim Rabbim,* 'Many Waters.' " *JBL* 74 (1955): 9–21.

Mazor, Yair. "The Song of Songs or the Story of Stories?" *Scandinavian Journal of the Old Testament* 1 (1990): 1–29.

McGinn, Bernard. "With 'the Kisses of the Mouth': Recent Works on the Song of Songs." *Journal of Religion* 72 (1992): 269–75.

Meek, Theophile J. "Canticles and the Tammuz Cult." *AJSL* 39 (1922–23): 1–14.

———. "Babylonian Parallels to the Song of Songs." *JBL* 43 (1924): 245–52.

———. "The Song of Songs: Introduction and Exegesis." In vol. 5 of *The Interpreter's Bible.* Ed. George A. Buttrick et al. Pp. 91–148. Nashville: Abingdon Press, 1956.

Merkin, Daphne. "The Woman in the Balcony: On Reading the Song of Songs." *Tikkun* 9 (May-June 1994): 59–64, 89.

Meyers, Carol. *Discovering Eve: Ancient Israelite Women in Context.* New York: Oxford University Press, 1988.

———. "The Drum-Dance-Song Ensemble: Women's Performance in Biblical Israel." In *Rediscovering the Muses.* Ed. Kimberly Marshall. Pp. 49–67, 234–38. Boston: Northeastern University Press, 1993.

———. "Gender Imagery in the Song of Songs." *HAR* 10 (1986): 209–23.

———. " 'To her Mother's House': Considering a Counterpart to the Israelite *Bet 'ab.*" In *The Bible and the Politics of Exegesis.* Ed. David Jobling, Peggy L. Day, and Gerald T. Sheppard. Pp. 39–51. Cleveland: Pilgrim Press, 1991.

Miller, Jonathan. "The Afterlife." In his *Subsequent Performances.* Pp. 19–72. New York: Viking, 1986.

The Mishnah. See Danby, Herbert.

Moldenke, Harold N., and Alma L. Moldenke. *Plants of the Bible.* 1952. Reprint. New York: Dover, 1986.

Momigliano, Arnaldo. *Alien Wisdom: The Limits of Hellenization.* Cambridge: Cambridge University Press, 1975.

Moore, Carey A. *Esther: Introduction, Translation, and Notes.* Vol. 7B of *The Anchor Bible.* Garden City, N.Y.: Doubleday, 1971.

Murphy, Cullen. "Women and the Bible." *The Atlantic Monthly* (August 1993): 39–64.

Murphy, Roland E. "Form-Critical Studies in the Song of Songs." *Interpretation* 27 (1973): 413–22.

———. *The Song of Songs: A Commentary on the Book of Canticles.* Minneapolis: Fortress Press, 1990.

———. "The Structure of the Canticle of Canticles." *CBQ* 11 (1949): 381–91.

———. "Towards a Commentary on the Song of Songs." *CBQ* 39 (1977): 482–96.

———. "The Unity of the Song of Songs." *VT* 29 (1979): 436–43.
Neusner, Jacob. *The Mishnah: A New Translation.* New Haven: Yale University Press, 1988.
O'Connor, M. *Hebrew Verse Structure.* Winona Lake, Ind.: Eisenbrauns, 1980.
Origen. *The Song of Songs: Commentary and Homilies.* Trans. R. P. Lawson. Ancient Christian Writers, no. 26. Westminster, Md.: Newman Press, 1957.
Orlinsky, Harry M. "The Canonization of the Bible and the Exclusion of the Apocrypha." In his *Essays in Biblical Culture and Bible Translation.* Pp. 257–86. New York: Ktav, 1974.
Ostriker, Alicia Suskin. *Feminist Revision and the Bible.* The Bucknell Lectures in Literary Theory. Cambridge, Mass.: Blackwell, 1993.
———. *The Nakedness of the Fathers: Biblical Visions and Revisions.* New Brunswick: Rutgers University Press, 1994.
Pagels, Elaine. *Adam, Eve, and the Serpent.* New York: Random House, 1988.
Pardes, Ilana. *Countertraditions in the Bible: A Feminist Approach.* Cambridge: Harvard University Press, 1992.
Parente, Paschal P. "The Canticle of Canticles in Mystical Theology." *CBQ* 6 (1944): 142–58.
Parmelee, Alice. *All the Birds of the Bible: Their Stories, Identification and Meaning.* New York: Harper and Brothers, 1959.
Patai, Raphael. *Sex and Family in the Bible and the Middle East.* Garden City, N.Y.: Doubleday, 1959.
Payne Smith, J. *A Compendious Syriac Dictionary.* 1903. Reprint. Oxford: Clarendon Press, 1967.
Pfeiffer, Robert H. "Canon of the OT." In vol. 1 of *The Interpreter's Dictionary of the Bible.* Pp. 498–520. Nashville: Abingdon Press, 1962.
———. *Introduction to the Old Testament.* 2nd ed. New York: Harper and Brothers, 1948.
Plaskow, Judith. *Standing Again at Sinai: Judaism from a Feminist Perspective.* New York: Harper and Row, 1990.
Pomeroy, Sarah. *Goddesses, Whores, Wives, and Slaves: Women in Classical Antiquity.* New York: Schocken Books, 1975.
Pope, Marvin H. *Song of Songs: A New Translation with Introduction and Commentary.* Vol. 7c of *The Anchor Bible.* Garden City, N.Y.: Doubleday, 1977.
Pound, Ezra, and Noel Stock, trans. *Love Poems of Ancient Egypt.* New York: New Directions, 1962.
Pritchard, James B., ed. *Ancient New Eastern Texts Relating to the Old Testament.* 3rd rev. ed. Princeton: Princeton University Press, 1969.

Rabin, Chaim. "The Song of Songs and Tamil Poetry." *Studies in Religion* 3 (1973): 205–19.

Rashi. "Commentary on the Song of Songs" (in Hebrew). In *Hamesh Megillot* (The Five Scrolls). The *Miqra'ot Gedolot* Commentary. Pp. 415–72. New York: Abraham Y. Friedman, n.d.

Rosenberg, Joel W. "The Garden Story Forward and Backward: The Non-Narrative Dimension of Gen. 2–3." *Prooftexts* 1 (1981): 1–27.

Rosenmeyer, Thomas G. *The Green Cabinet: Theocritus and the European Pastoral Lyric.* Berkeley: University of California Press, 1969.

Rosenthal, Franz. *A Grammar of Biblical Aramaic.* Rev. ed. Wiesbaden: Otto Harrassowitz, 1963.

Roth, Cecil. "Art: Antiquity to 1800." *Encyclopedia Judaica.* 1971 ed.

Rowley, H. H. "The Interpretion of the Song of Songs." In his *The Servant of the Lord and Other Essays on the Old Testament.* Pp. 195–245. 2d rev. ed. Oxford: Blackwell, 1965.

———. "The Meaning of 'The Shulammite.'" *AJSL* 56 (1930): 84–91.

Rozelaar, M. "The Song of Songs against the Background of Hellenistic Greek Erotic Poetry" (in Hebrew). *Eshkolot* 1 (1954): 33–48.

Rubenstein, Eliezer. *Ha-Ivrit Shelanu ve-ha-Ivrit ha-Qedumah* (Our Hebrew and Ancient Hebrew). Jerusalem: Ministry of Defense, 1980.

Rudolph, Wilhelm. *Das Buch Ruth, Das Hohe Lied, Die Klagelieder.* In vol. 17 of the Kommentar zum Alten Testament. Pp. 73–186. Gütersloh: Gerd Mohn, 1962.

Sappho. *See* Barnard, Mary.

Sarna, Nahum. "Bible: The Canon." *Encyclopaedia Judaica.* 1971 ed.

———. "The Interchange of the Prepositions *Beth* and *Min* in Biblical Hebrew." *JBL* 78 (1959): 310–16.

Sasson, Jack M. "Unlocking the Poetry of Love in the Song of Songs." *BR* 1 (Feb. 1985): 11–19.

Scheper, George L. "Reformation Attitudes Towards Allegory and the Song of Songs." *PMLA* 89 (1974): 551–62.

Schmidt, Nathaniel. "Is Canticles an Adonis Liturgy?" *JAOS* 46 (1926): 154–64.

Schneidau, Herbert N. *Sacred Discontent: The Bible and Western Tradition.* Berkeley: University of California Press, 1977.

Schoff, Wilfred H., ed. *The Song of Songs: A Symposium.* Philadelphia: Commercial Museum, 1924.

Scholem, Gershom. *Major Trends in Jewish Mysticism.* 1941. 3rd rev. ed. New York: Schocken Books, 1961.

———, ed. *Zohar: The Book of Splendor.* New York: Schocken Books, 1963.

Schulman, Grace. "The Song of Songs: Love is Strong as Death." In

Congregation: Contemporary Writers Read the Jewish Bible. Ed. David Rosenberg. Pp. 346–59. New York: Harcourt Brace Jovanovich, 1987.

Schwartz, Leo W. "On Translating the 'Song of Songs.'" *Judaism* 13 (1964): 64–76.

Scott, R. B. Y. *Proverbs and Ecclesiastes: Introduction, Translation, and Notes*. Vol. 18 of *The Anchor Bible*. Garden City, N.Y.: Doubleday, 1965.

Segal, M. H. *Grammar of Mishnaic Hebrew*. 1927. Reprint. Oxford: Clarendon Press, 1958.

———. *Mevo ha-Miqra* (Introduction to the Bible). 2 vols. Jerusalem: Kiryat Sefer, 1967.

———. "The Song of Songs." *VT* 12 (1962): 470–90.

———. *Torah, Nevi'im, Ketuvim* (Commentary on the Bible). 4 vols. Tel Aviv: Dvir, 1960.

Seiple, W. G. "Theocritean Parallels to the Song of Songs." *AJSL* 19 (1902–1903): 108–15.

Shea, William H. "The Chiastic Structure of the Song of Songs." *ZAW* 92 (1980): 378–96.

Simon, Maurice, trans. "Canticles Rabbah." In vol. 9 of *Midrash Rabbah*. Ed. H. Freedman and Maurice Simon. 1930. Reprint. London: Soncino Press, 1983.

Smalley, Beryl. *The Study of the Bible in the Middle Ages*. 3rd rev. ed. Oxford: Blackwell, 1983.

Smith, Morton. "Hellenization." In his *Palestinian Parties and Politics that Shaped the Old Testament*. Lectures on the History of Religions. New Series, no. 9. Pp. 57–81. New York: Columbia University Press, 1971.

Smith, R. R. R. *Hellenistic Sculpture*. London: Thames and Hudson, 1991.

Soulen, Richard N. "The *Waṣf*s of the Song of Songs and Hermeneutic." *JBL* 86 (1967): 183–90.

Speiser, E. A. *Genesis: Introduction, Translation, and Notes*. Vol. 1 of *The Anchor Bible*. Garden City, N.Y.: Doubleday, 1964.

Stadelmann, Luis. *Love and Politics: A New Commentary on the Song of Songs*. New York: Paulist Press, 1992.

Stanton, Elizabeth Cady. *The Woman's Bible*. 1895–1898. Reprint. New York: Arno Press, 1974.

Sternberg, Meir. *The Poetics of Biblical Narrative: Ideological Literature and the Drama of Reading*. Bloomington: Indiana University Press, 1985.

Stewart, Andrew. *Greek Sculpture: An Exploration*. 2 vols. New Haven: Yale University Press, 1990.

Stewart, Stanley. *The Enclosed Garden: The Tradition and the Image in*

Seventeenth-Century Poetry. Madison: University of Wisconsin Press, 1966.

Stillwell, Richard, et al., eds. "Ascalon," "Gadara," "Gaza," "Joppa (Jaffa)," "Marissa," "Ptolemais (Acre)," "Scythopolis." *The Princeton Encyclopedia of Classical Sites.* Princeton: Princeton University Press, 1976.

Stronach, David. "The Garden as a Political Statement: Some Case Studies from the Near East in the First Millennium B.C." *Bulletin of the Asia Institute* 4 (1990): 171–80.

Tannahill, Reay. *Sex in History.* New York: Stein and Day, 1980.

Tcherikover, Victor. *Hellenistic Civilization and the Jews.* Trans. S. Applebaum. Philadelphia: Jewish Publication Society, 1959.

Teresa of Avila. "Meditations on the Song of Songs." In vol. 2 of *The Collected Works of St. Teresa of Avila.* Pp. 205–60. Trans. Kieran Kavanaugh and Otilio Rodriguez. Washington, D.C.: Institute of Carmelite Studies, 1980.

Theocritus. *See* Gow, A. S. F., and Wells, Robert.

Trible, Phyllis. "Depatriarchalizing in Biblical Interpretation." *Journal of the American Academy of Religion* 41 (1973): 30–48.

———. *God and the Rhetoric of Sexuality.* Philadelphia: Fortress Press, 1978.

Urbach, E. E. "The Homiletical Interpretations of the Sages and the Expositions of Origen on Canticles, and the Jewish-Christian Disputation." In *Studies in Aggadah and Folk Literature.* Ed. Joseph Heinemann and Dov Noy. Vol. 22 of Scripta Hierosolymitana. Pp. 247–75. Jerusalem: Magnes Press, 1971.

Ussishkin, David. "King Solomon's Palaces." *BA* 36 (1973): 78–105.

Wagner, Max. *Die lexikalischen und grammatikalischen Aramaismen im alttestamentlichen Hebräisch.* Berlin: Alfred Töpelmann, 1966.

Waltke, Bruce K., and M. O'Connor. *An Introduction to Biblical Hebrew Syntax.* Winona Lake, Ind.: Eisenbrauns, 1990.

Waskow, Arthur. "The Bible's Sleeping Beauty and Her Great-Granddaughters." *Tikkun* 4 (March–April 1989): 39–41, 125–28.

Webster, Edwin C. "Pattern in the Song of Songs." *JSOT* 22 (1982): 73–93.

Wells, Robert, trans. *Theocritus: The Idylls.* Harmondsworth: Penguin Books, 1988.

Wenning, Robert. "Griechische Importe in Palästina aus der Zeit vor Alexander des Grossen." *Boreas* 4 (1981): 28–46.

———. "Hellenistische Skulpturen in Israel." *Boreas* 6 (1983): 105–18.

Wetzstein, J. G. "Die syrische Dreschtafel." *Zeitschrift für Ethnologie* 5 (1873): 270–302.

Whallon, William. "Formulaic Poetry in the Old Testament." *Comparative Literature* 15 (1963): 1–14.

White, John B. *A Study of the Language of Love in the Song of Songs and Ancient Egyptian Poetry.* Society of Biblical Literature Dissertation Series, no. 38. Missoula, Mont.: Scholars Press, 1978.

Williams, Ronald J. *Hebrew Syntax: An Outline.* Toronto: University of Toronto Press, 1967.

Winkler, John J. *The Constraints of Desire: The Anthropology of Sex and Gender in Ancient Greece.* New York: Routledge, 1990.

Wolkstein, Diane. *The First Love Stories: From Isis and Osiris to Tristan and Iseult.* New York: HarperCollins, 1991.

Wolkstein, Diane, and Samuel Noah Kramer. *Inanna, Queen of Heaven and Earth: Her Stories and Hymns from Sumer.* New York: Harper and Row, 1983.

Yoder, Perry. "A-B Pairs and Oral Composition in Hebrew Poetry." *VT* 21 (1971): 470–89.

Zakovitch, Yair. "Explicit and Implicit Name-Derivations." *HAR* 4 (1980): 167–81.

———. *Shir ha-Shirim im Mavo u-Ferush* (The Song of Songs: Introduction and Commentary). Tel Aviv: Am Oved, 1992.

Zeitlin, Solomon. "An Historical Study of the Canonization of the Hebrew Scriptures." In vol. 2 of his *Studies in the Early History of Judaism.* Pp. 1–38. New York: Ktav, 1974.

Zohary, Michael. *Plants of the Bible.* London: Cambridge University Press, 1982.

Index

Landsberger, Franz, 19 *n*
Landy, Francis, 22 *n*, 210
Lebanon, Mount, and area, 8, 122, 148, 174, 176, 177–78, 188, 203, 204
Leiman, Sid, 28 *n*
Lerner, Gerda, 167
lily, lilies, 14, 128, 148, 157, 173, 188
love, 137
  power of, 5, 131, 213–14
  symptoms of, 7
  personified, 130, 153, 204–205
  vs. worldly riches, 218
lover (the Shulamite's), 138, 139, 153, 154, 218
  his attractiveness, 138, 139
  as "brother," 6, 128–29, 209
  his companions, 6, 18, 179, 220
Luther, Martin, 31

Mahanayim, 199, 202
mandrakes, 124, 208
mare, as erotic metaphor, 39–40, 144–45, 195
Margolis, Max, 33 *n*
marriage, 175, 214
Masoretic Text (MT), 36, 135, 184, 186, 193, 200, 210, 211, 220
Mesopotamian art, 151–52
metonymy, 145, 206
Meyers, Carol, 159
Midrash, Midrashic usage, 161, 166, 180, 201
Midrash Rabbah, 22 *n*
milk, 185, 186
Moldenke, Harold and Alma, 148, 149
mother, 6
  house of, 6, 159, 210
  image of nursing, 128–29
  King Solomon's, 6, 22–23, 165–66
  the lover's, 6, 211–12
  "mother's sons," 6, 141
  the Shulamite's, 3, 5–6, 18, 19, 128–29, 159, 209
  as teacher of the arts of love, 6, 210
Murphy, Roland, 19 *n*, 29 *n*, 135, 143, 166, 192, 197, 199, 200, 201, 207

nature in the Song, 9
necklace, 171, 172, 175
New English Bible (NEB), 37, 143, 144, 151, 156, 162, 166, 172, 183, 184, 189, 200, 221
New Testament, similar elements in the Song, 209, 214, 219
nidgalot (6:4, 6:10), 37, 191–92
night, 147, 157, 163, 173, 180, 221

oral transmission, 20
orchard, 176–77
Origen, 30, 31
'oṭeyah (1:7), 142–43
"our," as used by the lovers, 8, 147, 153, 155, 208

parallelism, 191, 216
pardes (4:13), 24, 177
Passover Haggadah, 184, 190
pastoral elements, 8, 25–26
personification of abstract, 130, 204
Peshitta, 36, 138, 142, 163, 176, 179, 210
Pharaoh, 145
Pharaoh's daughter, 10, 32, 34, 163, 166
Philo, 31
place name symbolism, 203, 219
pools, 186, 202
Pope, Marvin, 29 *n*, 135, 142, 143, 145, 147, 148, 150, 151, 154, 155, 156, 163, 165, 166, 170,

saffron, 177
spikenard, 146–47, 177
spring, well, fountain, 176, 177, 202
springtime, 3, 19, 154
Stadelmann, Luis, 31 *n*
suitors, 214, 216
*susati (*1:9), 39–40, 143–45
Symmachus, 142, 168

Talmud, 163, 184
talpiyyot (4:4), 170–72
Tamar and Judah, 13, 142–43, 212
Targum, 31, 142
Tcherikover, Victor, 25 *n*
Teresa of Avila, Saint, 32
tesuqah (7:11), 206–207
Theocritus, *Idylls*, 25, 144, 157
Theodore of Mopsuestia, 32
Tirzah, city of, 188, 202
title of the Song, 137
Tower of David, 170–71, 172
Tower of Lebanon, 203
twins, 128–29, 169, 173

Ugaritic, 169
unity of the Song, 19–20

"veil," 5, 38-39, 119, 166–68
verb tenses, 39, 149, 152, 178, 205
vine, vineyard, 3, 6, 8, 18, 123, 141, 147, 155, 156–57, 176–77, 178, 192, 202, 207, 218–20
Vulgate, 36, 135, 142, 143, 144, 176, 179, 200

waṣf. See praise song
watchmen, 6, 18, 19, 158, 182, 183
waw-conversive, 24, 191
wedding, 20, 22–23, 33–34, 161, 163, 166, 175
wheat, 127–28, 201
"white and red," 184–85
wine, 127, 137, 148, 150, 176, 179–80, 185, 201, 206, 211
Wisdom literature, 152
Wolkstein, Diane, 37, 158
women in OT, 4, 5, 21
word order, 146, 158, 161, 174, 209, 218
wordplay, puns, 140, 154–55, 170, 179, 204, 207, 208, 219–20

Zakovitch, Yair, 182
zamir (2:12), 154–55
Zohar, 32, 163

ABOUT THE AUTHORS

ARIEL BLOCH is professor emeritus of Near Eastern studies at the University of California at Berkeley. His books and articles deal with classical Arabic, Arabic dialectology, biblical and Modern Hebrew, Ugaritic, Akkadian, and Aramaic. His books include *Die Hypotaxe im Damaszenisch-Arabischen; Damaszenisch-Arabische Texte; A Chrestomathy of Modern Literary Arabic;* and *Studies in Arabic Syntax and Semantics*. He translated and edited *The Window: New and Selected Poems of Dahlia Ravikovitch* in collaboration with Chana Bloch. Among his awards are a National Endowment for the Humanities Senior Fellowship, the president of the University of California's Research Fellowship in the Humanities, and a National Science Foundation grant. At the University of California he taught courses in Semitic linguistics, including Arabic dialectology and Aramaic, and a graduate seminar on the Song of Songs.

CHANA BLOCH is a poet, translator, scholar, and literary critic. She has published two books of poems, *The Secrets of the Tribe* and *The Past Keeps Changing;* three books of translations from Hebrew: *A Dress of Fire,* by Dahlia Ravikovitch, *The Selected Poetry of Yehuda Amichai* (with Stephen Mitchell), and *The Window: New and Selected Poems of Dahlia Ravikovitch* (with Ariel Bloch); translations of Yiddish poetry and prose; and a critical study, *Spelling the Word: George Herbert and the Bible.* Her awards include the Discovery Award of the 92nd Street "Y" Poetry Center, a Pushcart Award, the Poets & Writers Exchange Award, a National Endowment for the Arts fellowship in poetry, the Columbia University Translation Center Award, a National Endowment for the Humanities fellowship, and the Book of the Year Award of the Conference on Christianity and Literature. She taught Hebrew at the University of California at Berkeley, and is now professor of English and director of the creative writing program at Mills College, where she conducts poetry workshops and teaches courses on contemporary poetry, Shakespeare, and the Bible.

ABOUT THE TYPE

This book was set in Sabon, a typeface designed by the well-known German typographer Jan Tschichold (1902–74). Sabon's design is based on the original letterforms of Claude Garamond and was created specifically to be used for three sources: foundry type for hand composition, Linotype, and Monotype. Tschichold named his typeface for the famous Frankfurt typefounder Jacques Sabon, who died in 1580.

The Hebrew text was set in Narkis, a typeface designed by Bezelel Narkis.